Laboring and Dependent Classes
in Colonial America
1607-1783

AMERICAN CLASSICS

Laboring
and
Dependent Classes
in
Colonial America
1607-1783

MARCUS WILSON JERNEGAN

FREDERICK UNGAR PUBLISHING CO.
New York

First published 1931

Republished 1960 in the
AMERICAN CLASSICS SERIES

Printed in the United States of America

Library of Congress Catalog Card No. 60-13985

TO
MY WIFE

PREFACE

Though the essays included in this volume discuss a considerable variety of topics, nevertheless there is a bond of unity which warrants their inclusion under the general title chosen. Each study illustrates the attitude of the state and upper classes toward the lower classes; the place of the latter in society; their economic and social status; their treatment, efforts for their industrial, religious, or secular education, or their support.

The various studies presented have been published over a considerable number of years in several historical magazines. They are here presented with some revision, but no attempt has been made to elaborate the chapters on the basis of new studies or new materials, which, however, have been examined. It does not appear that many essentially new principles would emerge from such materials.

The researches have been made in many different libraries and archives—state, local, and private. These are too numerous to mention individually but special thanks are due the officials of the Library of Congress; the Newberry Library, Chicago; the American Antiquarian Society, Worcester; the Virginia State Library; the Virginia Historical Society; the Maryland Historical Society; the Charleston Library Society; the Massachusetts Historical Society; and the Connecticut Historical Society.

The officials of state and local archives were always very obliging in the use of material under their care. Special thanks are due to the officials of the state archives of Virginia, South Carolina, and Massachusetts and to the officials of the county archives of numerous counties in Virginia, and of Essex and Middlesex counties in Massachusetts.

Publication of this book is largely due to the interest, encouragement, and efforts of Dean Edith Abbott of the School of Social Service of the University of Chicago.

The author acknowledges, with thanks, the kindness of the editors and publishers of the various periodicals in which these studies originally appeared, indicated in the first note of each chapter. These publications are the *American Historical Review*, *Harper's Monthly Magazine*, the *School Review*, and the *Social Service Review*.

INTRODUCTION

This volume is designed as an introduction to the history of certain aspects of our colonial civilization which have been largely neglected by the historians of this period. The thirteen chapters here presented are studies illustrative of, rather than a history of, the subject as a whole. Indeed, if a comparative study were made for all of the colonies throughout the whole period, each chapter might well be expanded into a book. The studies presented relate, for the most part, to the conditions in the southern and New England colonies. Chapters might well have been included on similar topics illustrating conditions in the middle colonies. Such studies, however, would yield few new principles. In these essays may be found illustrations of the origin and early development of a number of major American problems relating to the laboring and poor classes of society: such as industrial training, immigration, racial relations, free education, and, especially, those two immediate and pressing problems, crime and poor relief.

In Part I, two aspects of the life of the negro slave are presented, with emphasis on the conditions in Virginia and South Carolina. It is believed that this account of the slave as an artisan and non-agricultural laborer typifies his life, in these respects, in other colonies; that it illustrates the reasons for, and the development of, plantation economy and illuminates the early history of numerous American industries and manufactures. Similarly, the study of the early religious life of the slave, mainly in these two colonies, illustrates conditions in other colonies.

Chapter III illustrates many of the important economic and social problems which arose in those colonies where the indentured servant system prevailed. This system was more widespread than the slavery system and even in the South it continued to be of great importance notwithstanding the large increase in the number of negro slaves in this section during the eighteenth century. This chapter, also chapters x–xii, illuminates the origin of the "new race," the mulatto, recently the subject of a special study.[1] The early history

[1] Edwin R. Embree, *Brown America. The Story of a New Race.* New York, 1931.

of miscegenation of whites and blacks probably received greater impetus through loose relations between indentured servants and slaves than through the relations of masters and slaves. These chapters also illustrate the emergence of the free negro, the forerunner of the emancipated slave.

The importance of the system of apprenticeship in our colonial history is now all but forgotten. In Parts II and III emphasis is placed on its educational rather than its industrial significance because the former is less well known than the latter. In the period before the general acceptance of the idea that the state or local governmental units should establish, administer, and support free public schools by taxes levied on all property-holders, the system of apprenticeship was the principal agency available, outside of the family, for providing poor children with the opportunity of securing the rudiments of an education. Though the studies presented are confined to New England and Virginia, they illustrate practices prevalent in the other colonies. This system was the foundation of, and the first effort to apply, the idea of the responsibility of the state, in the period considered, for the education of its future citizens. The fact that the system benefited only those apprenticed does not lessen its influence in the history of the idea. Though the laws were doubtless poorly enforced, it is clear from the study made for New England and Virginia in chapters viii and xi that the system was more than a theory, and that effort was made to make it an effective educational agency.

In Part IV two chapters are presented on the subject of public poor relief. This aspect of the history of poor folk has been greatly neglected by the historians of the colonial period. Here again a comparative study of the development of poor relief in all the colonies is greatly needed. But it is believed that the evolution of the principles and practices of public poor relief in these colonies illustrate similar developments in other colonies. It should be noted that only public agencies are here considered. Private philanthropy and aid for the poor were also of great importance, but no adequate account of this phase of poor relief in the colonies has yet appeared.

It is hoped that these essays will stimulate interest in American colonial history and lead to more comprehensive studies of the various topics considered.

TABLE OF CONTENTS

PART I. ECONOMIC AND SOCIAL ASPECTS OF NEGRO SLAVERY AND INDENTURED SERVANT SYSTEMS

PART II. FREE EDUCATION FOR POOR CHILDREN AND APPRENTICES IN NEW ENGLAND

PART III. FREE EDUCATION FOR POOR CHILDREN AND APPRENTICES IN THE SOUTH

PART IV. TYPES OF PUBLIC POOR RELIEF SYSTEMS

PART I

ECONOMIC AND SOCIAL ASPECTS OF NEGRO SLAVERY AND INDENTURED SERVANT SYSTEMS

CHAPTER I

SLAVERY AND THE BEGINNINGS OF INDUSTRIALISM[1]

One of the characteristic features of the evolution of the western nations in the last two centuries is the passing of comparatively simple agricultural societies through various stages to that condition known as industrialism. Reduced to their lowest terms, the chief factors which caused such changes were, first, increase in population, and second, exhaustion of the land, both in quantity and quality. These conditions led to diversification of industry, to an increase in the number and variety of artisans, trades, and occupations, not specifically agricultural. With a continued increase in population and a tendency toward compactness, with rapid exhaustion of the soil, with a growing scarcity of, and high prices for, food supplies, new lands were opened up and surplus population was either exported or, if not, it was diverted to manufacturing industries, trade, and commerce. This process was hastened in the Old World by the colonization of new lands overseas, and the resulting opportunities for the more rapid production of wealth through the development of the resources of these lands, the production of raw materials for use in manufacturing, or to supply other needs, and the establishment of markets for the sale of manufactured goods.

The American colonies supplied England with a portion of the new lands she needed in order to make the transition from agriculturalism to industrialism. Likewise, the colonies were compelled to depend on England, or some other country, in making a similar transition, for reasons to be noted. The influence of some of the factors mentioned, with others to be mentioned, caused the colonies to pass through the earlier stages of the process leading to industrialism even before independence was secured. This period of semi-industrialism is marked by a rapid increase of population, exhaustion of land and soil, and, in consequence, a tendency toward a diversification of farming and of occupations. Another important influence affecting this movement was the commercial policy of

England, which tended to stimulate as well as to retard certain manufactures. England, also, was in part responsible for scarcity or high price of imported manufactured goods, due to poor transportation facilities, or to the interruption or retardation of trade because of wars or for other causes. The colonial governments were thus led to stimulate manufactures by bounties and other methods in order that the colonists might meet pressing and immediate needs, and individuals were stimulated to manufacture for profit under such conditions. The high cost of transporting and marketing the bulky goods produced by the colonists, in connection with overproduction, especially of tobacco, and England's restrictive commercial and trade policy, often resulted in inability to ship goods, or in such low prices for the product as to make the colonists either unable or disinclined to purchase manufactured goods abroad. This also led to diversification of farming and of occupations, thus again stimulating certain forms of manufactures. In the decade preceding the Revolution, the movement for independence, in its economic as well as in its political aspect, stimulated manufactures. The colonists wished to avoid the payment of taxes on imported goods, both because of the principle involved and because of high prices. Patriotic motives, the desire for economic as well as political independence, the non-importation and non-consumption agreements, all these stimulated manufactures to supply pressing and immediate economic needs. In general, we may say that there was, in the generation or so preceding the Revolution, a rapid increase in the number of men who were convinced that it was more desirable, practical, and profitable to employ labor and to invest capital in industries or manufactures involving partial or complete transformation of raw materials into finished products, than to confine themselves exclusively to agriculture or to occupations involving only the production and transportation of purely raw materials. With the one exception of food supply, all the factors so far mentioned, viz., increase of population, exhaustion of land and soil, scarcity or high price of manufactured goods, encouragement of specific manufactures by England and by the colonial assemblies, low price of exported products, especially tobacco, the influence of the movement for independence, and the proportionate return to be obtained on capital invested—all of these factors were influential in producing a diversification of farming and occupations, and an increase in manufacturing in the southern colonies as well as in those of the North.[2]

In the so-called tobacco colonies of Maryland and Virginia, the general tendency of the tobacco régime was to make it more and more difficult because of overproduction and low prices[3] to make this product alone pay for the manufactured goods imported. Hence many a planter was faced with a loss of credit, heavy debt, or bankruptcy, on the one hand, or the necessity of finding a remedy to meet the situation, on the other. This remedy might be based on one or more of the following principles: that of decreasing the product, or using some other means of increasing the price of the same; that of raising other agricultural products for which a higher relative price could be obtained; that of purchasing fewer manufactured goods from abroad; or that of producing such goods at home. To counteract the bad effects of the English commercial policy, a few of the planters made the discovery, as early as the end of the seventeenth century, that it was more profitable to plant partly exhausted tobacco lands, and sometimes even fresh lands, with corn, wheat, or other cereals, or turn them into pasture lands for cattle and sheep, than to grow tobacco.[4] Moreover, much of the land unsuited to tobacco culture could be profitably used for such purposes, and, as the center of population moved westward, it became necessary, for the upland soil was lighter and more sandy. Such crops were also desirable and even necessary to supply food— corn, for example—for the rapidly growing population, and especially for the negro slave. Corn was also necessary to feed the cattle, as the practice of allowing herds to roam the woods proved too costly. There was thus some tendency toward a system of agriculture based on corn, wheat, and other cereals, cattle, sheep, and hogs, and later, farther to the south, cotton—products more suited to exhausted and poorer soils—rather than on tobacco, hemp, and flax, those products which both demanded a rich soil, and at the same time, exhausted it most rapidly.

We may now inquire what was the relation of these agricultural tendencies of the eighteenth century to other industries and occupations resulting, and particularly to the occupations of negro slaves. It is obvious that, with these raw materials present and plantation needs greatly extended, some needs might be satisfied by transforming a portion of these raw materials, through primary or secondary processes, into manufactured articles. If a surplus could be produced for purposes of export, the profit obtained could be used to supply other manufactured articles for which tobacco alone could no longer provide the funds. We know that, as the eighteenth century progressed, there was in all the southern colonies a large increase in the production of corn, wheat, and other cereals, and in the raising of cattle, sheep, and hogs. Likewise, we know that there was a large increase in mills for grinding grain, both for home consumption and for export. The production of cereal and animal products was stimulated by the opportunity for profit in provisioning ships, both English and colonial. The great increase in shipping in the eighteenth century called for large quantities of provisions, such as flour, ship-bread, beef, and pork; and, besides, there was a great demand for these articles in the West Indies, in exchange for molasses, sugar, and other products needed by the American colonies. For example, there were exported from the upper district of the James River, from October 25, 1763, to October 25, 1764, among other articles, 29,145 bushels of wheat, 3,003 pounds of bacon, 50 tierces of bread, 62,763 bushels of corn, 1,098 barrels of flour, and 920 barrels and 1,000 pounds of pork. We know, also, that the number of tanneries increased; that the southern colonies passed numerous laws to prevent the export of hides and leather in order to encourage the tanning of leather and allied industries; that leather manufactures, including especially the manufacture of the rougher grades of shoes, increased. We know that the textile industries—the weaving of cloth from flax, wool, and cotton—increased, both for home consumption and for neighborhood exchange.[5]

There was an increasing desire to secure a greater return from the capital invested by making greater use of the natural resources of the plantation, both because of necessity and for possible profits. Beverley had called the attention of the planters of Virginia, in 1705, to their wastefulness and lack of energy in this respect.[6] There were large supplies of raw materials on many plantations, the natural products of the land, especially forests, that led to occupations based on lumber products. The needs of England compelled her to stimulate the production of naval stores, and the southern forests were available for masts, spars, planks, and boards for building ships and boats of all kinds and for repairs on the same, as well as for the production of tar, pitch, and turpentine. There were, besides rough manufactures from the forests, other lumber products requiring more skill. We have evidence of a great increase in the manufacture of staves, hoops, and "headings," in order to provide for the enormous number of hogsheads, barrels, and tierces, containers for tobacco, rice, and other products to be exported. We know, besides, that great quantities of the above articles were manufactured for export to the West Indies and other countries, containers for molasses, sugar, etc. For example, from the upper district of the James River, October 25, 1763, to October 25, 1764, there were exported 566,800 staves, 9,250 hoops, 80,860 shingles, and 3,800 headings. From Charleston, November 1, 1763, to November 1, 1764, there were exported 1,553,365 shingles, 700 laths, and 228,015 staves and headings.[7] We know that various other industries were based on cultivated or natural products of the soil, such occupations as brewing, wine-making, and the production of bricks, rope, hats, salt, soap, candles, powder, potash, and a variety of domestic utensils and implements.[8] We know that the eighteenth century witnessed a rise in the standard of living; that there was a demand for better houses and a tendency to lath and plaster, to shingle and clapboard, to build brick houses in place of the earlier unfinished log or board structures.[9] The great increase of slaves and of production called for a larger output of lumber for building operations, for barns, tobacco-houses, outbuildings, landings, warehouses, etc. We know that as a result of these industries there was an increase in the number of artisans and craftsmen of all kinds; that effort was made by the colonial governments, particularly through the apprenticeship acts, to increase the supply,[10] that, as a result, there was an increase of millers, brewers, weavers, butchers, tanners, curriers, shoemakers, blacksmiths, sawyers, carpenters, shipwrights, brickmakers, masons, plasterers, and other skilled workers.

This diversification of farming and industry is the fundamental factor leading to the employment of the slave in non-agricultural labor and manufacturing processes. We have seen that the movement began in the latter portion of the seventeenth century, and was due principally to the shortage of goods from England, high prices for the same, and low prices for tobacco. The movement, however, had not made much headway by 1705, according to Beverley, though there is good reason for believing that he underestimated the amount of manufactures at this date.[11] The evidence of diversification of farming and of occupations increases rapidly after 1720. We have references to such in the reports of governors to the Lords of Trade, in reports of travelers, in the advertisements in newspapers, and in the statistics of the export trade in manufactured articles. We note diversification in the production of cereals in the increase of mills, of cattle and sheep and industries dependent on them. Further evidence of this tendency is seen in the legislation designed to increase the supply of artisans and in the acts to encourage manufactures and to prevent the export of raw materials. Such evidence proves that the industrial development of the southern colonies in the eighteenth century at least made possible the employment of the negro slave in non-agricultural occupations.[12]

It is evident that the part the slave might take in these rough manufactures would depend on the number of slaves available, their intelligence, and the relative profit to be obtained by use of this kind of labor; in other words, on the question whether it was possible, desirable, or necessary, practicable, and profitable. The eighteenth century witnessed a rapid and large increase in the number of slaves, both from importation and from births.[13] There was, therefore, a large possible supply. Negroes were of two general classes: first, "raw" or "Guinea" negroes, those imported directly from Africa; secondly, those "country-born." The latter might be imported from the West Indies or from some other colony; or they might be negroes born and brought up in the colony where they were employed. It is evident that the second class would constitute the most important possible sources for the supply of slaves who might be trained as artisans.[14] "Country-born" negroes would generally have greater intelligence and a better knowledge of the English language. They would be more docile, more adaptable to their environment, more familiar with the methods of production and, in general, more civilized than freshly imported negroes. Indeed, the latter were often judged, a priori, as nothing but brute creatures without intelligence.[15] The native-born negro came in contact with the civilization of the white man from birth and was disciplined, to some extent, in childhood and youth. Such discipline tended to develop the intelligence of this class of slaves, and it was from among them, by a process of natural selection, that the more capable were assigned to occupations requiring more intelligence than ordinary field labor; occupations usually calling for a certain degree of skill in handicraft. The "country-born" negroes were, however, subdivided into groups of varying degrees of ability. There were negroes of pure blood who, of course, varied in intelligence just as white persons do. But, from the first, there was the class known as mulattoes—negroes with more or less white blood in their veins.[16] It is quite generally admitted that the effect of crossing the races made most of the mulattoes more intelligent than the negroes of pure blood.[17] There were doubtless exceptions to the rule, but the percentage was small. This fact was reflected in the higher prices paid for mulattoes throughout the period of slavery.[18] There was thus a continual and increasing supply of this class, with a tendency to select from it the most intelligent for work requiring handicraft skill. Negroes of this class tended to increase in ability from generation to generation, both because of natural selection and because they were more favored. They had better opportunities for religious instruction and for closer contact with the white population.

It was natural for a planter to employ a slave to do a piece of work requiring skill or intelligence if he had one of suitable character. If, besides, such employment was necessary, he might make the attempt even at considerable cost. In fact, we know that there was throughout the colonial period a great scarcity of free artisans in the southern colonies. We know that indentured servant artisans were insufficient in number for the work to be done and were unsatisfactory for many other reasons; that frequently, perhaps generally, they gave up working at their trade, if they had one, in order to become farmers.[19] This scarcity of artisans made it almost necessary that the planter should put forth every effort to purchase or train slaves who had skill in some handicraft, particularly as he produced staple crops on a large scale, diversified his agriculture, or began to make use of the resources of his land, whether it produced forests, animals, minerals, or other things that could be profitably transformed into goods of greater value. If, at the same time, there was a shortage of manufactured goods from abroad, or the price was excessively high, or the planter had no funds for their purchase, or was in debt, these were additional and pressing reasons for the use of slaves in plantation manufactures. In other words, eighteenth-century plantation economy called for more careful use of all the resources available, both for greater profit and to avoid bankruptcy. If still further, there were facilities for training the slave in a trade, and all or many of the above reasons were operating, a planter would almost certainly make the effort. We may note that there was the opportunity to select from large numbers, and some would be available for training because of natural aptitude, or inherited tendencies. The indentured white servant artisan, as well as the free artisan, was always a possible source of instruction. Young negro slaves could be apprenticed by masters to free white artisans to learn particular trades. They were purchased by artisans, or those with skill in some handicraft, for the purpose of teaching them. Besides, slaves who had acquired skill could be used to instruct other slaves. Finally, masters could let or hire out young negroes to persons who would employ them in labor which would increase their intelligence and skill, or, if capable, masters could instruct slaves themselves.[20]

Let us now consider the early evidence for the actual employment of slaves in industries, other than those purely agricultural, up to about 1740. By 1649, one man, at least, had discovered that it was possible, practical, and profitable to train slaves to be artisans and to perform simple manufacturing processes. Thus the author of *A Perfect Description of Virginia* (1649) declares that

Worthy Captaine Matthews, an old Planter of above thirty yeers standing, one of the Counsell, and a most deserving Common-wealthsman, I may not omit to let you know this Gentlemans industry. He hath a fine house, and all things answerable to it; he sowes yeerly store of Hempe and Flax, and causes it to be spun; he keeps Weavers, and hath a Tan-house, causes Leather to be dressed, hath eight Shoemakers employed in their trade, hath forty Negroe servants, brings them up to Trades in his house. He yeerly sowes abundance of Wheat, Barley, etc. The Wheat he selleth at four shillings the bushell; kills store of Beeves, and sells them to victuall the ships when they come thither: hath abundance of kine, a brave Dairy, Swine great store, and Poltery. . . . .[21]

Here we have, in this remarkable document, an illustration of four tendencies, important and characteristic movements of the eighteenth century; first, diversified farming; secondly, diversified industry—provisioning and tanning; thirdly, manufacturing, linen cloth and shoes; and fourthly, the training of negro slaves as artisans and skilled workmen. In short Captain Matthews was a farmer, a rancher, a manufacturer, and a merchant. He ran a plantation and a factory at the same time. The inventory of Robert Beverley, Sr., shows that he had a negro carpenter valued at thirty pounds. John Carter, Jr., owned a negro cooper, and Ralph Wormeley, a negro cooper and carpenter, each valued at thirty-five pounds sterling.[22] The county records of Virginia of the seventeenth century, inventories and wills in particular, reveal the presence of many negro mechanics, especially carpenters and coopers, and negro women who had been taught to take part in domestic manufacture. Note also that Thomas Cocke (d. 1696) left by will a flour-mill and two tanneries, and mentioned by name one of his tanners, whom he bequeathed to his son James. Another mechanic at the mill was left "with all his tools" to his son Stephen.[23] The only other important source for artisans was the white, indentured servant mechanic. But when his term of service expired, usually in four or five years, another would have to be purchased in England. This constantly recurring necessity for supplying the place of white mechanics led the planters to have some of their slaves instructed in the trades, even in the seventeenth century.[24]

Owing to the rapid diversification of farming and of occupations after 1705, there was a corresponding increase in the variety of artisans. The increase in the number and variety of slave artisans may be judged from the statement of Hugh Jones in 1724, who said that "a good Negro" was "sometimes worth three (nay four) Score Pounds Sterling, if he be a Tradesman." He also says that negroes were taught to be "Sawyers, Carpenters, Smiths, Coopers, etc., and though for the most Part they be none of the aptest or nicest, yet they are by Nature cut out for hard Labour and Fatigue, and will perform tolerably well."[25] The frequent reference to negro artisans in the wills and inventories of the early eighteenth century is further evidence of the increase of this class. For example, note the will and inventory of Robert ("King") Carter, 1732. He bequeathed, among other slaves, "George the Cooper," and a negro boy who was being taught a trade by his cooper. His inventory mentions seven negro carpenters and three negro sawyers.[26] Richard Chapman writes in 1739 that he had a "couple of Young Slaves who are Carpenters and Coopers, who are just beginning to be of Great use to me." He then orders of his agent abroad axes, saws, coopers' tools, etc.[27]

It is desirable to study next the early development of these same tendencies in South Carolina, and then treat the general development of these two colonies together, from 1740 to the Revolution.

In South Carolina the use of the slave in non-agricultural occupations and the effort to train him as an artisan centered first on utilizing the resources of the forests. In a description of South Carolina published in 1761, the author states that slaves could be employed in the unused part of the year when "they will have some Time to spare for sawing Lumber and making Hogsheads, and other Staves, to supply the Sugar Colonies."[28] The bounties paid by England for the production of naval stores—masts, spars, and especially tar, pitch, and turpentine—would give great opportunity for the employment of slaves in this industry. Sawyers, carpenters, and coopers would be needed in large numbers to supply plantation needs—lumber for buildings and repairs, for staves, hoops, and headings, and for rice barrels. Staves, etc., were profitable for export to the West Indies to be made into barrels for sugar and molasses; and lumber products of all kinds—planks, boards, etc. Habersham wrote the Countess of Huntington (1775), "Last November I sent a fine young Fellow a Cooper to your Ladyship's Plantation to make Rice Barrels and teach two of your People that Business." An account of produce exported, in less than one year, from Charleston, November 1, 1751, to October 16, 1752, shows that it involved the production of 110,462 hogsheads, tierces, and barrels to hold the rice, pitch, tar, turpentine, skins, beef, and pork sent out. From November 1, 1753, to November 1, 1754, 110,714 barrels were needed for the export of similar products—i. e., a production of 221,176 barrels in a little less than two years. But, in addition, in this last period, there were exported 168,121 staves. The number of sawyers, carpenters, and coopers needed to produce this one type of article was quite considerable, and it is evident that a large portion must have been produced by negro slaves—artisans with a knowledge of the above trades. We may note in passing that there were also exported, in this last year mentioned, 952,880 shingles and 780,776 feet of scantling, plank, and boards, some of which it is likely were produced by negro slaves.[29]

In the files of the *South Carolina Gazettes*, 1732–76, we find evidence of slaves trained in and practicing at least twenty-eight different trades specifically so named.[30] Of woodworkers there were seven varieties; viz., sawyers, squares, coopers, house carpenters, ship carpenters or shipwrights, cabinet makers, and wheelwrights. Of leather workers, there were tanners, curriers, and shoemakers. Of cloth workers, there were spinners, carders, weavers, knitters, needleworkers or seamstresses, and tailors. Of those engaged in the building trades, there were brickmoulders and brickmakers, bricklayers, limemakers, plasterers, whitewashers, painters or glaziers, caulkers, blacksmiths, and even such a trade as that of a silversmith was represented. There were also miscellaneous occupations more or less connected with the production and distribution of non-agricultural goods. There were slaves who were navigators, pilots, boatmen, porters, etc. In the above statement no account is made of the use of the slave in occupations involving the partial transformation of raw materials into forms that involve rough or primary manufacturing operations, such as preparing rice, indigo, hemp, flax, and raw silk for export, the grinding of grain, packing of meat products, and other similar occupations, where slaves performed work not agricultural. The manufacturing industries carried on may be inferred from the trades represented, and these included manufacture of lumber, planks and boards, of staves, hoops and headings, hogsheads, and barrels; the making of buildings, ships, and boats of all kinds, and of furniture, wheeled vehicles, leather, shoes, cloth, clothing, socks, bricks, lime, domestic utensils, and implements.

The mechanical skill or knowledge possessed by the negro slave artisans was applied, and the production of manufactured goods accomplished, with slaves holding a variety of relationships with the person who for the moment profited by their labor. At least four distinct relationships were common. In the first place most artisan slaves, of course, applied their skill or produced goods when owned and kept as slaves by any free white or colored man or woman who wished to profit by such skill. Such an individual might be a rice or indigo producer, a planter, a farmer, a man or woman engaged in any of the trades or manufacturing industries mentioned above, or any other free person. Secondly, a slave might apply his knowledge or produce goods when apprenticed to some person. Thirdly, he might be hired out to some person by his owner by the day, month, or year, in town or country, for a stipulated amount. Fourthly, he might be allowed industrial freedom by his owner, or the privilege of working when and where he could find employment at his trade, either with or without previous agreement with the owner by the person employing such a slave. The condition on which the slave was allowed such freedom was that of turning over to the owner, at stated intervals, all or an agreed portion of the wages earned. A slave hired out or allowed freedom to work might be very profitable, since the return from the labor was practically all profit—a condition not possible when he was kept on the plantation and supported by the owner. Slaves might also be employed in considerable numbers by an individual or a group of persons who were producing goods in quantities. Such slaves might be owned, held as apprentices, or hired for the purpose.[31]

We may also note that five stages of production are represented in this industrial development of South Carolina, viz., first, plantation manufactures for home consumption; secondly, plantation manufactures for the purpose of disposing of a surplus within the colony; thirdly, plantation manufactures for export (the last two were known respectively as the domestic-commercial and commercial stages); fourthly, the stage in which individual artisans or others owned or hired slaves and employed them for the purpose of selling the whole of their product, or the whole of their time and skill, for a price specified; and fifthly, the shop and factory stage of producing manufactured goods wholly by slave labor with the purpose of disposing of the whole surplus.

Evidence of the first stage, home or plantation manufactures, is best illustrated by the advertisements offering at public sale, often at auction, large lots of slaves, usually in connection with the sale of a complete plantation, with lands, houses, equipment, stock, etc. Eighteen such notices, at least, are found in the *South Carolina Gazettes* before the Revolution, over half of them between 1760 and 1776. The total number of slaves in each case varied from about ten to seventy, the indefinite word "parcel" being used a number of times. In all these cases there is mention of the fact that some of the slaves are artisans, tradesmen, or skilled workers in some occupation. As the exact number of slaves of this character is seldom given, it is difficult to estimate the proportion having special skill. A typical advertisement reads as follows: "About Fifty Valuable Slaves, among which are sundry tradesmen, such as Bricklayers, Carpenters, Coopers, Sawyers, Shoemakers, Tanners, Curriers and Boat-men."[32] Another states that there would be sold "A Parcel of Slaves belonging to the estate of Mrs. Mary Frost, deceased, consisting of sawyers, mowers, a very good caulker, a tanner, a compleat tight cooper, a sawyer, squarer and rough carpenter."[33] One woman was a "washer, ironer and spinner." In another lot of twenty, mention is made of sawyers, a jobbing carpenter, and butcher, "and most of the fellows acquainted with lime making."[34]

Advertisements offering for sale one or more artisan slaves are numerous, especially ship carpenters and coopers.[35] Likewise there are numerous advertisements of persons who wished to purchase slaves skilled in some trade, such as house carpenters, ship carpenters, cabinetmakers, and blacksmiths.[36] Henry Laurens seems to have been in the business of supplying skilled negro artisans for the trade, for he advertises, in 1765, for two carpenters, two coopers, three pairs of sawyers, besides other workers, for field use and for indigo production.[37] Another striking example indicative of the supply of slave artisans is an offer in one advertisement to sell "five negro men, two of them tanners and three shoemakers."

A kind of advertisement which appears very frequently refers to runaway negro slaves, and many of this class were artisans. For example, as early as 1733, we find anxious masters seeking the following runaways: three negro sawyers, hired for work in Georgia; a mustee wench, who could spin, card, and do needlework; and two sawyers, for whose return a reward of £20 was offered for each one, an indication of the value of these men to the owner. Numerous examples of this sort could be given, involving the more common trades, e. g., a shoemaker and carpenter, a carpenter and cooper, and a ship carpenter.[38]

The practice of hiring out skilled workers must have been profitable, judging from the frequency of such advertisements. If such a man could be hired out, so that the cost of his upkeep would be met by the person who employed him, and a sum of money—say, ten pounds[39]—be paid, besides, for his work for one year, that would be a very profitable investment, the interest on a thousand dollars for a year at 5 per cent with practically no expense to the owner. We know that the practice was in existence from an early date. For example, a master offered to hire out a bricklayer and plasterer, by the month, quarter, or more or less time, in town or country.[40] Another offered a negro blacksmith by the month or year,[41] another a bricklayer and a carpenter, both "good workmen to be hired by the month or year."[42] The practice of allowing slaves industrial freedom, if the wages earned were given to the master, gave such artisans the opportunity to retain all or a part of the money they earned, and to work "clandestinely"—a common phrase of the owner when he forewarned everyone not to employ or hire his slave without previous agreement with the owner. Thus, in one case, two negro carpenters,[43] and, in another, a bricklayer, were claimed by the owner.[44] Another negro carpenter worked "clandestinely" about the town and defrauded his master of "several sums of money."[45] So also complaint was made that a ship carpenter and a whitewasher converted wages to their own use.[46]

Such an institution as the factory also existed in the pre-Revolutionary period. By this is not meant the factory system as developed later, but a building where goods were made by manual labor, usually requiring more equipment, several skilled workers of the same

trade, and some division of labor, more than would be the case on
the plantation or in the one-man shop. There were a number of
such establishments in operation before the Revolution, which exhibited these features to a greater or less degree. In some of these
institutions we find that the labor force consisted principally of
negro slave artisans. From one standpoint, of course, many of the
very large plantations, before the Revolution, were shops or factories, in the sense that they often manufactured goods in quantities,
had special buildings for the purpose, and made use of a number of
workmen skilled in some one trade. Captain Matthews of Virginia,
1649, has already been referred to. The carpenter's or cooper's
shop, where thousands of staves, hoops, headings, hogsheads,
tierces, or barrels were manufactured—containers for tobacco and
rice—represents a stage in advance of household production, the
making of a few articles in the family kitchen. When such articles
were made in quantities for shipment to the West Indies, they might
with good reason be classified as goods manufactured in the shop
or small factory.

Let us consider next the tanning and leather industries and the
making of shoes. We may note in passing that there were exported
from Charleston, in 1748, 10,356 pounds of tanned leather.[47] We
find, in 1764, that two "valuable" negro men, trained as tanners
and shoemakers, were offered for sale, "who can make any sort of
men's and coarse women's shoes; either of them can make two pair
of negro shoes a day."[48] If this statement is true it is evident that
these two slaves might produce twelve pairs of shoes a week, forty-
eight a month, or five hundred and seventy-six pairs in a year. If
we cut this production a third or more, we still have a considerable
output for a small shop or factory, with two workmen only, and it
is easy to see why it might pay to manufacture shoes of this type
rather than purchase them in England. Two years later, 1768, we
find that John Matthews proposed to give up his shoemaking business, and to sell two or three negro shoemakers—"Said negroes
have done all my business for nine years past, and are at least equal
to any negroes of the trade in this province; the eldest of them only
22 years old." Two months later we find that Richard Downes
will sell a negro shoemaker who "has been intrusted with the Care of

a Shoemaker's Shop, without any Assistance from a White Man, for several years."[49]

With the approach of the Revolution, we find that small factories were established for the manufacture of cloth. Washington had such an establishment in 1767–68, in which a variety of cloth —woollen, cotton, linen, etc.—was woven, both for his own use and for others. By the account for 1768 it appears that the weavers were one white woman, whom he hired for the purpose, and five "Negroe Girls," presumably his own slaves. In this "factory" there were spun and woven in the year 1768 for Washington's own use, 815¾ yards of linen and 1,355½ yards of woollen linsey, cotton, etc.[50] We find also that the "Manufacturing Society in Williamsburg" advertised in 1777 for weavers and "5 or 6 likely negro lads from 15 to 20, and as many girls from 12 to 15," with a note added to the effect that "Negro girls are received as apprentices."[51] There are also references to factories for weaving cloth, in which negro slaves were employed as weavers, in Maryland. Charles Carroll of Carrollton manufactured on his plantation coarse woollens and linen, woven in part by negro slaves.[52] We find also that Robert Carter had a similar weaving establishment at Nominy Hall. A document, dated 1782, shows that Carter had six negro weavers, boys of from thirteen to nineteen, and four negro winders, three of them girls of from fourteen to sixteen, and "Kate," of sixty-five years, all under the management of Daniel Sullivan, weaver, "at the Woolen and Linen *Factory* at Aires, belonging to Robert Carter, Esq. of Westm'd County."[53]

In South Carolina, also, negro slaves were employed in clothmaking. It is stated that the overproduction of rice in 1743, or the failure to market it because of war, "put the people [of South Carolina] upon trying to employ their negroes on sundry new manufactures of linen, woollen, etc., which they were before accustomed to take from Great Britain," but just at this time indigo-planting became profitable and it defeated their interest.[54] A remarkable proposition to teach slaves the art of linen-, woollen-, and cottoncloth manufacture occurred in 1766. The author of the advertisement says that he will teach slaves the raising of hemp and flax, "and the Spinning of both; he will take the Cotton, Flax and Hemp, from the Seed; and the Wool from the Sheep's Back and Compleat the whole." He had laid his scheme before the "Printer" and adds the following important bit of information: "The Above Person has Credentials from Pennsylvania and Virginia, where he has taught two Factories of this kind since the year 1749."[55]

Several questions are suggested by the data presented. First, is the evidence trustworthy? We may agree that without doubt slaves were trained to the trades, and worked at their calling. The evidence gives some general notion of the practice or proportion of slaves so trained, and, to a slight extent, indications of their efficiency. It is desirable, however, to check the newspapers from other sources because of the well-known tendency of those that have goods for sale to overstate their value and quality, especially in newspaper advertisements. Fortunately we have additional sources of information not open to this objection. It is well known that one of the most persistent inquiries of the Lords of Trade was that one which called for data on the kind and extent of manufacturing going on in the colonies. There were certainly good reasons for the royal governors to make reports which would underestimate the amount of manufacturing and to convey the impression that England had nothing to fear from the growth of manufacturing industries in the colonies. Two very interesting reports are available which give some notion of the extent of the practice of training slaves as artisans and their contribution to the production of manufactured goods. Governor Glen of South Carolina made a report of this kind in 1751.[56] He stated that there were forty thousand negroes in the province, which if valued as "New Negroes from Africa are now sold" would be worth £20 sterling per head; but this valuation did not satisfy him, considering that many of them were

Natives of Carolina who have no Notion of liberty. . . . have been brought up among White People, and by White People have been made, at least many of them, useful Mechanicks, as Coopers, Carpenters, Masons, Smiths, Wheelwrights, and other Trades, and that the rest can all speak our Language, for we imported none during the War, I say when it is Considered that these are pleased with their Masters, contented with their Condition, reconciled to Servitude, seasoned to the Country, and expert at the different kinds of Labour in which they are employed, it must appear difficult if not impracticable to ascertain their intrinsick Value. I know a Gentleman who refuses five Hundred Guineas for three of his Slaves, and therefore there is no guessing at the Value of strong seasoned handy Slaves, by the prices of weak Raw New Negroes.

We may note also that Lieutenant-Governor Fauquier of Virginia reported to the Board of Trade in December, 1766, as follows:

But to give your Lordships a true knowledge of this matter [manufacturers in Virginia] it is necessary I should add that every gentleman of much property in land and negroes have some of their own negroes bred up in the trade of blacksmiths, and make axes, hoes, ploughshares, and such kind of coarse work for the use of their plantations.[57]

Another convincing source of information is the fact that in South Carolina both free white laborers and the general assembly were greatly disturbed at the rapid development of the number of negro artisans, and respected their skill to the extent at least that they made vigorous complaint of the competition between white and slave artisans. For example, the *South Carolina Commons Journal*, of 1744,[58] contains an interesting petition of one Andrew Ruck, a shipwright, on behalf of himself and several other shipwrights. He complains that negro slaves worked in Charleston and other places near the same town, at the shipwright's trade, and were "chiefly employed in mending, repairing, and caulking of ships, other vessels and boats"; that, as a result, white shipwrights could meet with little or no work, were reduced to poverty, and would be obliged to leave the province if not relieved; that such a practice would discourage white shipwrights from settling in the province; and, therefore, the petitioners asked that relief be granted by the assembly. This petition was referred to a committee who reported that five other ship carpenters had sent in a petition denouncing Andrew Ruck and others, and declaring that there was no lack of work; that because of scarcity of white shipwrights slaves had to do the work; that the remonstrants were themselves, by trade, ship carpenters, and through diligence and savings had purchased several negro slaves, and had with great care and pains trained these slaves to be useful to them in the exercise of their trade, "and to be necessary for the support of them and their familys when by age or infirmity they became incapable of labor." The committee reported that the number of negroes hired out, "without a proportion of white men to do the business of shipwright or ship-carpenter, is a discouragement to white men of that business," advised a bill limiting the number of negro shipwrights, and suggested an inquiry to ascertain the wages of this class of white and negro artisans. A report of another committee in 1744,[59] appointed to suggest effectual measures for increasing the number of white persons in the province, complained that one hindrance to such increase was that "a great number of negroes are brought up to and daily employed in Mechanic Trades both in Town and Country," and proposed that the negro act be amended by introducing a clause to prohibit "the bringing up of Negroes and other Slaves to Mechanic Trades in which white persons are usually employed." But the interest of many persons who were profiting from this practice prevented the passage of such a bill. There was an attempt to limit the practice by a local ordinance of Charleston in 1751. This order declared "that no Inhabitant of Charlestown shall be permitted to keep more than two male Slaves, to work out for Hire, as Porters, Labourers, Fishermen or Handicraftsmen."[60]

A third source of information respecting the value of the slave artisan and the growing effect of his competition with white labor is the evidence contained in laws passed to prevent competition. Laws were enacted in South Carolina in 1712 and 1740 restricting the right of the master in hiring out his slaves unless the latter were under some person's care. It was also stipulated that the owner should receive all the wages earned by the slave.[61] A by-law of the trustees of Georgia, in 1750, forbade any artificer, except coopers, to take negroes as apprentices, or planters to lend or to let out their slaves "to be employed otherwise than in manuring and cultivating their Plantations in the Country."[62] Later, in 1782, Virginia forbade masters to hire out their slaves and receive the pay.[63]

Miscellaneous evidence of the value and efficiency of slave artisans is the testimony of Hugh Jones, in 1724, already quoted.[64] Governor Dinwiddie wrote in 1754 as follows: "I shall look out for Negro Coopers tho' I fear Success as the Owners of such do not care to part with them, but shall do my Endeavour. If you can purchase or hire, I shall be very well pleased."[65] A Virginia advertisement of a lottery, 1767, for disposing of lands and slaves, announced prizes of negro slave artisans with values, and certificates of the same, given by two men who appraised them. One was a "fine sawyer and clapboard carpenter" with his wife and child, valued at £180; another "was as good a sawyer as any in the colony, and understands clapboard work," valued at £100; a third, "A very fine Mulatto woman . . . . [who] understands all kind of needle work," valued at £100; and a fourth, a mulatto woman who was a "very good mantua maker," valued at £100, including her child.[66] On the other hand, there is some testimony to the effect that slave artisans were not efficient. Washington gives us an unfavorable impression of his negro sawyers and carpenters in 1760.[67]

Some advertisements indicate the artisan's degree of skill, in the opinion of the owner at least, or the amount of special training that he had obtained. For example, there were offered for sale "Four negro men sawyers that can whet, set and lay Timbers." Another offer mentions "two compleat Bricklayers—whose abilities in workmanship are inferior to none in this province, of their complexion, being brought up by a person well experienced in that business." More convincing of the possible skill of the negro slave is a "want advertisement": "Wanted in the Country immediately, on Hire by the Month or Year or job, two Negro Carpenters That can frame a Barn of any Dimensions or Plantation Out-Building on Sills." Negro artisans who had served a regular apprenticeship were of course likely to have the most skill in their trade. One such was offered for sale with this description, viz., a negro carpenter who had served seven years to one of the "Compleatest House-joiners in the Province."[68]

But whatever the shortcomings of the slave artisans, the weight of evidence shows that there was a great increase in numbers; that they were of much greater value than untrained slaves; that they were much sought after; that they did compete with free white labor, especially in the towns; and, finally, that they were the most important agency in the rise of plantation manufactures. It is certain also that the negro slave artisan was an important agency in the commercial development of the southern colonies, first, in relation to the necessary manufactures connected with the export of tobacco, rice, and naval stores—the making of staves, hogsheads, and barrels; secondly, in the manufacture of staves and lumber and other forest products for export; thirdly, in the tanning industries—the making of leather for home consumption and for export. He was also a not inconsiderable factor in offsetting the evils of the English commercial system, in helping the planters to diversify farming and occupations, and in helping them to solve the most pressing problem of trade with England—that of avoiding almost certain debt and perhaps bankruptcy. By raising products more valuable than tobacco and manufacturing at home many articles resulting from the new sources of raw material, and by utilizing the natural resources, the tendency to get more and more heavily in debt to English merchants was lessened. Indeed, it is hard to see how the eighteenth-century plantation could have survived if the negro slave had not made his important contributions as an artisan, in the building and other trades, calling for skill in transforming raw materials into manufactured articles. The self-sufficiency of the southern colonies, made necessary by the Revolution, was more successful than it could have been if the negro slave artisan had not been developing for generations before. We may also believe that the relation of the negro slave to the later history of the plantation régime in the southern colonies, in its industrial as well as its agricultural aspect, was greatly influenced by the industrial training the slave received before the Revolution. Finally, we may conclude that the evidence given of the industrial training of the negro slave is important in estimating the development of his intelligence and his capacity for the acquisition of mechanical skill. The industrial discipline which the slave received in the pre-Revolutionary period both prepared the way for his freedom, and no doubt lessened the shock when it came, and laid the foundation for his later status in a modern industrial and agricultural society.

CHAPTER II

RELIGIOUS INSTRUCTION AND CONVERSION OF NEGRO SLAVES[1]

From the time of Christian Rome to a period within the memory of many now living, slavery has flourished in Christian lands and nowhere, in modern times, to such an extent as in our own country. Even before the Revolution probably a million negroes had lived as slaves within the boundaries of the American colonies. But, in spite of the fact that religious motives were so prominent in the settlement of these colonies, and religion was a subject which occupied the thought and effort of private individuals, denominations, missionary societies, and even legislative bodies to an extraordinary degree, most of the slaves lived and died strangers to Christianity, and with religious and moral ideals but little better than those developed under the pagan and superstitious beliefs prevalent in their native-land. With comparatively few exceptions the conversion of negro slaves was not seriously undertaken by their masters. On the contrary, many of them strenuously and persistently opposed the Church of England and the Society for the Propagation of the Gospel in Foreign Parts, the agencies most active in promoting conversion. The conflict between these forces forms an interesting chapter in the history of slavery and Christianity in the American colonies. The following study considers for the most part one aspect only of this struggle, viz., the more direct agencies and forces which promoted or hindered the conversion of the negro slave, and the progress made up to the opening of the American Revolution.

One of the arguments offered in defense of the modern slave-trade was that which justified the enslavement of the negro on the ground that he was an infidel. In the ancient world all men were considered equally capable of becoming slaves; but, with the conversion of the people of Northern Europe to Christianity, the custom of enslaving prisoners of war gradually ceased as between Christian na-

24

tions, though between Christians and Mohammedans the practice continued.[2] Thus at the time when America was first colonized, the opinion was widely held that the inhabitants of an infidel nation could be rightfully made slaves by those of a Christian nation. Some believed that heathens and barbarians were placed by the circumstance of their infidelity without the pale of spiritual and civil rights and that their souls were doomed to eternal perdition.[3] Others, more charitable, brought forward another argument, perhaps to quiet their consciences and enable them to share in the profits of the slave-trade. They declared that the enslavement of the negro was an act of mercy, because only through slavery could large numbers be brought to Christ. Some of the papal bulls of the fifteenth century granted to Catholic princes the privilege of making war on the Saracens and other infidels, for this reason;[4] and European monarchs sometimes allowed companies of discoverers, commercial adventurers, etc., the right to trade in slaves, partly because conversion might thereby be promoted.[5]

This religious sanction for slavery raised many troublesome questions. It appears that some believed that the conversion of a negro to Christianity entitled him to freedom, on the ground that one Christian should not hold another as a slave; others asserted that after conversion he should at least have certain religious privileges that were conferred on other persons because they were Christians or members of a Christian state.[6] The question giving most trouble was that which concerned the effect of conversion or baptism. If proof of heathenism legalized the enslavement of a negro, would his subsequent conversion to Christianity be a reason for enfranchisement? The practice of certain European nations favored enslavement even after conversion. Thus Mohammedan slaves in Spain and Portugal were not often freed when Christianized.[7] The French *Code Noir* of 1685 obliged every planter to have his negroes baptized and properly instructed in the doctrines and duties of Christianity.[8] In Mohammedan states conversion of a slave from a different faith to Islam was not usually a legal cause for enfranchisement.[9] But in England and her colonies many believed that such conversion or baptism should be a cause for manumission. The lawfulness of the enslavement of negroes in England came before the courts on several occasions but the cases are in conflict. A few decisions seem to have been based on the principle that infidel negroes could be held as slaves, but when baptized and domiciled as inhabitants they should be enfranchised.[10] At any rate, there arose in the minds of many American colonists the notion that under English law a baptized slave might claim freedom. Conscientious masters thus found themselves in a dilemma: to deny conversion and baptism would retard Christianization; to favor it might cause them the loss of their property. To avoid this dilemma, some of the colonial assemblies altered the religious sanction for slavery and based its validity frankly upon race. While positively denying that conversion or baptism was a sufficient reason for enfranchisement and insisting that all slaves must serve for life, they at the same time called upon masters to use their efforts to convert slaves to the Christian religion.

Thus between 1664 and 1706 at least six of the colonies passed acts affirming this principle. Maryland (1664) declared that all slaves must serve for life in order to prevent damage which masters might sustain if their slaves pretended to be Christians and so pleaded the law of England.[11] Again in 1671, because some had feared to import, purchase, convert, or baptize negroes or slaves, owing to a belief based on an "ungrounded apprehension that by becomeing Christians they and the Issues of their bodies are actually manumitted and made free and discharged from their Servitude and bondage," it was declared that the conversion or baptism of negroes or other slaves before or after their importation should not be a cause for manumission.[12] A Virginia act of 1667 declared that slaves by birth were not freed when baptized. The preamble states that it was passed because doubt had arisen in the minds of owners of slaves on this point, and "that diverse masters, ffreed from this doubt, may more carefully endeavour the propagation of christianity by permitting children, though slaves, or those of greater growth if capable to be admitted to that sacrament."[13] Virginia now proceeded with the notion that a negro Christianized before importation could not be enslaved for life. By the act of 1670 only those imported by shipping and not already Christians were to be slaves for life.[14] This act was repealed in 1682 because it allowed a Christian slave to be sold "for noe longer time then the English or other christians are to serve," and was thus a great discouragement to bringing in slaves.[15] This act with that of 1705[16] made all imported servants slaves, excepting those who were Christians in their native country or free in some Christian country before their importation, thus practically confining slavery to the negro races. North Carolina, South Carolina, New York, and New Jersey all affirmed the principle by denying that freedom resulted from baptism.[17] Those colonies which do not appear to have taken action were Georgia, Pennsylvania, and Delaware, and all the New England colonies.[18] It is clear, however, that the assemblies in colonies where slaves were most numerous were anxious to remove the doubt respecting the effect of baptism, and at the same time encourage the conversion of slaves.

The forces thus far mentioned promoted to a greater or less degree the conversion of imported negroes, even though they were compelled to live in a state of bondage. For the removal of large numbers from an environment in which paganism and superstition were the ruling forces, even though accomplished through slave-traders, to one in which Christianity prevailed, made probable the conversion of a greater number of negroes than would otherwise have been possible. The removal by legislative action of doubt as to the effect of baptism, and the favorable attitude shown toward conversion by the assemblies, doubtless encouraged some masters to withdraw opposition to conversion. However, as the matter was still uncertain, even after 1704, the opinion of Yorke and Talbot, attorney and solicitor-general, respectively, was asked. They replied (1729) that baptism did not alter the status of the slave.[19]

We may now consider other influential agencies and forces which promoted the conversion of slaves, first, with respect to English official bodies. As early as December 1, 1660, instructions were given by the king to the Council for Foreign Plantations, one of which was:

And you are to consider how such of the Natives or such as are purchased by you from other parts to be servants or slaves may be best invited to the

Christian Faith, and be made capable of being baptized thereunto, it being to the honor of our Crowne and of the Protestant Religion that all persons in any of our Dominions should be taught the knowledge of God, and be made acquainted with the misteries of Salvation.[20]

Instructions to governors of the colonies frequently contained a clause urging them to use their efforts to have slaves Christianized. For example, Governor Dongan of New York was instructed on this point (1686): "You are alsoe with the assistance of Our Council to find out the best means to facilitate and encourage the Conversion of Negros and Indians to the Christian Religion." Similar instructions were given to later governors of New York and other colonies. Culpeper, governor of Virginia, was enjoined in his instructions (1682) to inquire what would be the best means of facilitating the conversion of slaves, but was warned not to throw in jeopardy individual property in the negro or to render less stable the safety of the colony.[21] Some of the governors urged the assemblies to pass bills for this purpose,[22] and used their efforts to promote conversion in other ways. Thus a communication by the governor to the council of Maryland, March 18, 1698-99, called attention to his instructions relating to the conversion of negroes and Indians, and because of information that several hindered and obstructed their negroes from attending church, though baptized, advised that a law should be recommended to the assembly to remedy the evil.[23] The replies of the governors to queries of the Lords of Trade show that some of them reported progress in this work.[24] Through such efforts the assemblies were influenced to pass bills furthering the conversion of negroes, as already pointed out. Some of them also passed acts to prevent masters from working their slaves on Sunday[25] and to prevent them from hindering their slaves attending church on Sunday.[26]

More important than these agencies of the state were the religious denominations and forces which promoted conversion. The Church of England stands first in importance, working through unofficial and official agencies. Morgan Godwyn, at one time a rector in Virginia, published a book in 1680 called *The Negro's and Indians Advocate*. It is a severe criticism of the masters of slaves in the plantations; and in the dedication to the Archbishop of Canterbury the author implores relief "for those Myriads of hungry and distressed Souls abroad . . . . our Peoples Slaves and Vassals, but from whom also the Bread of Life is most sacrilegiously detained."[27] From 1679, the Bishop of London exercised considerable jurisdiction over the Church of England in the colonies, and from this date was active in its interest.[28] He appointed, in 1689, Rev. James Blair as commissary for Virginia, and, in 1696, Rev. Thomas Bray for Maryland.[29] The former urged upon a committee of the House of Burgesses, who had in hand a revision of the laws, a proposition "for the encouragement of the Christian Education of our Negro and Indian Children."[30] The latter, on his return to England in 1700, succeeded in procuring a charter for the S.P.G. (1701), destined to be the most important single agency in furthering the conversion of the negro.[31] He had previously prepared a plan of a society for carrying on work "Amongst that Poorer sort of people, as also amongst the Blacks and Native Indians."[32] The Bishop of London stimulated interest in the conversion of negroes, in 1724, through his queries to the clergy of several colonies,[33] and again in 1727 through three published letters:[34] one to masters and mistresses of slaves; another to the missionaries commanding them to distribute copies of this letter and use their efforts to promote conversion; and a third to "Serious Christians," asking for money to promote the work of conversion among the slaves.

An agency of still greater importance was the missionary society of the Church of England founded in 1701, "The Society for the Propagation of the Gospel in Foreign Parts."[35] From 1702 to 1785 it sent to the American colonies numerous missionaries, catechists, and schoolmasters with instructions to promote the conversion of negro slaves.[36] Indeed, the catechists were appointed for this express purpose.[37] Besides, the society distributed sermons, catechisms, and other literature, to aid the work,[38] and established several schools especially for religious instruction of negroes.[39] Appeals were made by the society for funds to be used for Christianizing the negro, and by 1741 they amounted to about £2,500.[40] The society also prepared a bill, to be offered to Parliament, to oblige masters to cause children of slaves to be baptized.[41] The annual sermons preached before the S.P.G. by noted clergymen of the Church of England were printed, together with abstracts of the proceedings of the society; and both were effective agencies in furthering interest in the conversion of negro slaves.[42]

Other agencies include a society closely allied to the S.P.G., founded in 1723 by Dr. Bray, and called "Associates of Dr. Bray," whose authority was ratified by a decree in Chancery, June 24, 1730.[43] One of its objects was to give religious instruction to negroes and supply missionaries with books to this end. A school for negroes was opened in Philadelphia in 1758, and in 1760 similar schools were established in New York, Newport, Rhode Island, and Williamsburg, Virginia, all of which were in operation up to 1775.[44] Two other societies aided to some extent the conversion of slaves. First, the Society for Promoting Christian Knowledge. It helped to maintain missionaries to the Salzburgers in Georgia (1738–76), who made great efforts for the conversion of slaves.[45] The Society for Promoting Christian Learning sent books, catechisms, etc. (1755–61) to Samuel Davies of Virginia, for distribution among negroes.[46]

We may now consider more in detail the attitude and work of the principal religious denominations as organized bodies. It is obvious that many troublesome questions would arise if Christian slaves were to be granted the same religious privileges as Christian free persons. The religious denominations were confronted with such problems as the following: the right of a church member to hold a slave; the endowment of churches with slaves; active efforts toward their conversion; formal religious instruction; church attendance; attitude toward baptism; admission as communicants in full standing; conduct after admission; grants of other privileges incident to church membership; and the relative responsibility of clergy and masters with respect to many of these particulars. The attitude of the principal religious denominations shows a considerable variety of beliefs and practices on such questions.

The Church of England did not raise the question of the right of its members to hold slaves, denied that there was any inconsistency between Christianity and slavery, and made no effort to emancipate negroes because of religious scruples. Indeed the Bishop of London has declared, in 1727, that Christianity did not make "the least

Alteration in Civil Property; that the Freedom which Christianity
gives, is a Freedom from the Bondage of Sin and Satan, and from
the Dominion of those Lusts and Passions and inordinate Desires;
but as to their outward condition they remained as before even after
baptism."[47] The clergy held slaves[48] themselves, and the churches
accepted them as a form of endowment.[49] On the other hand, the
Church of England made great efforts toward the conversion of
slaves, favored formal religious instruction by both clergy and masters, urged the clergy to persuade masters to allow their slaves to
attend church, and baptized and admitted them as communicants.[50]

Of the various dissenting sects, the Friends alone, before the
Revolution, seriously questioned, because of religious scruples, the
right of church members to hold slaves. The Society of Friends
was the only denomination that gradually forced members who held
slaves to dispose of them or suffer expulsion from the church.[51] It
also favored the conversion of slaves. As early as 1657 George
Fox urged the right of slaves to religious instruction,[52] and in 1693
George Keith advised members to give their slaves "a Christian
Education."[53] A minute of the yearly meeting of Pennsylvania,
1696, urged those who had negroes to be "careful of them, bring
them to meetings, or have meetings with them in their families, and
restrain them from loose and lewd living, as much as in them lies."[54]
The yearly meetings in the southern colonies sometimes raised the
question whether Friends instructed their slaves in the principles
of the Christian religion, for example, in Virginia in 1722.[55] In
North Carolina, 1752, the yearly meeting urged masters to encourage negroes to attend church,[56] and in 1758 it was agreed that meetings should be held at specified times at four designated places for
the benefit of slaves.[57] The New England yearly meeting, 1769,
advised Friends to take them to places of religious worship and
give such as were young "as much learning that they may be capable
of reading."[58] While the official pronouncements of the yearly
meetings indicate a strong interest in the religious welfare of slaves,
in practice, many Quakers held slaves, and it was not until just before the Revolution that severe measures were adopted to disown
such members. Many refused to follow the suggestion of the yearly
meetings and even the elders and ministers were holders of slaves.[59]

George Ross reported in 1727 that the Quakers of his parish in Delaware left their slaves, in respect to instruction in the Christian religion, to "the natural light."[60] Mr. Wetmore declared, February 20, 1727/28, that at Rye, New York, the Quakers in his parish refused to allow slaves religious instruction.[61] It appears, moreover, that slaves were not allowed to participate in the meetings, at least in Pennsylvania.[62]

The attitude of Puritans and Congregationalists as a whole cannot be easily determined, because of the absence of any general representative body or head. Each church might determine for itself all the questions involved with respect to the relation of its members to slaves. There seems to have been little effort among the early Puritans to Christianize them. John Eliot protested against the treatment of negroes in Massachusetts, and, according to Cotton Mather's report, "had long lamented it with a Bleeding and Burning Passion, that the English used their Negro's but as their Horses or their *Oxen*, and that so little care was taken about their immortal Souls." Eliot declared that masters prevented and hindered their instruction, and proposed that those having negroes within two or three miles of him should send them to him once a week for catechizing and instruction.[63] The Congregational clergy held slaves without scruple, and the town of Suffield, Connecticut, even voted (1726) their pastor, Rev. Mr. Devotion, "£20 towards the purchase of his negroes."[64] A few churches seem to have taken action against slavery; for example, that of Newport, Rhode Island (1769), under Dr. Samuel Hopkins.[65] Moreover, slaves were often baptized and admitted to the churches as communicants.[66] However, the fear that freedom might result from baptism is shown by a petition of certain ministers of Massachusetts to the General Court in 1694, asking the passage of a bill expressly denying that baptism conferred freedom, because masters deprived their slaves of this privilege.[67] In Connecticut (1738) there was a meeting of the "General Association of the Colony," at which an inquiry was made whether infant slaves of Christian masters might be baptized in "their masters right: Provided they Suitably Promise and Engage to bring them up in the Ways of Religion." Another inquiry was whether it was the duty of masters to offer such children and promise as provided for in the first query. To both of these inquiries an affirmative reply was given.[68]

The first Presbyterian church in Philadelphia was organized in 1698. A Presbytery was formed in 1705, and rival synods of New York and Philadelphia existed from 1741 to 1758, when they were united. The right of members to hold slaves was not questioned in any of these bodies, nor did they take official action toward the emancipation or conversion of slaves before 1774.[69] Individual clergymen, like Samuel Davies, made efforts to Christianize slaves and urged masters to send them to church and have them baptized. Davies himself baptized and admitted slaves as communicants.[70] The diary of Colonel James Gordon, a Presbyterian of Lancaster County, Virginia, shows that slaves attended the church of Mr. Todd; and that some of them were admitted as communicants.[71] In one case at least, a Presbyterian church was presented with a slave as an endowment.[72]

The Methodists had an early advocate for slavery in the person of George Whitefield, who pleaded with the Georgia trustees in 1751 to allow the introduction of slaves into Georgia. He had no doubt of the lawfulness of keeping slaves and declared that he would consider himself highly favored if he could "purchase a good number of them, to make their lives comfortable, and lay a foundation for breeding up their posterity in the nurture and admonition of the Lord."[73] Wesleyan Methodism was represented by societies formed in Maryland about 1766. The first conference was held at Philadelphia in 1773, attended by Francis Asbury and nine other English preachers acting under due authority from John Wesley, but no action was taken on slavery.[74] Individual clergymen, however, were against slavery, like Freeborn Garrettson, who manumitted his slaves;[75] and, especially, Francis Asbury, who writes in his *Journal*, June 23, 1776, "after preaching . . . . I met the class, and then met the black people, some of whose unhappy masters forbid their coming for religious instruction."[76]

There were comparatively few Baptists and Lutherans in the South before 1774, and fewer still held slaves. We have evidence that one Baptist church in Virginia, in 1758–59, had admitted them as members.[77] In 1766, Mr. Barnett, a missionary of the S.P.G., wrote to the secretary from Brunswick, "New light baptists are very numerous in the southern parts of this parish—The most illiterate among them are their Teachers even Negroes speak in their Meetings."[78] The attitude of the Lutherans is best shown by the Salzburgers who settled in Georgia in 1738. They were at first opponents of slavery,[79] but, owing to the want of suitable white laborers, their pastor Boltzius yielded on the ground that the negro might be given moral and spiritual advantages.[80] He expressed joy when his first purchase proved to be "a Catholic Christian." The slaves were given freedom from labor on Sunday, and other church festivals, nor was labor required which would prevent them from attendance upon any week-day service. One of the plans of Boltzius was to buy a large number of young children and place them in the hands of thoroughly trustworthy Salzburgers for religious instruction. He baptized a number of negro children.[81] Heinrich Muhlenberg and his associates in Pennsylvania also endeavored to give negroes religious instruction.[82]

It thus appears that the dissenting sects were interested to a greater or less extent in the conversion of slaves, and were generally willing to baptize and admit them into their churches. Only the Friends, however, could see any inconsistency in the holding of slaves by church members.[83] Though so many forces in state and church were favorable to the conversion of slaves, progress was nevertheless exceedingly slow, and the results attained at the opening of the Revolution were comparatively meager. Before tracing the actual progress it may be well to examine the reasons for continued opposition to the conversion of slaves, and consider other hindrances which interfered with the work.

With the introduction of slaves in large numbers, pressing problems of an economic, political, and social nature arose, which influenced masters to continue their opposition to conversion. Of great importance was the belief that religious instruction would impair their economic value. As early as 1680, Morgan Godwyn pointed out that the state of religion in the plantation was very low, and asserted that men knew "No other God but Money, nor Religion but Profit."[84] A writer in the *Athenian Oracle* says, "Talk to a *Planter* of the *Soul* of a *Negro*, and he'll be apt to tell ye (or at least his Actions speak it loudly) that the Body of one of them may be worth twenty Pounds; but the Souls of an hundred of them would not yield him one Farthing."[85] Among the principal arguments against conversion of slaves was, first, that it would increase the cost of maintenance. Time would be consumed in instructing them, and especially in their attending church. Sunday labor was common; some masters required their slaves to work on Sunday as on other days, or compelled them to work for their own support on that day, in order to lessen the cost of maintenance.[86] Another and more serious effect of conversion was the alleged change in the attitude and character of slaves. It was asserted that conversion developed notions of religious equality, and made slaves haughty and dissatisfied, and increased the danger of insurrections. The notion was widespread that the converted negro became intractable and ungovernable, because of increased knowledge obtained through religious instruction.[87] A third objection was on social grounds. The belief was common that imported African negroes were hardly above beasts,[88] and the appearance of many negroes must have given ground for such a notion. Savages of the lowest types were quite different in appearance and character from the negro of the present generation, so much changed by infusion of white blood and contact with a Christian civilization. From a social standpoint, association with the imported negro was extremely objectionable. To mingle with him in church, or to receive him on terms of equality at the communion table, was not only undesirable but positively dangerous.[89] Kalm, the Swedish traveler, notes (1748) that masters feared to have their negroes converted because they would grow proud "on seeing themselves upon a level with their masters in religious matters."[90]

Besides the specific reasons mentioned, one must consider those of a more general character. In the colonies where slaves were most numerous, a vital interest in religion was lacking. The form rather than the substance was most emphasized.[91] There was also a lack of clergymen and missionaries to carry on the work, and very often those sent to the colonies were not particularly interested in the welfare of the negro slaves.[92] In the character of many of the clergy in question one sees still other causes for low religious life.[93] Missionaries and clergymen write of the indifference of masters to their own religious welfare.[94] If they were not interested in religion for themselves, it is certain that they would not be anxious for the religious welfare of their slaves. Indeed, this indifference on the part of the masters was the occasion for many of the complaints of missionaries. It appeared in several forms. Sometimes masters did not offer positive objection or opposition, but were so little interested that they would not take the time or trouble to give religious instruction themselves,[95] or encourage their slaves to attend church,[96] or aid the clergyman or missionary by showing interest in the religious life of the slave after his conversion.[97] When the masters were positively hostile,[98] of course nothing could be done by the missionaries. Under such circumstances clergymen, who were willing to give part of their time and effort to religious instruction of slaves, were often afraid even to mention the subject because of the fear of incurring the ill-will of the masters.[99]

A not inconsiderable hindrance to the work was the divided responsibility for religious instruction of slaves. It is evident that this would fall in part on the clergy, in part on the masters. Owing to the large number of negroes, it was usually impossible for the clergyman of a parish to assume the whole burden himself. Bishop Fleetwood's sermon in 1711, and the address of the Bishop of London in 1727, held that masters were responsible for the religious instruction of their slaves.[100] The answers to the latter's queries on this subject (1724) show that the clergy were inclined to place the burden of instruction on their parishioners, while most of the latter, who were not opposed, expected the clergy to do all the work.[101]

Another hindrance to religious instruction of many slaves was their inability to understand, or profit by, the Christian religion, due to mental incapacity, lack of knowledge of the English language, or disinclination to accept a new religion in place of their heathen rites. The question of mental capacity was a matter of some dispute. Many planters, either because of real conviction or for other motives, declared that their negro slaves were only beasts, incapable of instruction, and besides, as some asserted, were without souls.[102] It was quite generally agreed among missionaries that most of the adult imported negroes, "Guinea" negroes as they were often called, could not be converted successfully.[103] A sharp distinction was drawn, however, between this class and those born in the colonies. Not only were the former stupid, but many adult imported negroes failed to learn the English language well enough to appreciate or profit by religious instruction, a fact frequently commented on by the clergy.[104] On the other hand, those born in the country were considered more intelligent, and generally could learn English well enough for such purposes.[105] Perhaps the statement of Mr. Williamson, rector of St. Paul's, Kent County, Maryland (1731), describes a condition on many plantations. He divides negroes into three classes: first, those so grossly ignorant that there was no possibility of successful religious instruction; second, those capable, that is, able to answer questions of the church catechism, but so egregiously wicked as to render baptism ineffectual; third, those duly qualified and of exemplary lives.[106]

The character and environment of the average negro slave was an almost insuperable obstacle to his conversion. One should remember that the negro brought with him from Africa conceptions of morality, truthfulness, and rights of property, usually quite out of harmony with the teachings of Christianity. Then, too, conditions inherent in the slavery system hindered his moral and religious progress, even if he were well disposed toward conversion. Severe punishments, usually the result of his own conduct, excessively hard physical labor, and the practical reduction of the slave to a mere chattel, led to a life of deception in order to avoid labor and punishment.[107] The environment of most slaves was hostile to a normal religious life. There was little direct religious instruction on the plantations, while the conversations which a slave heard and the scenes that were frequently enacted before his eyes, in his one-room shack called "home," were for the most part positively evil influences.[108] The almost universal immoral relations between the sexes, unchecked by laws to safeguard the institution of marriage; indeed, the encouragement of polygamy and fornication, because of the law that the issue of a slave-mother remained a slave—all provided an environment almost as bad as could be imagined.

But even if the factors which have been mentioned had been

favorable to the conversion of the slaves, the physical conditions in
the southern, and to a considerable extent in the middle, colonies,
would have been a great obstacle to the success of this work. The
extent of territory often included in a southern parish,[109] and the
fact that plantations were ordinarily at considerable distances from
each other, made it very difficult for the clergy to visit families, or
for slaves to attend church or assemble easily at one place for religious instruction. Even as late as 1761 a missionary of the S.P.G.
in North Carolina writes that most of the negroes of his parish
were heathen, "it being very impossible for the Ministers in such
extensive Parishes to perform their more immediate Duties in
them, and find time sufficient for those poor Creatures Instructions,
and very few if any of their masters will take the least Pains about
it."[110] Some of the colonies passed acts which hindered the Christianization of slaves, such as laws to prevent them from assembling
in numbers, at places outside their master's plantation.[111] Even
where there were laws to the contrary, the working of slaves on
Sunday[112] was a common practice. In both cases, the opportunity
of the slave to meet for religious purposes was more or less restricted.

Keeping in mind the two groups of factors which promoted and
hindered the conversion of slaves, we may now consider the progress
made before the Revolution. The testimony of Morgan Godwyn
in 1680, and that of David Humphreys in 1730, agree to the effect
that the state of religion in the southern colonies was very low.
If this was true of the white inhabitants, then the situation of the
slaves must have been still worse. A declaration of the House of
Burgesses of Virginia in 1699 denies that religious progress is possible in the case of *imported* negroes, because of the "Gros Bar-
barity and rudeness of their Manners, the variety and Strangeness
of their Language and the weakness and shallowness of their
Minds."[113] In North Carolina, Mr. Taylor reported in 1719 that
masters were on the whole opposed to the conversion, baptism, and
salvation of their slaves;[114] and other missionaries make the same
complaint.[115] The letters from Mr. Thomas, 1703-06, show that
there were about 1,000 slaves in the colony of South Carolina at
this time, but he reports only 4 as Christianized and 1 baptized.[116]
Rev. Mr. Pownal reported in 1722 that there were about 700 slaves

in his parish (Christ Church) a few of whom understood English, but very few "knew any Thing of God or Religion";[117] and Mr. Hesell of St. Thomas Parish wrote in 1723/4 that there were 1,100 negroes and Indian slaves and 20 free negroes in his parish, with "about 12 negroes baptiz'd, some of them free, and some Slaves."[118]

The first extensive survey of the religious conditions of negroes in the southern colonies was made in 1724, when the Bishop of London sent queries to the clergy respecting the condition of the parishes. One of these queries reads, "Are there any infidels, bond or free, within your parish and what means are used for their conversion?"[119] An analysis of the replies from twenty-nine parishes in Virginia shows that slaves were accustomed to attend church in eleven of them, but in most cases only a few were allowed this privilege, largely those born in this country who understood English. Likewise, comparatively few were given religious instruction. According to nine replies a few of the masters undertook the work themselves, and a few allowed the clergy to do so, especially in the case of the more intelligent; but it appears certain that the great bulk of the slaves neither attended church nor received religious instruction. A still smaller number were baptized and made communicants.[120] On the whole it appears that the sentiment of masters toward Christianization of slaves was distinctly hostile in about one-third of the parishes reported, hostile in the remainder for imported negroes and those who understood little English, and favorable for a few of their slaves who they believed might profit thereby. A petition from various persons, urging the Christianization of negro children "borne in this Country," was presented to the House of Burgesses in 1723, but the report of the committee to whom it was referred reads, "Resolved that the same be rejected being at present impracticable."[121]

Replies from South Carolina are available from eight parishes.[122] In St. James (Santee) parish, it is declared that there are many slaves, but only one negro man is mentioned as a Christian. In St. John's parish there were "no means used for their Conversion." In St. Philip's parish there were about 2,000 black and Indian slaves, but "no means are used for their Conversion." In St. James (Goose Creek) parish there were about 2,000 negro slaves, but the rector reports that "the best means are used for their Conversion which the present posture of affairs will admit of which will I hope hereafter have a more prosperous aspect than at present." In Christ Church parish there were about 700 negro slaves "all of them in Infidelity. Both public preaching and private exhortation I have used with their Owners, but all those methods at present are ineffectual." In St. Andrew's parish, though there were a great number of slaves, "all the means I use for their conversion is to show their Masters their obligations, but few or none will be prevailed on." In St. Dennis parish, the rector replied: "All Infidels in my Parish are Bond Servants and their Masters will not consent to have them instructed." In Dorchester, St. George's parish, it is stated, "I have hitherto indeavored in vain to prevail with their masters to convince them of the necessity of having their slaves made Christians." It will be seen that these reports for South Carolina are much more discouraging than those of Virginia or Maryland, a situation that was apparently maintained throughout the colonial period.

From 1724 to 1776 there was less opposition on the part of masters toward both conversion and baptism, and a larger number of conversions and baptisms are reported than in the earlier period. But it must be remembered that in the later period the increase in the slave population was very large, especially by importation. The figures seem to show that there was no very great increase in the proportionate number of slaves Christianized. The letters of Samuel Davies and other Presbyterian ministers in Virginia, 1750–1761, show some progress. Davies reports in 1750 that there were as many as a thousand negroes in Virginia converted and baptized, about one hundred belonging to Presbyterians.[123] In this same letter he writes that he himself had baptized forty in a year and a half, and had admitted seven or eight to full communion.[124] In 1756 he said "the Protestant dissenters lie under an odium in this colony—yet the Negroes in these parts are freely allowed to attend upon my ministry";[125] but he laments "upon the almost universal neglect of the many thousand of poor slaves . . . . who generally continue Heathens in a Christian Country."[126] So a report of a yearly meeting of Friends in Virginia (1764) declared that "more care should be taken to instruct negroes in the Christian religion."[127] Other evidence points in the same direction.[128]

In South Carolina we may judge of progress from a letter of Rev. Mr. Harrison (1759) of St. James (Goose Creek) parish, who said that he had two hundred families in his parish, and his congregation generally consisted of 150 whites and 50 to 60 negroes. His communicants numbered 31 whites and 26 negroes.[129] The inhabitants of this parish were, however, unusually favorable to the conversion of slaves. Rev. Mr. Clark, rector of St. Philip's, Charleston, said in 1757–58 that there was great negligence among white people respecting the religious education of negroes, and laments that there was not one "Civil Establishment in the Colony for the Christian Instruction of fifty Thousand negroe Slaves." He says, moreover, that the duties of the clergy, "besides many other Difficulties and Obstructions" prevent them from remedying the evil.[130] Hewatt writes discouragingly of conditions in South Carolina at the opening of the Revolution. He says that the negro slaves were "excluded in a manner from the pale of the Christian Church"; that the S.P.G. had, a few years before, "no less than twelve missionaries in Carolina with instructions to give all assistance in their power for this laudable purpose; but it is well known that the fruit of their labors has been very small and inconsiderable."[131]

In the middle colonies and in New England we are concerned with a very much smaller number of slaves throughout the period. However, much the same opposition to conversion came from masters,[132] and progress was not marked. Although there were about 1,400 negroes and Indian slaves in New York City (1725/6),[133] the catechist of the S.P.G. writes that from 1732 to 1740 but 219 had been baptized, only 24 of whom were adults.[134] In 1770 30 communicants were reported.[135] The replies[136] made in 1724 from seven parishes in New York show considerable opposition to conversion as in Rye and Staten Island, with very few reported as baptized or as communicants,[137] and later reports do not indicate much improvement.[138] In New England the early period shows negligence,[139] though, after 1730, reports are somewhat more favorable.[140]

This survey of the colonies points to the conclusion that the number of slaves who were even nominal Christians bore a small proportion to the total number, while it is certain that a very much smaller number can be said to have lived Christian lives. It is evident that the comparatively few clergymen and missionaries, who took an interest in the conversion of slaves, could make little impression on the whole slave population. This threw the main responsibility on the masters; but the testimony respecting their general hostility or negligence is almost unanimous, from both the clergy and other witnesses. Moreover, in considering the figures based on reports of the clergy some discount must be made, due to their well-known enthusiasm for favorable accounts of conversion, church attendance, etc., and the fact that many of the baptisms mentioned were those of infants.[141] We should also remember that a Christian life was not a necessary result of this ceremony. Then, too, the tendency of the clergy of the established church to rely on outward forms rather than inward regeneration, as a test of Christianity, is too well known to need comment.[142] Those who described their methods usually laid stress on ability to say the creed, repeat the ten commandments, or the catechism, as the main test for baptism.[143] The actual effect of nominal, or even real, conversion upon the conduct of slaves was in dispute. Many asserted that conversion made them worse than before.[144] On the other hand, there is contrary evidence, though much of this is theoretical rather than concrete.[145] It must be admitted that the conditions which often surrounded the negro slave made it very difficult for him to lead a real Christian life.

It is impossible to assert how many slaves were even nominally converted. David Humphreys, the historian of the S.P.G., reported in 1730 that some hundreds had been converted.[146] Dean Berkeley said in 1731: "The religion of these people [slaves], as is natural to suppose, takes after that of their masters. Some few are baptized, several frequent the different assemblies, and far the greater part none at all."[147] Peter Kalm, the Swedish traveler, declared in 1748: "It is likewise greatly to be pitied that the masters of the Negroes in most of the English colonies take little care, of their Spiritual welfare and let them live on in their pagan darkness."[148]

We must conclude from all the evidence that the struggle between the contending forces had, on the whole, resulted in a victory for those who were antagonistic to the conversion of negroes. John Griffith, a Quaker missionary to Virginia, declared in 1765: "It is too manifest to be denied, that the life of religion is almost lost where slaves are very numerous; and it is impossible it should be otherwise, the practice being as contrary to the spirit of christianity as light is to darkness."[149] If Griffith's observation is true, then the institution of slavery must be considered a primary cause, not only in greatly hindering the conversion of the negroes, but also, where slaves were numerous, in preventing important religious advances among the whites. Thus the heart of the difficulty is apparent. As one missionary states, "It can hardly be expected that those should promote the spiritual welfare of this meanest branch of their families who think but little (if at all) of their own eternal salvation."[150]

The reasons for the failure of the clergy and missionaries to accomplish more have been well expressed by Hewatt in accounting for conditions in South Carolina at the opening of the Revolution. He says:

Whether their small success ought to be ascribed to the rude and untractable dispositions of the negroes, to the discouragements and obstructions thrown in the way by their owners, or to the negligence and indolence of the missionaries themselves, we cannot pretend to determine. Perhaps we may venture to assert, that it has been more or less owing to all these different causes. One thing is very certain, that the negroes of that country, a few only excepted, are to this day as great strangers to Christianity, and as much under the influence of Pagan darkness, idolatry and superstition, as they were at their first arrival from Africa.[151]

It is evident that much of the difficulty lay in the system of slavery itself. The lack of a sufficient number of earnest workers was a second great difficulty. But much greater progress could undoubtedly have been made but for the low state of religion among the masters and the positive hostility to conversion of slaves on the part of a large number of them. One of the chief reasons for this opposition seems to have been economic in character. Thus one can understand how ideals growing out of a desire for material gain triumphed, for the most part, over those religious and moral in character. In explanation of this economic reason it must be recognized that many were convinced that the conversion of slaves would inevitably lead to increased demands from the negro for equality—religious, social, and political—a situation that would not only reduce the economic value of the slave but might seriously endanger those conventions between master and slave which were deemed necessary for effective control. Thus fundamentally the contest between the opposing forces involved, in the opinion of many, the life of the institution of slavery itself, and perhaps the very existence of southern society so far as it was based on this system.

CHAPTER III

ECONOMIC AND SOCIAL INFLUENCE OF THE INDENTURED SERVANT

Could we draw the curtain which conceals the life of prehistoric people, we should see that the servant problem is as old as the human race. Indeed, if it were possible for extremes to meet, cave-dwellers and denizens of twentieth-century skyscrapers would doubtless converse sympathetically on this never-ending problem. Its existence is due to the universal desire of man to use the strength of others for his own profit and pleasure—an unchangeable trait of human nature.

During the colonial period of our history, service was performed in the main by two classes—the negro slave and the indentured white servant.[1] The white servant, a semi-slave, was more important in the seventeenth century than even the negro slave, in respect to both numbers and economic significance. Perhaps the most pressing of the early needs of the colonists was for a certain and adequate supply of labor. It was the white servants who supplied this demand and made possible a rapid economic development, particularly of the middle and southern colonies. In 1683 there were twelve thousand of these semi-slaves in Virginia, composing about one-sixth of the population, while nearly two-thirds of the immigrants to Pennsylvania during the eighteenth century were white servants. Every other colony made greater or less use of them, and it is likely that more than a quarter of a million persons were of this class during the colonial period.[2]

Such a widespread and important institution has great significance for the social and economic history of Europe and America in the seventeenth and eighteenth centuries. Moreover, the story is full of human interest because of methods used to supply the demand, similar to methods in the slave-trade: the classes of people from which some servants were drawn—convicts, paupers, and dissolute persons of every type; the stormy life of many servants, and the

45

troublesome moral and social problems which their presence en-
gendered, such as intermarriage with negro slaves; the runaway
criminal servants, and their influence on moral standards and on
other phases of life in the colonies.

White servitude developed rapidly because of favorable conditions—a large demand for servants coupled with a large supply.
The economic theory of European states in the seventeenth century called for a large population in their colonies, in order that
trade and commerce might develop rapidly. The colonists were to
supply food and raw materials, and the home country was to develop
manufactures. Means, therefore, must be devised, first, to attract
settlers who would develop the economic resources of the colonies,
and, second, to provide them with an adequate supply of labor.
There were vast areas of rich virgin lands, which, in the southern
and middle colonies, were usually granted in a manner to promote
rapid increase of population and extension of cultivated tracts. This
method was known as the "head-right" system. Anyone emigrating
was rewarded with a gift of land—about a hundred and fifty acres.
Since labor was needed to clear and work this land, anyone importing
a servant was entitled to an additional allotment, a "head right."
To induce laborers to emigrate, a similar allotment was promised to
them after each had served a term of years as a servant. Thus free
land solved the two most pressing problems mentioned above.[3]

Fortunately, the enormous demand for white servants came when
economic conditions had created a large supply. In the sixteenth
century, English agriculture was giving way to sheep-raising, so that
a few herders often took the place of many farm laborers. As a
result, the unemployed, the poor, and the criminal classes increased
rapidly. Justices, who were landowners, had the power to fix the
maximum wages of farm laborers. Sometimes they made them very
low, hardly a shilling a day; for the lower the wage the greater the
profits of the tenant farmer, and, therefore, the greater his ability to
pay higher rents demanded by the landowner. Thus, while wages
remained practically stationary, wheat multiplied in price nearly
four times in this period, 1500–1600. In other words, a man worked
forty weeks in 1600 for as much food as he received in 1500 by working ten weeks. To prevent scarcity of farm laborers, the statute of

apprentices (1562) forbade anyone below the rank of a yeoman to withdraw from agricultural pursuits to be apprenticed to a trade. Moreover, the poor laws passed in this period compelled each parish to support its poor, and provided penalties for vagrancy. Thus the farm laborer had no chance to better himself. Conditions were almost beyond description, and in dear years people perished from famine. Sheffield in 1615, with a population of 2,207, had 725 relying on charity, 37.8 per cent of the population. As a result, the colonies were regarded as a convenient dumping-ground for undesirable citizens. Velasco, the Spanish minister in England, wrote his sovereign, 1611, "Their principal reason for colonizing these parts is to give an outlet to so many idle, wretched people as they have in England, and thus prevent the dangers that might be feared of them."[4]

It is evident that if this surplus population could be transferred to the American colonies, both the mother country and the colonists would profit. One of the earliest proposals was made by Sir George Peckham, 1582. He declared that there were such great numbers living in penury and want that they might be willing to "hazard their lives and serve one year for meat, drinke, and apparell only without wages, in hope thereby to amend their estates."[5] It was natural for men and women, in order to secure free transportation to America, to bind themselves by written contract, called an indenture, to serve some individual for a term of years.

There were three main classes of servants.[6] One who entered into such a contract with an agent, often the shipmaster, was called an indentured servant. The shipmaster reimbursed himself, on arrival in America, by selling the time of the servant to the highest bidder. The second class included the "redemptioners," or "free-willers." They signed no contract beforehand, but were given transportation by the shipmaster with the understanding that on arrival they were to have a few days to indenture themselves to someone to pay for their passage. Failing this, the shipmaster could sell them himself. The free-willer then was at a great disadvantage. He had to bargain in competition with many others, and was so much at the mercy of the buyer or shipmaster that laws were passed by several colonies limiting his time of service and defining his rights.

The third class consisted of those forced into servitude, such as convicts,[7] felons, vagrants, and dissolute persons, and those kidnapped or "spirited" away by the so-called "spirits" or "crimps." Convicts were often granted royal pardon on condition of being transported. For example, Charles I, in 1635, gave orders to the sheriff of London to deliver to Captain Thomas Hill or Captain Richard Carleton nine female convicts for removal to Virginia, to be sold as servants. At an early date judges imposed penalties of transportation on convicted criminals and others. Thus Narcissus Luttrell notes in his diary, November 17, 1692, that the magistrates had ordered on board a ship lying at Leith, bound for Virginia, fifty lewd women out of the house of correction and thirty others who walked the streets at night. An act of Parliament in 1717[8] gave judges still greater power by allowing them to order the transportation of convicts for seven years, known as "His Majesty's seven-year passengers," and, in case the penalty for the crime was death, for fourteen years. Those agreeing to transport convicts could sell them as servants. From London prisons, especially Newgate and the Old Bailey, large numbers were sent forth, the latter alone supplying not far from 10,000 between 1717 and 1775. Scharf, the historian of Maryland, declares that 20,000 felons were imported into that colony before the Revolution. At least nine of the colonies are known to have received felons as servants, so that the total number sent was not far from 50,000.[9] Lists of felons ordered transported were often printed in the *Gentleman's Magazine;*[10] one of May, 1747, numbering 887. Remembering this, perhaps, Dr. Johnson said in 1769, "Sir, they are a race of convicts, and ought to be content with anything we may allow them short of hanging."[11]

The colonists became alarmed as early as 1670.[12] At that date Virginia passed an act prohibiting the importation of convicts. The preamble speaks "of the great nombers of felons and other desperate villaines sent hither from the several prisons of England." Later, communications which appeared in the newspapers show great indignation. One writer speaks of the practice as a "vile importation" and comments particularly on the bad moral effects of such persons.[13] Even at an earlier date Lord Bacon had commented on the injustice and fallacy of this policy as follows: "It is a shameful and unblessed thing to take the scum of people and wicked, condemned men to be the people with whom you plant."[14] And Benjamin Franklin, in reply to the arguments of British authorities that it was necessary to get rid of convicts, asked whether Americans for the same reason would be justified in sending their rattlesnakes to England![15] For a brief period Great Britain listened to the complaints of the colonists, confirmed the Virginia Act of 1670, and made it apply to other colonies. But in 1717 Parliament in effect repealed it by the act of that date mentioned above,[16] and, throughout the eighteenth century, convicts were a never-failing source of supply for white servants. In this connection it has been suggested that American genealogists in search of missing data to complete their family tree would find a rich mine of unexplored material in the archives of Newgate and Old Bailey, the latter filling 110 manuscript volumes![17]

The reasons for sending so many convicts were several. It is obvious why Great Britain was particularly anxious to rid herself of this class of her population. Criminals were not only unproductive but entailed a great expense on the country. Economists urged their transportation, while others argued that in a new country many criminals would forsake their old habits and become good citizens.[18] Some of the colonists were certainly not averse to convicts as servants, since their term of service was longer. The committee of trade for New York even petitioned the authorities, 1693, to send them all the prisoners who were to be transported from Newgate.[19] It should be remembered, too, that the word felon in the seventeenth and eighteenth centuries conveyed a different meaning from that at present. The penal code of England in 1600 provided a death penalty for hundreds of offenses, many of which were of a trivial nature,[20] and even just before the American Revolution Blackstone states that there were some one hundred and fifty capital crimes. Thus many persons called "felons" were less objectionable as servants than might be supposed, and there was good reason to expect that a number would become respectable when transported.[21]

One of the most interesting sources of supply was kidnaping.[22] The profits gained by such practices were so great that this developed as a regular business in London and seaport towns like Bristol.

"Spirits" would pounce on all classes of persons and entice them on board ships bound for the colonies, and even children were induced to go by offers of sweetmeats. The county court records of Middlesex[23] give evidence of this practice. A record for November 7, 1655, states that Dorothy Perkins accuses Christian Chacrett, alias Sacrett, "for a Spirit, one that taketh upp men and women and children and sells them on a shipp to bee conveyed beyond the sea, having entised and inveagled one Edward Furnifull and Anne his wife with her infant to the waterside and put them aboard the shipp called *The Planter* to be conveyed to Virginia." Parliament passed an act in 1671 providing a death penalty for this crime.[24]

Analogous to the spirits were the "newlanders," or "soul-sellers." The great German immigration to America in the eighteenth century developed this class of agents, who traveled up and down the Rhine Valley, persuading peasants to sell their belongings and migrate to the colonies. They pretended that they were rich merchants from Philadelphia, dressed in costly clothes, and wore wigs and ruffles. They would seek acquaintance with a merchant in Holland and agree with him upon a sum for every person persuaded to remove. They described Pennsylvania as a land of Elysian fields flowing with milk and honey, where gold and silver could be picked up on the hills, and servants could become independent and live like noblemen. The simple German peasant would often sell his belongings and trust himself to the mercy of the soul-seller. Many were forced to become servants by indenture, because the excessive charges imposed for transportation from the Rhine Valley to the port of departure used up their small capital.[25]

The voyage over often repeated the horrors of the famous "middle passage" of slavery fame. An average cargo was three hundred, but the shipmaster, for greater profit, would sometimes crowd as many as six hundred into a small vessel. Picture to yourself several hundred people of all ages with only six feet by two feet allotted between decks for one adult person, with no privacy whatever, wearing the same clothing for the whole voyage—from four weeks to four months or even more—and often lying flat for whole days at a time when the ship was tossed by terrific storms. Imagine the vile atmosphere in an unventilated space containing hundreds of people, many ill with all manner of contagious diseases, living and dead side by side, without medical attendance, moaning and shrieking, praying and crying, and perhaps crazed by famine and thirst.[26] John Harrower, an indentured servant, describing in his diary a scene between-decks during a storm, says, "There was some sleeping, some daming, some blasting their leggs and thighs, some their liver, lungs, lights, and eyes, and for to make the scene the odder, some curs'd Father, Mother, Sister, Brother." When food ran short it was doled out at the rate of three ounces of bread a day.[27] Mittelberger, an eye-witness, says that spoiled biscuit were given the passengers, "dirty and full of red worms and spiders' nests." When such vile stuff called food was lacking, rats and mice were eaten.[28]

The mortality under such circumstances was tremendous, sometimes more than half of the passengers dying of hunger and privation. Children from one to seven rarely survived. Mittelberger says he saw thirty-two little children thrown into the ocean during one voyage.[29] It must be remembered, of course, that a safe, short passage of thirty days was not uncommon. Still, conditions were so terrible that several colonies passed laws regulating food, the number of passengers to be carried, and care of the sick.[30] Philadelphia and other ports were exposed to constant dangers from contagious diseases. Sickness continued after landing, so that much legislation was necessary respecting quarantine, inspection of vessels, and the building of pesthouses.[31]

When the vessel finally made her port,[32] no one was permitted to leave unless the passage had been paid for. The sick and old always fared worst, the very ones whose misery ought to have been relieved first. Parents were forced to sell their children to service, perhaps never to see them again. Husband and wife were often separated. Children under five were sometimes given away to serve until they were twenty-one. "Soul-drivers" would purchase fifty or more servants from the captain of one of these ships, and drive them through the country like a drove of cattle, offering them for sale to the highest bidder.[33] They were protected, in part, however, first by their indenture, which specified the term of service, lodging, food, and apparel; and, second, by "freedom dues," which were provided for by law, and included such things as clothing, corn, a gun, and sometimes a fifty-acre tract of land.[34]

Most of the servants were unskilled laborers, though many artisans and some in the professions bound themselves to service. The following advertisement in the *Virginia Gazette* for March 28, 1771, will give one an idea of their occupation.[35]

> Just arrived at Leedstown, the Ship *Justitia*, with about one
> Hundred Healthy Servants.
>
> Men, Women and Boys, among which are many Tradesmen—viz. Blacksmiths, Shoemakers, Tailors, House Carpenters and Joiners, A Cooper, a Bricklayer and Plaisterer, a Painter, a Watchmaker and Glaizer, several Silversmiths, Weavers, a Jeweler, and many others. The Sale will Commence on Tuesday, the 2d of April, at Leeds Town on Rappahannock River. A Reasonable Credit will be allowed, giving Bond with Approved Security to
>
> THOMAS HODGE.

The advertisements for runaway servants are numerous,[36] give descriptions of their appearance and dress, mention little peculiarities, and bring before us vividly the personality of these servants. Richard Kinnersley, an English servant-man, had "a pretty long visage of a lightish complexion, and thin-flaxen hair; his eye tooth sticks out over his lower teeth in a very remarkable manner." James Murphy, an Irish servant-schoolmaster, was "somewhat long visaged, with sharp nose, much pitted with the small pox, flaxen hair, reddish beard, sometimes ties his hair behind with a string, a very proud fellow, loves drink and when drunk is very impudent and talkative, pretends much, and knows little, was sometime in the French service and can talk French." Then there was the fat pock-broken tailor with a "hard look," the carpenter who wore his own black hair, the convict servant-woman who could knit and spin, the shoemaker and fiddler who "loves to be at frolicks and taverns and is apt to get in liquor and when so is subject to fits."

The variety of dress was astonishing. We read of cinnamon-colored vests, blue, green, and yellow coats with brass buttons, and breeches with silk puffs. Shoes were of all styles, square-toed and peeked-toed, with buckles and without. An Irish runaway servant-man, Daniel Macdonald, had "a double-breasted cape-coat, with white metal buttons, a little flowered on the top, an ozenbrigs shirt, tow-linen trousers, and an old jacket of a bluish color, good shoes, and large white buckles, had no stockings except he stole them."[37]

The general character of the servants varied in different colonies according to the class from which they came.[38] Of course, not much could be expected of the criminal classes. On the other hand, there were honest artisans and German peasants, seeking a new home for wife and children. The runaway servants represented the worst element, and frequently had stolen horses, clothing, or silver. One was described as "so prodigious a lyer that if observed he may easily be discovered." A tract published in London, in 1708, entitled "The Sot Weed Factor or a Voyage to Maryland,"[39] is a poem by a tobacco agent, Ebenezer Cook, describing the manners and customs of the ruder elements of Maryland society at this date. In picturing a coarse group of female servants who had gathered about the fire-side to play games, he says:

> To fire-side I did repair;
> Near which a jolly Female Crew,
> Were deep engag'd at *Lanctre-Looe;*
> In Night-rails white, with dirty Mein,
> Such Sights are scarce in *England* seen;
> I thought them first some Witches bent,
> On Black Designs in dire Convent.
>
> .   .   .   .
>
> We scarce had play'd a Round about,
> But that these *Indian* Foes fell out.
> D—m you, says one, tho' now so brave,
> I knew you late a Four-Years Slave;
> What if for Planter's Wife you go,
> Nature designed you for the Hoe.

The main work[40] of the servant was to clear the land and cultivate the crop, though artisans, of course, worked at their trades. Boucher asserts[41] that two-thirds of the persons employed as schoolmasters in Maryland just before the Revolution were either indentured servants or convicts. A letter[42] from Washington's overseer complains of the fact that his servants were difficult to manage because of a liking for liquor. The "Sot Weed Factor" makes one of the female servants "who passed for a chambermaid" speak thus:

> In better Times, e'er to this Land
> I was unhappily Trapann'd;
> Perchance as well I did appear,
> As any Lord or Lady here,
> Not then a Slave for twice two Year.

> My cloaths were fashonably new,
> Nor were my Shifts of Linnen Blue;
> But things are changed, now at the Hoe,
> I daily work, and Barefoot go,
> In weeding Corn or feeding Swine,,
> I spend my melancholy Time.
> Kidnap'd and Fool'd, I thither fled,
> To Shun a hated Nuptial Bed,
> And to my cost already find,
> Worse Plagues than those I left behind.

Interesting phases of the institution of white servitude appear in the laws regulating their status.[43] Unlike the slave, the white servant could bring suit for justice. The court could order his freedom or lessen his term of service. It could require the master to provide the servant with medical attendance, see that freedom dues were paid and that he had sufficient food and clothing. On the other hand, his time belonged to his master, and severe work could be exacted. His privileges and freedom of movement were restricted. He could not absent himself from his master without permission. He could be whipped for disobedience. He was not allowed to buy or sell anything without leave. Tavern-keepers could not entertain him or sell him liquor. He could neither marry without his master's consent, nor could he vote or hold office, but he could be sold or seized to satisfy an outstanding debt.

The treatment and condition of servants varied widely in different colonies and at different periods, depending on the nature of the work and the character of the servant and the master.[44] In general, their treatment was better in New England and the middle colonies than in the southern. Harrowing tales of cruelty and abuse of white servants are common, but the same kind of treatment was meted out to servants in England during this period. In the court records of Middlesex County, England, 1673, we find that Thomas Tooner was cited to answer to the charge of inhumanly beating his female servant with knotted whip-cords, so that "the poor servant is a lamentable spectacle to behold." The lash was likewise the usual mode of correction in the colonies. Eddis, writing in 1769–77, declares that servants in Maryland groaned beneath a worse than Egyptian bondage. Runaway servants were severely punished, and elaborate laws were passed to secure their arrest and punish all who aided them to freedom.[45]

Some perplexing moral problems[46] were caused by white servants. The question of intermarriage between servant and slave arose, as well as that of restraining looser relations between these classes. Nearly all the colonies were forced to pass laws to prevent such relations between servants, between free men and servants, and between negro slaves and servants. A great increase of illegitimate mulatto children in the eighteenth century is one evidence of low moral standards. In Virginia, the parish vestry books record large sums expended for the support of such children. Laws were passed to prevent intermarriage of black and white. For example, the preamble of the Virginia Act of 1691 states that it was enacted "for the prevention of that abominable and spurious mixture which hereafter may increase in this dominion as well by negroes intermarrying with English or other white women as by their unlawful intercourse with one another." A Maryland act provided that the children of a servant-woman resulting from intermarriage with a negro slave should be slaves to her master for life. But since unprincipled masters urged the marriage of their servant-women to slaves, the law was repealed. Nevertheless, miscegenation continued.[47]

It is obvious that the economic significance of the white servant was very important. Benjamin Franklin said in 1759, "The labor of the plantations is performed chiefly by indentured servants brought from Great Britain, Ireland, and Germany, because the high price it bears cannot be performed in any other way." Free labor on a wage system was impossible because of both high wages and scarcity of labor. Few would work for hire when land could be had for almost nothing. The certainty of supply, the power of control, its economy, and the large profits resulting, made the system superior to other forms until the negro slave was imported on a large scale.[48] John Pory, of Virginia, wrote in 1619 that "one man by the means of six servants hath cleared at one crop [tobacco] a thousand pounds English . . . . our principal wealth consisteth of servants."[49]

Socially, the white servant was an important factor in helping to build up a landed aristocracy in the South, because he made possible the cultivation of extensive areas of land.[50] But in the course of a few years he became a free citizen and owner of a small estate. Thus was developed a yeoman class, a much-needed democratic element in the southern colonies, while at the same time settlers were secured for the back lands, where they were needed to protect the frontier. Nevertheless, they did not form a distinct class after becoming freedmen. Some were doubtless the progenitors of the "poor white trash" of the South, but it is likely that environment rather than birth was the main factor in producing this class. While comparatively few rose to prominence, yet there are some notable examples to the contrary. Two signers of the Declaration of Independence—George Taylor and Mathew Thornton—and Charles Thompson, the Secretary of the Continental Congress, had all been white servants. It is certain also that many became successful planters, and perhaps the majority, respectable and desirable citizens.

On the whole, the effects of the institution were beneficial. Great Britain was relieved of her undesirable citizens; many German peasants were given the opportunity to better their condition; the colonies were supplied with laborers for the rougher work, and servant-artisans supplied wants impossible to meet in any other way.[51] That the white servant was useful, even after the Revolution, is seen by the fact that large numbers continued to come to Pennsylvania, where the institution existed until 1831. By that time various causes were leading to its abolition. Opposition developed in Europe because of the drain of the labor supply to America. In the South the negro slave had tended to supplant the white servant, while in the North labor-saving machinery was doing so much of his work that he was no longer needed.

PART II

FREE EDUCATION FOR POOR CHILDREN AND
APPRENTICES IN NEW ENGLAND

CHAPTER IV

INFLUENCES PROMOTING FREE EDUCATION

The study of the origin and evolution of American institutions, though interesting and profitable, is beset with numerous difficulties. For some were inherited directly from Great Britain or the Continent and reproduced with but little or no change; others were more or less modified by the new environment; still others were essentially new products devised to meet needs and conditions often peculiar to some particular colony or section.[1]

American colonial education well illustrates these principles. Some of its main features, together with the means employed to carry on the educational process, were a direct inheritance from Great Britain, Netherlands, or other European countries. The colonies were settled by civilized peoples who were inheritors of educational ideals, institutions, and practices, which had been developing for a thousand years or more.[2] Among these may be mentioned the belief that the important subject matter to be employed in the later educational processes should be Latin and Greek, keys to the literature of the peoples who used these languages. From the medieval world came the notion that education should be, normally, under control of the church and clergy, and that the inculcation of religious ideals and beliefs should be one of the principal motives in education.[3] The Renaissance intensified the former and the Reformation the latter of these two ideals. With the opening of the modern era, the notion developed more rapidly that it was the duty of the state to control or aid education in the interest of religion or good citizenship,[4] the former, in particular, where there was a close union between church and state; the latter, because of a growing belief that education was an insurance against ignorance or a relapse to barbarism and a necessary means to preserve and pass on to future generations the experience and knowledge of the race. Still another inherited notion was that of private philanthropy. From an early date, generous individuals had dedicated a portion or all of their wealth

59

to the cause of education.[5] The motive was sometimes religious, sometimes secular. Besides these more general principles, the colonists inherited, not only many of the forms of organized institutions for education, such as the grammar,[6] parish, and charity school, but also the machinery for administration, such as charters, statutes, officials, etc. To a great extent they were dependent on imported teachers, English and European notions of the curriculum, methods of instruction, textbooks, educational theories, etc.[7]

In the case of other features of colonial education, the original forms were often modified by the new environment. For example, chartered schools endowed with lands, so common in England, were less important in the colonies, because land was plentiful, cheap, and failed to produce an income sufficient to defray school expenses. Again, the apprenticeship system was unimportant in England as a means of education, but in certain of the colonies it was, for a time, almost the only means whereby poor children could obtain the rudiments of education. An example of one new feature was the principle set forth in the educational act of Massachusetts, 1647, that when a territorial division, the town, had a specified number of families, it must set up certain types of schools. This principle was unique, for never before had any legislative body enacted just such a law and enforced it with suitable penalties. Of the principles mentioned, those inherited were not reproduced by all the colonies in exactly the same form. Indeed certain features prominent in one colony do not appear at all in others. Again, some were modified by one colony more than by another.

During the colonial period, there were certain forces which hindered uniformity in educational development, such as diverse racial elements, environment, economic conditions, and religious beliefs. We must consider the variety of institutions, customs, and ideals brought over by the English, Dutch, Scotch-Irish, and Germans, the great planter of the South, the patroon of New Netherland, and the small farmer of New England. We must remember the antagonism between Puritan and Quaker, Anglican and Presbyterian, Lutheran and Catholic, and note that all these forces tended to produce a diversity which would hinder educational unity, particularly in certain of the colonies.

On the other hand, there were forces promoting uniformity in education. Within each section, environment, economic conditions, and intermarriage tended to modify racial differences. Political and judicial control were in the hands of the English, and hence each colony was under one system which tended toward a common type. Most of the printed matter produced in the colonies as well as that imported was in the English language. The English occupied the seaboard while other racial elements were largely in the back country—the frontier. Thus the former controlled the best lands, the slavery system, trade and commerce, with the opportunity to unify diverse elements through laws, courts, newspapers and books, and higher institutions of learning.

Our conception of what factors may have influenced the progress of education before the Revolution is largely determined by our notions of what is meant by the term "education." A conventional view would confine the subject to the origin and description of organized institutions of learning, subject matter and methods of instruction, and the theory or philosophy underlying the educational systems. Often histories of education consider little more than this last phase. But they should be called, more properly, histories of educational theory. They bear much the same relation to educational history that the history of economic theory bears to economic history.

To explain satisfactorily the origin and evolution of all phases of education in the American colonies, one must consider many influences, such as physical, racial, economic, political, social, literary, intellectual, and particularly religious factors—all of which tend to perpetuate, modify, or change prevailing practices. The ideals of the teaching force, the methods and textbooks used, and the curriculum as a whole are, to a large extent, the product of ideals and achievements of previous generations. It is clear, then, that to enumerate the factors that influence the progress of education one must take into consideration a great variety of facts and forces. This view implies that educational development is dependent on all the factors which influence human life and progress.

The most important contributory factors which influenced the educational development of each of the American colonies were

ethnic or race elements—including inherited ideas or practices and
the spirit of the race; environment—including geographical conditions, climate, and physiography; economic conditions—including
distribution of land and population, industrial organization, and
economic well-being; religion—including the relation of church and
state, religious motives for education, and the influence of religious
sects in promoting and controlling education; political conditions—
including the relation of the state and education, the influence of
forms of local government, such as town or parish; social conditions—including home influences, social classes and groups; intellectual conditions—including the proportion of educated men
to the total population, average intelligence of the race, and the
means of distributing knowledge, such as printing, libraries, and
newspapers. The progress of education is dependent on all these
factors and others not mentioned. In short, to understand its real
development, we must know the reaction of geographical, economic,
religious, political, social, and intellectual influences on education
in its narrower meaning. In the light of what has been said, it is
obvious that any detailed study of colonial education requires a
survey of Old World social and intellectual conditions, as well as
educational theories and practices, particularly in England. We
must know what notions and traditions the colonists started with,
in order to determine how far the educational institutions of the
New World were reproductions, how far modified by new conditions,
and what features were wholly new. Then the conditions within
each group of colonies must be studied to determine the features
of the educational system common or peculiar to each, with the
reasons therefor, how far the groups influenced each other by law
or custom, and the processes by which educational uniformity was
attained, or for what reasons variations persisted.

We may now consider in detail the more important factors
which influenced the beginnings of public education in New England. The number and character of its educational institutions,
as well as the rapidity with which they were established, warrant
a careful study of the conditions and forces which account for
such a development. By 1660 three of these colonies, Massachusetts, Connecticut, and New Haven, had passed a remarkable

series of educational acts and established agencies for education which, in comparison with other colonies at the same date, were truly extraordinary. Indeed, we may say that by this date several essential principles of elementary and secondary education had been formulated and the foundation of the American public school laid.

To understand the reasons for and nature of these institutions, one needs to keep in mind those more general influences already mentioned, viz., inherited features from the ancient and medieval world, intensified by the Renaissance and the Reformation, the philanthropic movement in England, 1550-1640, with the attendant increase in the civil control of education, the inherited types of educational institutions, methods, organization, and administration, and the content and theory of education. But such inherited notions and characteristics did not of themselves always lead to further activity, else it would be difficult to account for the educational history of Plymouth or Rhode Island, where progress was so slow. We must consider, then, those special conditions which influenced the character of public education in New England.

One group of important factors centers about the personality and character of the settlers. This involves such questions as their general motives in migrating, relative strength of contending motives after settlement, average intelligence, and the proportion of educated leaders, particularly clergymen. Then one must consider how far harmonious or contending religious, social, and political groups aided or retarded the development of public education, and how far the forms of local political and economic organization made it easy to legislate for the common good in educational matters. It will be found that even in such a homogeneous population as that of New England, these principles varied not only in the different colonies but even in the different towns of the same colony. Another important group of factors centers around environment and economic conditions—climate, extent of territory, the character and distribution of the land, nature of occupations, and particularly the distribution of population in relation to centers where educational agencies could be established and intelligence easily transferred.

Bradford and Winthrop have told us the reasons for the early settlement of New England. Suffice it to say, they go deep into

English history, religious, economic, and political. That great upheaval of the sixteenth century, the Reformation, bred religious and political dissent from established authority in church and state. It placed emphasis on the worth of the individual man and encouraged the right of private judgment, especially with respect to the interpretation of the Scriptures. Sectarianism, a product of this principle, became one of the strongest forces which promoted intellectual development. For the desire to read and study the Bible and to have their children brought up in the faith of their fathers was one of the most important characteristics of the dissenters. The struggle between churchmen and dissenters and the flood of controversial literature which it brought forth furnish evidence of the increased mental activity resulting from sectarianism. This was intensified by the determination of such men as James I and Archbishop Laud to put down insurgency in church and state. Thus we can understand why one of the principal motives actuating the New England settlers, both before and after their settlement, was religious, and how closely it was related to education.

First in importance was the Massachusetts Bay colony. In the number, character, distribution, and quality of her educational institutions, she was pre-eminent, and established precedents which greatly influenced other colonies. The Puritan migration to Massachusetts was unique in colonial history for several reasons. The racial stock was almost pure English, for the most part of one sect, and of excellent quality. Rev. William Stoughton, in his election sermon of 1668, declared that "God sifted a whole Nation that he might send choice Grain over into this Wilderness."[8] Again, the proportion of educated leaders was higher than in any other colony. Over one hundred graduates of Oxford and Cambridge settled in New England before 1650, most of whom acted as pastors of churches. The progress of education depends in large part on the ability and energy of leaders, and in this respect Massachusetts was most fortunate. Nearly three-fourths of these educated clergymen were from the University of Cambridge. More than twenty of them were educated at Emanuel College, Cambridge, and were contemporaries of such men as John Robinson,

Oliver Cromwell, and John Milton, who had also received a portion of their education in this institution. Among these leaders were John Cotton, Nathaniel Ward, Thomas Shepard, and John Harvard. John Winthrop, the elder, attended Trinity, and Henry Dunster, the first president of Harvard, graduated from Magdalen College.[9] The migration to New England to 1643 is commonly reckoned at about 20,000, or 4,000 families. Thus there would be about one person in 40 families, or one for every 200 or more emigrating, who had received university training. It is estimated that Massachusetts had a population of about 9,000 in 1639.[10] Moreover, a large proportion of her university men lived within a short distance of Boston or Cambridge. It is safe to say that such a concentration of educated men in a new settlement has never been duplicated. They were the intellectual leaders who gave the community its educational ideals. They doubtless influenced the passage of the educational acts and urged their enforcement. Knowing these facts, we can understand why a public school, a printing press, and a college were established in Massachusetts before 1640.

Unlike the leaders of the planter aristocracy of the southern colonies, the religious leaders of the Massachusetts Bay colony believed that the state was responsible for the education of the rising generation without respect to particular classes. Through the act making church membership the basis of the franchise,[11] their views would greatly influence legislation. It should be noted that almost without exception it is stated or implied in the early educational acts of New England that the principal reason for their passage was the desire to promote religion. By the acts compelling all persons to support and attend church, the people of the towns were brought together weekly. The ministers, so generally university men, had unusual opportunities to influence them in favor of public education. This weekly meeting also furthered social solidarity and community interest—an aid to public support of education.

As environment and general economic conditions have always played an important part in molding human institutions, so we find that these factors had an influence upon education in New England. It so happened that the climatic conditions, physiography, the land, and economic forces all favored the group plan of settlement. The severe winters, poor soil, and lack of extensive areas of fertile land prohibited the production of great staple crops. The environment rather favored a society of small farmers, fishing communities, traders, and manufactures, especially as the population increased and the margin of productivity of the land diminished. These factors influenced settlement in groups rather than as individuals.

Another important factor aiding the cause of public education in Massachusetts was the land system. Methods of distributing land have had a powerful influence on the development of American institutions.[12] The formation of a community group, occupying a comparatively small area, was a natural consequence of the desire of the people to be near each other because of the habit of living in villages in England. It was further intensified by the strong religious motive which led to weekly meetings at the church as well as the need of protection from the Indians. The General Court of Massachusetts favored the principle of group settlement because it made easier the enforcement of the religious and moral principles involved in the Puritan ideals of a spiritual commonwealth.

These tracts of land, or townships, averaged about forty square miles each and were usually laid out contiguous to each other. Individuals were compelled to settle within the boundary of one of them.[13] Ordinarily, a small group of men petitioned the General Court for a township; if the petition was granted, the "proprietors," as they were called, could admit others persons and divide up the land as they wished. Usually the greater part of the land was held in common, undivided, until needed. This common land was of great importance, because it could be used for the common good, and, in the early period, portions were often granted to aid in the support of religion and education.

Still further, this land system promoted the distribution of population, compelling a density quite remarkable when compared with that in the southern colonies. This aided in the development of the principle of taxation of all the people for the support of education. The difficulty of securing agreement on matters of public interest in towns with a widely scattered population, as was often the case in the eighteenth century, will be a subject for later comment.

The system of local government also had much influence on educational development and warrants close study. Indeed, the town meeting promoted many aspects of community life—political, religious, social, economic, and intellectual. The word "town" was a name applied to a territorial division containing a group of people who had associated themselves for political, religious, and other purposes in order to satisfy their needs. The state gave this group corporate existence and powers of great importance in promoting public education.[14]

Certain acts passed by the General Court between 1630 and 1638 have an important bearing on the powers of the towns with respect to the subject of education. Up to 1636 the groups of people who had associated themselves at various places met in extra-legal assemblies of their own and passed orders for the common good. At this time, March 3, 1635/36, the General Court sanctioned the town system of government by passing an order giving particular powers to towns, such as the power to dispose of lands, make orders for the well-being of the town, lay fines and penalties for breach of orders, choose officers, etc.[15] In 1638 it ordered that every inhabitant should be liable to contribute to all charges both in church and commonwealth, "whereof hee doth or may receive benefit"; and every inhabitant not contributing in proportion to his ability to all common charges, "as well for upholding of the ordinances in the churches as otherwise," should be compelled to do so by assessment and distress.[16] It thus appears that the towns had ample powers conferred upon them to provide for public education if they were so inclined.

By 1642, when the first educational act was passed, twenty-one towns had been founded in Massachusetts and the population had increased to about 9,000.[17] Most of them had a church and a settled minister who was a university graduate. By this date children were doubtless becoming numerous and growing up with meager opportunities for even elementary education. In 1636 the General Court appropriated £400 toward the founding of a college,[18] and two years later John Harvard bequeathed half of his estate for its advancement.[19]

The influence of the educated ministers already mentioned in the founding and nourishing of Harvard College in its early history is of great importance in accounting for the development of elementary and secondary education in Massachusetts, and even in New England as a whole. It was realized that the group of clergymen educated àt Cambridge and Oxford would for the most part pass away in a generation. Accordingly there was great fear that an illiterate or uneducated ministry would take their places.

> After God had carried us safe to *New England*, and wee had builded our houses, provided necessaries for our liveli-hood, rear'd convenient places for God's worship, and setled the Civil Government; One of the next things we longed for, and looked after, was to advance *Learning*, and to perpetuate it to Posterity; dreading to leave an illiterate Ministry to the Churches, when our present Ministers shall lie in the Dust.[20]

A failure to found a college within a generation or two would thus have been a great calamity from the Puritan standpoint. Not only would educated leaders soon be lacking, but a great stimulus toward the founding of public elementary and secondary schools would have been wanting. It will be seen later that the passage of the Massachusetts Act of 1647 was greatly influenced by the desire to provide a school system which would supply the college with students who could be fitted to carry on the work of the group of clergymen educated in England.

But in spite of the extraordinary number of favorable influences and factors, educational progress was slow up to 1647, not only from our standpoint, but, as the evidence shows, quite unsatisfactory to the leaders interested in a more rapid advance. Yet it is the period before 1647, the date of the first act of Massachusetts which compelled towns to set up schools, that needs careful study. For a number of them had, by that date, established some of the important principles of the American public-school system.

CHAPTER V

THE BEGINNINGS OF FREE PUBLIC SCHOOLS[1]

The terms "public school" and "free school" have had various meanings historically. In many cases the English endowed grammar schools were "public" only in the sense that they were open to all classes, and "free" only for a limited number of pupils. When these terms were transferred to New England they were used sometimes as in England, and at other times in a quite different sense. In tracing the beginnings of our system of public education in this chapter, we are concerned primarily with the action of New England towns in their corporate capacity; as the inhabitants voted in town meeting respecting the establishment, management, and support of town schools. A public school in this sense involved, first, establishment by the town; that is, initiating it by vote in town meeting; second, management by the town either directly or by delegating power to the selectmen or appointed committees; third, support by means of town property—often public lands set aside as an endowment for schools, or funds obtained by taxes levied on all or a portion of the property in the town. It will be seen later that the early history of public schools shows many combinations involving mixed systems of public and private establishment, management, and support. There were, of course, other agencies for education besides town schools, such as privately endowed schools, private schools, private tutors, education through the apprenticeship system, and parental education. But such agencies are reserved for future treatment.

Although some of the essential principles of our public-school system were in operation in New England before 1647, it is difficult to determine precisely their origin and evolution. At this date there were six separate colonies,[2] containing at least sixty towns,[3] in all stages of development. Some were mere clearings in the forest —small frontier settlements; others were in a later period of growth, but still in the early stages of their institutional beginnings, with a population of perhaps thirty or forty families each, or even less. Scarcely one-third of the towns could have had as many as one hundred or more families, and nearly all of these were situated on or near the coast.[4] How many are known to have established and supported town schools before 1647?

The principal original sources for this information are town records. But here, as is often the case, the historian is confronted with records that are unsatisfactory. Some are missing, others imperfect, and still others survive as incomplete copies of originals. We thus have good reasons for believing that surviving records reveal the minimum rather than the maximum extent of the educational activity of the towns in this period. Nevertheless, we must base our conclusions only on evidence supported by existing data. With respect to Massachusetts, it appears that out of thirty-two towns established, the records of at least six are entirely missing for this period, while others are imperfect. Of the twenty-six towns which have records, nineteen fail to record action on schools before 1647. This leaves only seven in which there is a record of a town vote on this subject.[5] In New Haven colony we find only two towns, in Connecticut only one, and in Rhode Island only one, in which there are votes concerning schools. Not a single town in Plymouth, Maine, or New Hampshire, took action before the date in question.[6] We have then only eleven towns to consider.[7]

There are many interesting questions concerning the origin of certain features of our public-school system. For example, one would like to know which town first established and opened a public school, and supported it in whole or in part out of public property or by the levy of a tax on a portion or all of the property-holders; which first appointed a schoolmaster and fixed his salary, or established a school committee; which first made the school free in part, or for all classes, etc. Then there are other questions, such as those involving the development of administration, supervision, and support; the content of the curriculum, and the means taken to make public education effective and general.

But there are numerous difficulties which hinder satisfactory answers to such questions besides the lack of complete data already mentioned. Would a mere proposal for a town school, or the date

set for its opening, or proof that it was actually in operation, mark
the date of its establishment? A school might be established by
a vote in a regular town meeting, but its support and management remain wholly in private hands; or it might be privately established and receive occasional aid from the town. Would a voluntary contribution, decided upon in a town meeting, but unenforced,
warrant the assertion that a school had been established by the
town and was supported by public taxation? Is it proper to speak
of a "free school" which was free only to the poor, or which derived
a considerable portion of its support from tuition fees? In the brief
account of the eleven schools, which follows, there will be illustrations of these problems. We shall consider what educational
principles were established and endeavor to award credit to the
towns which were responsible for them.

April 13, 1635, the town of Boston voted that "our brother
Philemon Pormont, shalbe intreated to become scholemaster, for
the teaching and nourtering of children with us." With no subsequent vote on this particular matter, we cannot assert that the
school was opened, or, if opened, that it was supported by the town.[8]
Indeed, there is no vote respecting a town school for nearly seven
years.[9] January 10, 1641/2, it was voted, at a general town meeting,
that "Deare" Island, granted to the town by the General Court in
1634/5,[10] should be improved "for the maintenance of a free schoole
for the Towne" or for other purposes, "the sayd schoole being sufficiently Provided for."[11] The island was not rented until December
30, 1644, and then for three years only at the rate of £7 a year.[12]
These votes mark a change in policy on the part of the town, and
show that the previous method of support had become unsatisfactory. The principle of granting public land as a permanent endowment for education had been one of the main sources of support
in England, and was now being tried out in New England, in several
towns, even before Boston adopted the plan. A few weeks before the
vote to rent the island, the selectmen, at one of their meetings,
ordered the constables to pay to Deacon Eliot (one of the selectmen)
for Mr. Woodbridge, "eight pounds[13] due to him for keeping the
Schoole the Last yeare."[14] This also indicates a change of policy and
shows that the town was assuming more responsibility for support

of the school. It is uncertain from what source this money came, though the order seems to indicate some contract with the school-master, whereby the town through the selectmen had agreed to grant him a stipulated sum, perhaps in part payment for his services. The money was probably drawn from general funds obtained by taxes levied for town purposes.[15] Yet it is possible that it represents a voluntary contribution, collected by the constables. Winthrop has a note on school support under date July 3, 1645, which has often been quoted, but part of which is not confirmed by other evidence. His version is:

> Divers free schools were erected as at Roxbury (for maintenance whereof every inhabitant bound some house or land for a yearly allowance forever) and at Boston (where they made an order to allow forever 50 pounds to the mas-ter and an house, and 30 pounds to an usher, who should also teach to read and write and cipher, and Indians' children were to be taught freely, and the charge to be yearly by contribution, either by voluntary allowance, or by rate of such as refused, etc., and this order was confirmed by the general court . . . .). Other towns did the like, providing maintenance by several means.[16]

Neither the town records of Boston nor those of the selectmen con-tain any such order, nor is there any such reference in the records of the General Court at this date; nor is there any evidence of the appointment of an usher, or more than one teacher, until 1666.[17] An order was made in 1650 to pay "Mr. Woodmansey, the School-master," £50 by rate, but no usher is mentioned.[18] There is, there-fore, doubt concerning Winthrop's statements. Apparently he has confused events of a later date with those of 1645 or before. It should be noted that he says nothing of the rental of Dear Island, which, according to the town's vote of three years before, might be improved for the use of the school, and which was actually rented six months before the date of Winthrop's entry.

The records fail to show that the town of Boston appropriated any funds for the support of the school between 1635 and December 2, 1643. There is, therefore, very meager evidence to substantiate the claim that the town of Boston, in its corporate capacity, sup-ported the first public school in America. We are, therefore, forced to the conclusion that its support must have arisen from private sources, and that Mr. Pormont and Mr. Maud, assuming that the school was in operation in this period, were maintained in the manner common in such cases, by contributions[19] and tuition fees.

On June 3, 1636, the town of Charlestown voted as follows: "Mr. Wm. Witherell was agreed with to keepe a schoole for a twelve monthe" to begin August 8, and have £40 "this year."[20] February 12, 1637/8, a committee was appointed by the town to settle Mr. Witherell's wages "for the yeare past in pt. and pt. to come."[21] These two items indicate that the town established, opened, and supported a town school. The agreement is definite, including the salary and the date of beginning and ending the service—a full year. The town assumed responsibility for payment of the salary, and appointed the first committee—the germ of the school committee—in any New England town to manage school affairs. The power to settle the wages due for work already done and work to be done is good evidence that the school had been in operation for a considerable period and was to be continued.[22] If kept a year from August 8, 1636, as the first vote provided, for which, however, we have no direct evidence, and for the "yeare past," viz., from August 8, 1637, as the second vote indicates, the school would have been in continuous operation for eighteen months. No other New England town can show as good evidence as Charlestown on these points within the dates mentioned. The exact method of raising the salary is not mentioned, but both votes indicate that the money was collected and administered by officials appointed by the town. On January 20, 1646/7 the town adopted a more complex system of support. It was agreed "that A Rate" of £15 should be "gathered of the Town towards the schoole for this yeare"; secondly, that £5 due the town for rent of Lowell's Island should be paid for the use of the school by the town; thirdly, that the town's part of "Misticke Ware" should be appropriated "ffor the Schoole fforever."[23] This vote is important, for it is the first recorded in Massachusetts which provides for raising a definite sum by rate; viz., by taxation to be levied, presumably as other taxes, on all property-holders. In the margin of the record we find the words, "Allowance granted for the Towne Schoole,"[24] additional evidence of the use of this important principle of school support. It should be noted also that Charlestown voted to open her school August 8, 1636. There is no evidence that the Boston vote of 1635 resulted in the opening of a school. The date of the subscription for a free school in Boston was August 12, 1636, with no proof of the date when it was opened. Therefore, the date set for the opening of the Charlestown School was four days before the meeting of the richer inhabitants of Boston, who subscribed for a free school. Note also that the vote of Charlestown was taken in town meeting more than two months before this agreement of private individuals was made.

On May 20, 1639, the town of Dorchester voted to impose an annual rent of £20 forever on "Tomson's" Island,[25] to be paid by every person having property there, and proportionate to the amount held by each, toward the maintenance of a school. The sum mentioned was to be paid to a schoolmaster, chosen by the freemen, to teach "English, latin and other tongues, and also writing." The elders and seven men (selectmen) were given power to decide whether "maydes shalbe taught with the boyes or not." A refusal to pay the rent imposed subjected the owner to a levy by distress or a forfeit of his land.[26] On February 7, 1641/2, because of the difficulty of collecting rent from no less than "Sixscore or theraboute," and because the rent when collected was not alone "sufficient maintenance for a Schoole, without some addicon thereunto," the owners bequeathed the island to the town, "Towards the Maintenance of a free schoole in Dorchester aforsayd for the instructinge and Teaching of Children and Youth in good literature and Learninge."[27] It was to be let to not more than ten persons, by the inhabitants or their agents, for its full value; and the sum realized was to be paid only for the use of the schoolmaster, a condition stipulated by the donors. On March 14, 1645/6, rules and orders were presented to the town for the government of the school and confirmed.[28] Three men, called wardens or overseers, chosen by the town for life, were made a permanent committee to manage the school; viz., to collect and lay out its income and account for the same to the town, supply the schoolmaster, with the consent of the town, pay his wages, and keep the schoolhouse in repair. The support was to come from the "school stock," or in case of need the wardens might "repayre to the 7 men of the Towne for the time being who shall have power to taxe the Town," to an amount sufficient to pay for the repair of the schoolhouse. They were to provide firewood for the school and tax the scholars for this purpose. Finally, they were to see that the schoolmaster instructed all pupils sent to him, whether their parents were "poore or rich not refusing any who have Right and Interest in the Schoole."[29]

The vote of 1639 thus provided for a permanent school, with the amount and method of support definitely fixed. The town did not grant its own public land at this date or provide for the taxation of persons who might later become inhabitants of the town. Indeed, the levy did not fall necessarily on all the property-holders in the town at this date. It may be regarded as a forced contribution imposed on all the owners of the land by a majority vote in town meeting, the owners being bound by the town vote to pay the contribution even if later they were disinclined to keep the agreement. It is perhaps reasonable to call this a species of public support, especially in view of the fact that refusal to pay subjected the owner to a levy by distress or forfeiture, as in the case of failure to pay other taxes, and because a large number of the inhabitants held the land in question. But the case lacks certain of the important elements of real public support. On the other hand, however, we must bear in mind that this plan was a failure. The deed of gift, February, 1642, by the proprietors of the island, was a voluntary contribution, and its tendency was to relieve property-holders to some extent of a possible annual tax for school support, since the income from the rent of the island was to be used for the main support of the school. This gift was not made by a vote in town meeting, but was a bequest of land owned by certain individuals. Although there were at least 120 who had rights in the island at this date, only 71 signed the document (about 60 per cent of those who were owners) conveying the land to the town. Between 1642 and 1647, then, the school at Dorchester was a privately endowed school, not supported by public taxation, and not even endowed by the town with its own property.[30] The gift was made necessary because of neglect or refusal of some to pay their dues, and perhaps the disinclination of the town to levy by distress. No provision was made by the town within these dates for additional income, except the right of the selectmen to lay a tax for the repair of the schoolhouse if requested to do so by the wardens. We have no evidence that such a tax was laid. Indeed, there seems to have been little inclination to raise money by taxation, even after the town lost the island in 1648 by a decision of the General Court. In a petition (1648) for more land, the town complained that the school was "like to faile" for want of land to support it.[31] The school was a town school, because managed by the town. It was public, open to all classes, and, in theory at least, was free. But provision was made for a tax on pupils for firewood, and the complaint in 1648 that the school was "like to faile" does not indicate that town support had developed much by that date. We have no record of the amount received from the rental of "Tomson's" Island but, as has been seen, Dear Island, Boston, was let at only £7 in 1644, and Lovell's Island, Charlestown, for £5, apparently, in 1647. It is quite possible even that tuition fees or gifts were resorted to, to help support the school in this period.

The method of management by a permanent committee, wardens or overseers, was distinctly English, and similar committees, "feoffees," were proposed by both Dedham and Ipswich, before Dorchester.[32] The wardens may be considered a type of school committee, though not apparently the source of the town school committees developed later. While the town delegated certain powers to this body, it took care to reserve to itself the final power in appointing new wardens, requiring an accounting of their management, approving the schoolmaster chosen, and levying a tax through the selectmen for repair of the schoolhouse. The wardens did not exercise power in the later history of the school to the extent one would expect.

The Dorchester school appears to have been in operation by October 31, 1639, Thomas Waterhouse[33] being the first master, and, apparently, continuously throughout the period to 1647. It appears then that Dorchester gave less public support for education between 1642 and 1647 than Boston, and showed less inclination to raise money by taxation than either Boston or Charlestown.

Salem thus records a vote at a general town meeting in February, 1639/40: "Young Mr. Norris Chose by this Assemblie to teach skoole.[34] At the quarterly court, March 30, 1641, "Col. Endecot brought up the matter of a ffree skoole and therefore wished a whole town meeting about it"; whereupon it was decided "that goodman Auger Warne a towne meeting the second day of the week."[35] The next vote of the town occurred September 30, 1644, as follows: "Ordered that a vote be published one [sic] the next Lecture day that such as have Children to be kept at schoole would bring in their names and what they will give for one whole year and Also That if any poore body hath children or a childe to be put to Schoole & not able to pay for their schooling That the Town will pay it by a rate."[36] These items show that the town of Salem was depending on voluntary contributions, in the main, for the support of the school. The principle of taxation by rate was adopted only for the education of the children of those parents unable to contribute. This policy of school support, viz., distributing the burden partly on parents of pupils sending children and partly on the whole body of inhabitants paying taxes, was often adopted by other New England towns in the seventeenth century. It may be noted that this is the first mention of the word "rate" in a town record of Massachusetts, though we have no evidence that it was actually laid at this time for the purpose stated.[37]

Under the date November, 1642, the Ipswich town records declare: "The town votes that there shall be a free school."[38] On October 3, 1643, the town voted that in view of a former grant respecting the establishment of a free school, "now there should be XI£ per annum raised as the Committee in that case provided, shall determine. And that there shalbe Seven free schollars, or soe many as the Feoffees (to be chosen) from tyme to tyme shall order," but the number was not to be more than seven.[39] As there is no further vote between 1643 and 1647, and little seems to be known concerning the history of the school at this date, it is uncertain whether the vote of 1643 was carried out.[40] It provides for an expenditure of £11, but the amount was not necessarily to be raised by taxation. It shows that a committee, to be appointed by the town, was to raise the money and that feoffees, apparently to be chosen by the town, should be a permanent committee.

On January 2, 1642/3, the town of Dedham voted unanimously to set apart land for public use, "for the Towne, the Church, and A fre Schoole, viz: 40 acres at the leaste or 60 acres at the most."[41]

On January 1, 1644/5, because of "the great necessitie of providing some meanes for the Education of the youth in or said Towne,"
Dedham voted unanimously to raise £20 annually to maintain a
schoolmaster to keep a free school. It was also voted that this
sum, together with the land already set apart for public use, should
be intrusted to "Feofees" chosen by the town, who should improve
the same for the use of the school; and that as the profits arose from
the land "everyman may be proportionably abated" of his proportion of the £20, "freely to be given to ye use aforesaid." The "Feofees" were given power to make a rate for the necessary charges in
improving the land, accounting for the same to the town. Five men
named were chosen feoffees, three of whom were on the board of selectmen for this year.[42] This plan evidently contemplated support by
voluntary contributions, until the income from the land increased
sufficiently to support the school without such contribution. The
vote lacks the element of a tax, for nothing is said about a levy by
distress in case of a failure to pay, as occurred in the case of Dorchester in its first vote of 1639. The phrase "freely to be given"
indicates a disposition to avoid giving any power to force a man to
support the school, as a tax levied by distress would do. Again,
the notion evidently was to provide eventually for an endowed
school. Dedham thus established a public town school, free in
theory at least, supported in part by contributions, voluntarily
granted in town meeting and apparently by the most of the property-
owners and in part from income to be derived from town land.
As in the case of Dorchester, however, it lacks all the elements of a
real tax, since the contribution in question cannot be considered
compulsory. Nevertheless, the right to tax every property-holder
for the improvement of the school land is provided for, and thus
there might be partial support by general taxation, somewhat
like the case of Dorchester, and preceding the latter by more than
three months. But we have no evidence that such a tax was laid.
Dedham also, it may be noted, like Boston, granted town land for
the endowment of the school.[43]

The schools at Cambridge and Newbury were apparently private.
The former was not aided by the town before 1647,[44] and the latter
was aided only once within this period and then for a single year.[45]

The school at Roxbury was not a town school, and was neither established, managed, nor supported by a vote in town meeting before 1647.[46]

Under date of February 25, 1641/2, at a General Court held at New Haven, it was ordered that a free school should be set up in the town, and the pastor Mr. Davenport, with the magistrates, should consider "Whatt yearly allowance is meete to be given to itt out of the common stock of the towne, and also whatt rules and orders are meet to be observed in and about the same."[47] Owing to a doubt as to the accuracy of the records kept by Secretary Fugill, the General Court ordered a revision of the colony and town records, February 24, 1644/5. In the minutes given under this order the following appears,

For the better trayning upp of youth in this towne, that through God's Blessinge they may be fitted for publique service hereafter, either in church or commonweale, it is ordered, that a free schoole be sett upp, and the magistrates with the teaching elders are intreated to consider what rules and orders are meete to be observed and what allowance may be convenient for the schoolmars care and paynes, which shalbe paid out of the towns stocke. According to wch order, 20 £ a yeare was paid to Mr. Ezekiell Cheevers, the present schoolemaster for 2 or 3 yearse at first, but that not proveing a competent maintenance, in August, 1644, it was inlarged to 30 £ a yeare and soe contineweth.[48]

It seems evident that the vote of February 25, 1641/2, had been put into effect soon after its passage, and that Mr. Cheevers must have received an allowance of £20 out of the "Common Stock" of the town as early as the spring or summer of 1642—the phrase "two or three years" not allowing us to set an exact date.

Guilford, in New Haven colony, was founded in 1639, and a school supported by contributions appears to have been established in 1643.[49] The first town vote on the subject, October 7, 1646, provided for a committee of three to collect contributions for the salaries of Mr. Whitfield (pastor) and Mr. Higginson.[50] The record continues:

It is ordered that whoever shall put any child to schoole to Mr. Higginson shall not pay for lesse than a quarter's time at once and so shall be reckoned with all quarterly, though they have neglected to send all the time, at the rate of four shillings by the quarter to the Treasurer. It is agreed and ordered that ye additional sum toward Mr. Higginson's maintenance, with respect to the schoole, shall be paid by the Treasurer, yearly, out of the best of the rates in due season, according to our agreements.

This vote shows that the support fell partly on the parents sending children to the school and partly "out of the best of the rates in due season." The meaning of this phrase is not clear, but it seems to indicate that an additional sum to make up a salary agreed upon was raised by rate. This is the fifth New England town to use the word "rate" in connection with the support of a town school before 1647.[51]

On December 6, 1642, the town of Hartford voted as follows: "It is agreed that thurte pownd a yeer shall be seatled upon the Schoole by the towne for efer."[52] But in April, 1643, this plan was greatly modified, by ordering Mr. Andrews, the teacher, to teach one year from March 25, 1643, for £16, to be paid by the parents sending their children in proportion to the time sent, at the rate of 20 shillings a year. But those unable to pay should give "notes" to the selectmen, who would pay the teacher at the town's charge. Mr. Andrews was to keep the record and send "Nottes" and demand payment. If then his wages did not amount to the sum specified, the selectmen were to collect and pay what was lacking "at the Townes Charges."[53] The first vote evidently provided for a free school established and supported by the town. The second provided for most of the income by tuition fees, and the rest by taxation, first for the education of poor children, thus preceding Salem by seventeen months, and, secondly, to make up a contingent remainder which might arise from a small number of pupils. If we assume that Mr. Cheevers, at New Haven, did not receive his allowance from the town until after December 6, 1642, then Hartford would have the honor of proposing the first public free school supported by a general tax, provided we admit that the £30 was to be raised in this way. It is not so stated, however, and, moreover, it is very unlikely that New Haven did not grant money out of the "common stock" before the date in question. Although the word "rate" or "tax" is not used in the New Haven records, there is hardly any other way to account for the payments to Mr. Cheevers than by means of a tax.

According to a statement of John Callender,[54] Robert Lenthal,[55] who had been pastor at Weymouth, Massachusetts, came to Newport, Rhode Island, and was admitted a freeman August 6, 1640. On August 20, he was

by vote called to keep a public school for the learning of youth, and for his encouragement there was granted to him and his heirs one hundred acres of land, and four more for an house lot, it was also voted that one hundred acres should be laid forth, and appropriated for a school, for encouragement of the poorer sort, to train up their youth in learning, and Mr. Robert Lenthal, while he continues to teach school, is to have the benefit thereof.[56]

Nothing further is known concerning this school.

To award the honors to each town is not easy, but the following observations seem warranted from the evidence submitted. Boston was the first town to choose a schoolmaster in town meeting (April 13, 1635). Charlestown was the first to vote to establish a town school (June 3, 1636), appoint a schoolmaster with salary and length of service fixed, set a date for opening the school (August 8, 1636), and appoint a temporary school committee (February 12, 1637/8). It is the first to give good evidence that it had a town school in continuous operation for a considerable period (August 8, 1636, to February 12, 1637/8). There is no evidence to show whether the £40 voted in 1636 was raised by general taxation, yet the votes show that the town made itself responsible for payment, and the next year appointed a committee in town meeting to settle the wages of the master for past and future work. This seems to be reasonably good proof that Charlestown should have the honor of establishing the first town school, because all the steps involving the establishment, management, and support were taken in town meeting. Dorchester was the first to provide for a permanent town school, with the annual income fixed and the method of raising it determined (May 20, 1639), though the payments to be made by individuals fell only on persons holding certain property. Nevertheless, since these payments could be collected by distress, it is fair to call it a tax-supported school, though the tax was not raised by a rate or general levy on all property-holders. Salem was the first town in Massachusetts (but see Hartford) to vote to support a town school in part by a rate on all property-holders (September 30, 1644), though such support was for poor children. Dedham was the first to vote to raise a definite sum annually (January 1, 1644/5), "freely to be given," presumably by "everyman" ("everyman may be proportionally abated," etc.). This is support by voluntary contribution. It is impossible to say what the town would have done in case a contributor later refused to contribute. Without another vote it seems that compulsion could not have been used. There is no evidence that such a vote was taken or even that it was necessary. This school, therefore, cannot be considered a tax-supported school, as this word is ordinarily used. Dedham was also the first town to elect a permanent committee to manage school property, "feoffees" (February 4, 1644/5), though Ipswich was the first to propose such a committee (October 3, 1643). Newbury was the first to grant public or town land to a schoolmaster, expressly for his "encouragement" to keep school (1639). Newport was the first to set apart a large tract of town land as a permanent endowment for a school (August 6, 1640), though the income was, by the vote, to be used for the "poorer sort." New Haven was the first which gives satisfactory evidence that it supported a town school out of "town stock," meaning, presumably, money raised by a general tax levied on all property-holders (1642). This view, however, rejects the vote of Charlestown as inconclusive on the method of raising the £40 voted in 1636. Hartford was the first to vote an annual sum, for the support of the school, "by the towne for efer" (December 6, 1642); the intent being, apparently, to raise the money by taxation on all property-holders. It was also the first to vote to provide for the education of poor children "at the Townes Charges"; viz., evidently by taxation (April, 1643).

We may conclude then that certain towns in New England had, before January 21, 1647, voluntarily established, managed, and supported town schools, and developed the following important principles: First, certain towns in their corporate capacity took the initiative in establishing town or public schools, and in aiding those already established. Secondly, they assumed responsibility for the support of schools out of public property, partly through gifts of land to schoolmasters, partly by setting aside tracts of land as a permanent endowment and partly through what may be called forced contributions from certain property-owners. Thirdly, they voted to levy a rate or tax on property-holders for the partial support of the school. This method was proposed, and the word "rate" used, by at least six of the eleven towns mentioned before January 21, 1647, and taxation is implied in two others. Thus the foundation for the famous act of 1647 had been well laid by voluntary effort of the towns in question. Nevertheless, the action of a few of the larger towns must not blind us to the fact that this accounts for less than one-fifth of all the towns that had been established in New England at this date. Even allowing for the fact that a few more would probably be added if the records were complete, yet they could accommodate but a very small proportion of the pupils of school age. New England had a population of at least 25,000 by 1647,[57] and at that time we do not have evidence of more than eleven town schools in operation. If other towns had schools they were private rather than public. In most cases, no doubt, the people were depending on parental education. Indeed, the Massachusetts act of 1642 does not mention schools, but complains that there was "great neglect in many parents and masters in training up their children in learning and labor . . . . especially of their ability to read and understand the principles of religion and the capital laws of the country."[58] Thus, at this date, the school was not considered by the General Court, or even by most of the towns, as a matter of public concern, to be supported by the town, as was the church, for example. The school as an organized public agency for carrying on education was fighting for recognition, and great efforts would have to be made before the principles established voluntarily by a few towns would become general. The General Court of Massachusetts recognized this in 1647, and took the next important step in public education by compelling towns with a certain number of families to establish both elementary and secondary town schools.

CHAPTER VI

EDUCATIONAL LEGISLATION FOR POOR CHILDREN AND APPRENTICES, 1642–1671

The history of compulsory free education in America is of great interest, because fundamentally such a system is the surest foundation for the ultimate success of that great experiment in democracy to which we are dedicated.[1] As the working out of the principle of democracy has been one of the greatest single forces in American history, so now it is perhaps the most important issue at stake in the present world-controversies over its virtues and defects.

The development and extension of the principle of compulsory education as a foundation for democracy are justified because democracy depends on public opinion; and it is only through an enlightened public opinion that a government by democracy can succeed. For the more universally the people are educated, the less need there is of restraint and the greater is the check against corruption and unjust or unwise legislation by the people's representatives.

The original idea underlying the establishment of our state systems of public instruction was the responsibility and duty of the states to make education available and free to all children at public expense. The notion that it was also the duty of the state to compel all children to acquire a minimum of education was of slower growth, and it is only in comparatively recent times that all the states have passed laws embodying this principle.

Compulsory education must be distinguished from compulsory schools. Obviously either could exist independently of the other, and such was the case for long periods in some of the colonies and states. We should also distinguish between two forms or agencies of compulsory education. As now thought of, it is nearly synonymous with compulsory attendance of all children, between certain ages, for a definite time, at organized institutions of learning usually called schools.[2] But the first important legislation involving this principle did not mention schools as the agency but rather parents or the "master" or "governor" of a family, or a "guardian." The word "master" was usually applied to one who held a child as an apprentice or servant and who, from the standpoint of the law, was considered as acting in the place of a parent. Hence every parent and master was looked upon as an agency for the compulsory education of the child. Later legislation recognized "others"—for example, a tutor—as a proper agency, and still later we have the phrase "schoolmaster, or other helps and means," thus including organized institutions of learning.

Compulsory education is now principally associated with the idea of secular book education. In its earliest development, however, the emphasis was distributed and included instruction in a trade, in religion, and· in the rudiments of education. The inherited notions of the colonists would have limited their legislation almost entirely to compulsory vocational education for certain classes of children, following the practice of England and the two great acts of 1562 and 1601—the Statute of Artificers and the poor law, respectively.[3] But, as in many other cases, the colonists modified an English institution to fit their peculiar needs or environment, and thus developed a peculiarly American institution.

Another important difference connected with the early development of compulsory education is the fact that the cost, as well as the actual responsibility, was placed chiefly on the parent or master rather than on the state or the people of any local unit. This now results in the general taxation of the property of every individual. Some modification of this theory was made in practice, but on the whole the cost fell on the parent or master.

Any system of compulsory education, to be effective, must be based on general mandatory laws passed by the central governing body of the state, with adequate provisions for their enforcement. This includes either specific mention of the officers and courts responsible for enforcement and penalties for neglect, or it is implied in the law that such machinery exists and will be used. It is obvious that we cannot consider acts of a permissive or advisory character as compulsory. Even laws which use the word "shall" rather than "may" must often be classed as permissive acts when the responsibility for enforcement or the penalty for neglect is so vague or uncertain that the law may easily become a dead letter. The educational legislation of the states, like other types of legislation, includes many such examples. It is the purpose of this and the following chapter to trace the legislation and practice of the New England colonies on this important subject.

Colonial legislation appears in a variety of forms, and the utmost care is needed to determine the course of legislation as well as the law in force at a particular time. Committees appointed from time to time by the various assemblies for the revision of the laws were given the power, not only to include the laws in force, but to repeal, amend, and even make new laws. When their work was finished, the assembly adopted the revision as a whole. Consequently, a law may appear in a code which can be found nowhere else; for example, in the so-called "colonial records" or in the session laws or in the journals of either house. The one attempt to bring together the important educational legislation of the colonies omits important educational acts because of a failure to examine these codes. This is also necessary for the purpose of determining how long a law remained in force. In the book referred to important educational legislation found in the codes is omitted. There is no account, for example, of the educational legislation of Plymouth colony. It may be noted that the laws of 1648, 1655, and 1671, given below, appear only in the codes published, respectively, by Massachusetts in 1648, New Haven in 1656, and Plymouth in 1672. Moreover, the same is true of the Connecticut law of 1650 and 1672, and that of Massachusetts of 1658, published, respectively, Connecticut in 1822 and 1673, and Massachusetts in 1660. In other words, in no case is the above legislation to be found in the "colonial records" of these colonies, or in their session laws published separately. In every case both the original and amended law were the work of a committee appointed to prepare the code, and their work was ratified as a whole.[4]

In an examination of the educational legislation of the New England colonies, we find that certain underlying factors helped to determine the character of this legislation—those leading to centralization of power in the state, and those emphasizing the power of the local unit, such as the town or county and later the district. Because of the fact that the states have imposed requirements on the local units and their officers and taken from them certain powers, efficient school systems have been made possible. A general compulsory law operates over a wide area and makes for uniformity; for more equal and progressive development. Permissive acts which allow each local unit to do as it pleases make general progress haphazard. There is a lack of uniformity which may result even in retrogression. It is the New England colonies that furnish us with the first examples of the former tendency.

The educational legislation of these colonies shows that the various assemblies sought two main ends, namely, compulsory education and compulsory schools. The first contemplated a minimum of education for all children, to be given by parents, masters, or someone employed by them for this purpose. The Massachusetts act of June 14, 1642, was the first general colonial act of this character. It reads as follows:[5]

This Court, taking into consideration the great neglect in many parents and masters in training up their children in learning, and labor, and other imployments which may bee profitable to the common wealth, do hearupon order and decree, that in every towne the chosen men appointed for managing the prudencial affaires of the same shall hencefourth stand charged with the care of the redresse of this evill, so as they shalbee liable to bee punished or fined for the neglect thereof, upon any presentment of the grand jurors, or other information or complaint in any plantations in this jurisdiction; and for this end they, or the greater part of them, shall have power to take accompt from time to time of their parents and masters, and of their children, concerning their calling and impliment of their children, especiallity of their ability to read and understand the principles of religion and the capital lawes of the country, and to impose fines upon all those who refuse to render such accompt to them when required; and they shall have power (with consent of any Court or magistrates) to put fourth apprentice the children of such as shall not be able and fitt to employ and bring them up, nor shall take course to dispose of them, of such as they shall find not to bee able and fit to imply and bring them up, nor shall take course to dispose of them themselves; and they are to take care that such as are set to keep cattle bee set to some other impliment withall, as spinning up on the rock, knitting, weveing tape, etc.; and that boyes and girles bee not suffered to converse together, so as may occasion any wanton, dishonest, or immodest behavior, and for their better performance of this trust committed to them, they may divide the towne amongst them, appointing to every of the said townsmen a certeine number of families to have speciall oversight of; they are also to provide that a sufficient quantity of materialls, as hempe, flaxe, etc. may bee raised in their severall townes, and tooles and implements provided for working out the same; and for their assistance in this so needful and beneficiall impliment, if they meete with any difficulty or opposition which they cannot well master by their owne power, they may have recourse to some of the magistrates, who shall take such course for their help and incuragment as the occasion shall require, according to justice; and the said townsmen, at the next Court in those limits, after the end of their yeare, shall give a breife account in writing of their proceedings hearin; provided, that they have bene so required by some Court or magistrate a month at least before; and this order to continue for two yeares, and till the court shall take further order.

Briefly, this law declared that there had been great neglect by many parents and masters in training their children in learning and labor and other employments which might be profitable to the commonwealth; and that, therefore, the chosen men (selectmen) of every town should redress the evil or suffer a fine for neglect thereof, upon presentment by the grand jury or on other information or complaint. To this end they were given power to take account of parents and masters concerning the calling and employment of their children, especially of their ability to read and understand the principles of religion and the capital laws of the country; to impose fines on all those refusing to render such account when required; to "put forth" as apprentices, with the consent of any court or magistrate, the children of parents not "able and fitt to employ and bring them up." These phrases cover three points: first, bringing a child up to work at some employment or trade; second, maintaining him, so that he would not become a charge on the town; and third, seeing that he was taught to read.

The first desire was to have all children taught some definite calling or trade—"imployments which may bee profitable to the commonwealth." There was hope that skilled labor would, as stated in the English Statute of Artificers, 1562, help "banishe Idlenes, advance Husbandrye and yeelde unto the hired person bothe in the tyme of scarsitee and in the tyme of plentye a convenient proporčon of Wages."[6] Secondly, there was the notion of checking pauperism. Unskilled labor not only was not so profitable to the state but it was often a direct expense, because it led to unemployment, idleness, and poverty. Even caring for cattle was not in itself an occupation, and selectmen were ordered to "take care that such as are set to keep cattle bee set to some other impliment withall, as spinning up on the rock, kniting, weveing tape, etc." The fear of the growth of a poor class was justified, considering the experience of England in the previous century, and the power granted to the selectmen to bind out children as apprentices was partly for the purpose of reducing pauperism. The fact that the selectmen were parties to the contract, that the phrase "not able and fitt to employ and bring them up" suggests poverty, and finally that indentures often fail to specify a trade, merely stating that the master shall "keep" or "maintain" or "shall have," or that the child "shall dwell" with him—all this shows that the motive was in part poor relief; that is, it was hoped that the system of apprenticeship would relieve the town of expenses incident to the care of the poor, for which the town was by law responsible.[7] The third motive was educational; that is, to compel every parent and master to be a school teacher, to teach every child to read. This duty was based first on religious grounds, that the child might understand the principles of religion, and secondly, on the ground of good citizenship which demands, according to the law, a knowledge of the capital laws. The desire to have all children read was not unique, but the provision for making this degree of education compulsory was so. It was the evident intention of Massachusetts to provide for the compulsory universal free education of all children, first, through parents and, secondly, through masters by the system of apprenticeship. The penalties specified for neglect were introduced by act of an assembly for the first time. We have here one of those cases where an essentially new institution was created, and it is this fact which makes the act of 1642 so important and the glory of Massachusetts so secure. So far as the author knows, Massachusetts was the first organized state in history to enact such a law.

The details of this act are of very great interest because of the variety of educational principles included and the inference we may draw from it with respect to the state of education in Massachusetts at this date.[8] We may note first that the agency for educating the child is the parent or master. No mention is made of schools or schoolmasters. At least five different parties are concerned in its enforcement: selectmen, grand jurors, magistrates, courts, parents, and masters. Besides, "any court" might give its consent to an apprenticeship, and any person might make complaint, presumably to a court or any one of the officials named. This multiplication of officials to enforce a law is characteristic of the Puritan scheme of government and shows a desire to make the law really compulsory. The principle of penalizing the parents or masters for refusal to report concerning the education of their children, and what amounted to a severe penalty for failure to "bring them up" properly, viz., the removal of the child by apprenticing him or her, as well as the provision for a fine on the selectmen for neglect of duty—this whole system of penalties was unique. It does not appear that any legislative body had ever before provided for similar penalties.[9] The content of the education to be given is specified. It included secular and religious features, and in certain cases provided for vocational training, and, besides, mention was made that care should be taken against boys and girls conversing together "so as may occasion wanton, dishonest, or immodest behavior."

The great significance of the act, in comparison with the attitude of states before this time, is, of course, the recognition of the responsibility of the state for the education of all children within its boundaries. In general, we may say that previous to this date most states considered that either the church, a religious denomination or society, or private agencies were responsible for education. True, states were often willing to encourage, and often gave direct support to, or assisted in the management of, education. On the whole, however, responsibility for education rested with other agencies than the state. We may note also that the minimum standard set for the kind and amount of education was based on the needs of the state and church, and that the state made itself responsible for enforcement and instructed local bodies and officials to carry out its will.

The act of 1642 was to continue two years "and till the Court shall take further order." A failure to appreciate this clause has resulted in errors and omissions in the principal accounts of the compulsory educational legislation of the Massachusetts Bay colony. This is due to a number of causes, some of them already mentioned. We may note especially that, up to a recent date, a copy of the code of laws enacted by the General Court of Massachusetts in 1648 was not known to be in existence, and since its discovery no one, to the writer's knowledge, has made known the fact that it contains an important revision of the act of 1642, which act was thereby repealed. After long search by collectors of Americana, this book was found in a small private library in England. It was purchased for a large sum and is now owned by the Huntington Library of California, the only copy known to be in existence. In the reprint of the code of 1660, in the introduction by Mr. Whitmore, there will be found the history of the legislation leading up to the preparation of the code of 1648. The important point to note is the fact that the amendments, changes, etc., made in the act of 1642 were the work of the committee which prepared the code and that it was ratified by the General Court as a whole. This accounts for the absence of this new law in the *Records of the Company of Massachusetts Bay.* Under the title "children" there occurs the law in question. The title page of the code reads:

Book of the General Lawes and Libertyes concerning the inhabitants of the Massachusetts collected out of the Records of the General Court for the severeal years wherein they were made and established. Cambridge, Printed according to order of the General Court, 1648. And are to be solde at the shope of Hezekiah Usher in Boston.

"CHILDREN

"Forasmuch as the good education of children is of singular behoof and benefit to any Common-wealth; and wheras many parents and masters are too indulgent and negligent of their duty in that kinde. It is therefore ordered that the Select men of everie town, in the severall precincts and quarters where they dwell, shall have a vigilant eye over their brethren and neighbours, to see first that none of them shall suffer so much barbarism in any of their families as not to indeavour to teach by themselves or others, their children and apprentices so much learning as may inable them perfectly to read the english tongue, and knowledge of the Capital lawes; upon penaltie of twentie shillings for each neglect therein. Also that all masters of families doe once a week (at the least) catechize their children and servants in the grounds and principles of Religion, and if any be unable to doe so much: that then at the least they procure such children or apprentices to learn some short orthodox catechism without book, that they may be able to answer unto the questions that shall be propounded to them out of such catechism by their parents or masters or any of the Select men when they shall call them to a tryall of what they have learned in this kinde. And further that all parents and masters do breed and bring up their children and

apprentices in some honest lawful calling, labour or imployment, either in husbandry, or some other trade profitable for themselves, and the Commonwealth if they will not or can not train them up in learning to fit them for higher imployments. And if any of the Select men after admonition by them given to such masters of families shal finde them still negligent of their dutie in the particulars aforementioned, wherby children and servants become rude, stubborn and unruly; the said Select men with the help of two Magistrates, or the next County court for that Shire, shall take such children or apprentices from them and place them with some masters for years(boyes till they come to twenty-one, and girls eighteen years of age compleat) which will more strictly look into and force them to submit unto government according to the rules of this order, if by fair means and former instructions they will not be drawn unto it. [1642]."[10]

It will be observed that the law of 1648 differs from that of 1642 as well as that of 1660, with respect to both additions and omissions. We may note first that it is much more specific and makes compulsory book and religious education more certain for apprentices as well as children. Children and apprentices were to be taught to read, etc. Children and servants were to be catechized in the principles of religion. Children and apprentices were to learn a catechism and answer questions propounded. Selectmen could take children and apprentices from masters of families for failure to teach them to read and bring them up properly, and could then place them with other masters who would treat them "according to the rules of this order." The power of the selectmen, it will be noted, was limited, as the help of the magistrates or "the next County Court" was specified. This accounts for the fact that some indentures appear in the town and others in the county court records. There is an enlargement of the educational qualification from mere ability to read to "perfectly to read the english tongue," and the penalty laid upon the selectmen for neglect of duty was made specific; that is, twenty shillings "for each neglect therein." Besides, learning is a "higher" employment, and husbandry is also mentioned as an employment. Selectmen are given powers of inspection and might "admonish" parents for neglect of duty. The phrase, "teach by themselves or others," recognizes the teachers appointed in towns of fifty families and up as required by the act of 1647, and also private teachers. On the other hand, the selectmen are deprived of power to fine parents for refusal to make reports, the industrial features are less complete, and the machinery for enforcement is less specific. The clause concerning the dividing of the town for purposes of inspection and that calling for a written report of the proceedings of the selectmen are both omitted.

Effective compulsory education depends in part on compulsory support of education by the people in their corporate rather than their individual capacity. The provision which compelled masters to teach apprentices to read and that which made the selectmen subject to a penalty of twenty shillings for neglect of duty compelled the latter to see that indentures contained an educational clause, when they bound out children as apprentices, unless the child already knew how to read. But the supply of children to be apprenticed might exceed the demand. Ordinarily the selectmen would naturally endeavor to persuade someone to take a child as an apprentice without expense to the town. But if no one could be found to do this, it was necessary to offer inducements. This usually took the form of a fixed sum of money which the selectmen promised to pay a master as a bonus for taking a child as an apprentice. Such sums had to be taken from the town treasury; that is money raised by general taxation. An indenture, then, which contained a clause requiring the master to teach the apprentice to read, and which also involved money paid by the town to the master, may be thought of as providing for partial compulsory town support of education by general taxation. It is perhaps possible to draw this conclusion from the act of 1642, though there is some doubt whether an apprentice under this act was on exactly the same basis as a child not apprenticed, with respect to book education. This is due to the omission of the word "apprentice" in connection with the word "children." It is not clear from the wording of the act of 1642 that selectmen could take an apprentice from a master for failure to teach him to read, unless such a clause had been inserted in the indenture. But there was no law compelling selectmen to include such a clause in the indenture. On the other hand, it seems to have been the intention of the framers of the act to have apprentices taught to read and to have the selectmen fined for neglect of duty in this respect. If this is a correct interpretation, then the word "children" must be interpreted to include apprentices. Considering the English practice of not paying attention to book education of apprentices, it would have been natural for the framers of the act of 1642 to stress the industrial efficiency of the apprentice and the provision for his maintenance rather than book education. It is evident that there was doubt on this question, for the revision of the law in 1648 was very specific on this point and removed this ambiguity, because possible payments to a master out of the town treasury made the compulsory education of apprentices more certain, and helped establish the principle of partial support of education by the town through the agency of general taxation.

The law of 1648 remained in force until the next revision of the laws, which was made in 1658 and published as the code of 1660.[11] The new law on education is entitled "Children and Youth," and is with a few minor changes, a copy of the law of 1648.[12] Because of neglect of this law, an enforcing act was passed in 1668.[13] Clerks of the county courts were directed to send an order to the constables of the towns in their county to execute it. This was to the effect that the General Court would require the selectmen to enforce the law, "the prevalency of the former neglect notwithstanding." Constables were ordered to take a list of the names of "those young persons" in towns and adjacent farms who "do not serve their Parents or Masters, as Children, Apprentices, hired Servants or Journey men ought to do," and return the same to the next court, viz., county court. If then the return showed that selectmen had been negligent in their duties—namely, in seeing that all children and youths under family government were taught to "reade perfectly the English Tongue"; that they had knowledge of the capital laws; that they were taught some orthodox catechism and brought up to some honest employment; that "Family Governours," after admonition and neglect of the provisions of the law, had their children and apprentices taken from them and apprenticed to others—then the court was to proceed against them by "Admonition, or fine, as the merit of the case may require." This enforcing act appears in the code of 1672, as well as that entitled "Children and Youth," without essential change.[14]

The colony of Connecticut copied, in her code of 1650,[15] almost verbatim, the Massachusetts law of 1648 regarding children, so that it is not necessary to comment further on this act. The important point to note is the fact that Massachusetts, not Connecticut, as has often been asserted, was responsible for the numerous changes in the law of 1642. This is one of the early examples of the manner in which our public-school system has evolved and approached something like uniformity, and this in spite of the fact that the colonies, and later the states, have always been entirely independent in establishing their educational systems. Connecticut found that the Massachusetts law of 1648, revised from that of 1642, fitted her needs, and thus considered that there was no need of spending time and effort in drafting a new law. She also adopted the compulsory school act of 1647 entire, as given with minor changes in the code of 1648, besides taking much other legislation from this same code.

The New Haven colony was entirely independent of Connecticut from its foundation in 1638 to 1665, when it was formally united with Connecticut under the charter of 1662.[16] Though a small colony consisting of only a few towns,[17] it passed important educational legislation. The law regarding compulsory education appears in the code of 1655,[18] and was evidently based in part on the Massachusetts acts of 1642 and 1648, but includes some entirely new principles.

CHILDREN'S EDUCATION

Whereas too many Parents and Masters, either through an over tender respect to their own occasions, and businesse, or not duly considering the good of their Children, and Apprentices, have too much neglected duty in their Education, while they are young and capable of learning, It is Ordered, That the Deputies for the particular Court, in each Plantation within this Jurisdiction for the time being; or where there are no such Deputies the Constable, or other Officer, or Officers in publick trust, shall from time to time, have a vigilant eye over their brethren, and neighbours, within the limits of the said Plantation that all parents and Masters, doe duly endeavour, either by their own ability and labour, or by improving such Schoolmaster, or other helps and means, as the Plantation doth afford or the family may conveniently provide, that all their Children, and Apprentices as they grow capable, may through Gods blessing, attain at least so much, as to be able duly to read the Scriptures, and other good and profitable printed Books in the English tongue, being their native language, and in some competent measure, to understand the main grounds and principles of Christian Religion necessary to salvation. And to give a due Answer to such plain and ordinary Questions, as may by the said Deputies, Officers, or others, be propounded concerning the same. And where such Deputies or Officers, whether by information or examination, shall find any Parent or Master, one or more negligent, he or they shall first give warning, and if thereupon due reformation follow, if the said Parents or Masters shall thenceforth seriously and constantly apply themselves to their duty in manner before expressed, the former neglect may be passed by; but if not, then the said Deputies, or other Officer or Officers, shall three months after such warning, present each such negligent person, or persons, to the next Plantation Court, where every such Delinquent upon proof, shall be fined ten shillings to the Plantation, to be levied as other fines. And if in any Plantation, there be no such Court kept for the present, in such case, the Constable or other Officer, or Officers, warning such person or persons, before the Freemen, or so many of them as upon notice shall meet together, and proving the neglect after warning, shall have power to levy the fine as aforesaid: But if in three months after that there be no due care taken and continued for the Education of such Children or Apprentices as aforesaid, the Delinquent (without any further private warning) shall be proceeded against as before, but the fine doubled. And lastly, if after the said warning, and fines paid or levied, the said Deputies, Officer or Officers, shall still find a continuance of the former negligence, if it be not obstinancy, so that such Children or Servants may be in danger to grow barbarous, rude and stubborn, through ignorance, they shall give due and seasonable notice, that every such Parent and Master be summoned to the next Court of Magistrates, who are to proceed as they find cause, either to a greater fine, taking security for due conformity to the scope and intent of this Law, or may take such Children or Apprentices from such Parents or Masters, and place them for years, Boyes till they come to the age of one and twenty, and Girles till they come to the age of eighteen years, with such others, who shall better educate and govern them, both for publick conveniency, and for the particular good of the said children or Apprentices.

Briefly, this law declares that too many parents and masters had too much neglected their duty in the education of their children and apprentices, "either through an over tender respect to their own occasions and businesse, or not duly considering the good of their Children and Apprentices"; therefore, deputies for the particular court in each plantation, or the constable or other officers in public trust, where there was no deputy, were to see that parents and masters, either by their own ability, or "by improving such Schoolmaster, or other helps and means, as the plantation" offered, taught all their children and apprentices "at least so much, as to be able duly to read the Scriptures, and other good and profitable books in the English tongue," and to understand the main principles of the

Christian religion, so that on the asking of questions concerning the same by the above officers "due answer" might be given. An elaborate system was provided for the enforcement of the act. When by information or examination such officers found that any parent or master, one or more, was negligent, warning was to be given, and, if reformation followed, the neglect could be passed by. But if there was still neglect, then three months later the officers must present the negligent person or persons to the next plantation court where, on proof, the delinquent "shall be fined ten shillings to the Plantation to be levied as other fines." If after three months there was still neglect, the delinquent must be proceeded against as before and the fine doubled. Finally, if after three months more there was still neglect, after warning and the fines were paid and levied and the officers believed that children or servants might grow "barbarous, rude, and stubborn, through ignorance," they could summon the parent or master to the court of magistrates, who could either increase the fine, "taking security for due conformity," or "take such Children or Apprentices from such Parents and Masters" and place them with other masters, boys to twenty-one and girls to eighteen years of age, who "shall better educate and govern them."

This act has better machinery for locating negligence on the part of the parent, and the penalties are more severe for continued neglect than those of Massachusetts and Connecticut. Even the court of magistrates might take a hand in compelling some erring parent to see to the education of his child. For the first time in the colonies, and apparently in any community, a money penalty was placed directly on the parent or master, after the first warning, for failure to educate a child or apprentice, and this was levied and made and collected as other fines. The education demanded was broader than that in Massachusetts and Connecticut, and the emphasis was placed on mental development. There is no special mention of trades. We may note also that the principal officer responsible for enforcement was the deputy, a colony or state rather than a local official like the selectmen or grand-jurymen. The principal weakness of the law is the failure to penalize the officials responsible for enforcement if they neglected their duty. An important amendment to this law was made May 30, 1660,[19] when, for the first time, a colonial assembly, or indeed any government, provided that "the sonnes of all the inhabitants within this jurisdiction, shall [under the same penalty] be learned to write a ledgible hand, so soone as they are capable of it." It is evident that the New Haven colony had, in theory at least, developed the most comprehensive system of compulsory education of any New England colony up to 1660 and should, therefore, have the credit for such a system. Because overshadowed by Massachusetts in size, and in the zeal of the latter's historians, the New Haven colony has never received proper credit for this remarkable law providing for the education of all boys in both reading and writing and of girls in reading. As Connecticut absorbed the New Haven colony in 1665, the latter became subject to the former's educational code of 1650.[20]

Plymouth colony in its revision of the laws in June, 1671,[21] introduced a section entitled "Education of Children."

EDUCATION OF CHILDREN

Forasmuch as the good Education of Children and Youth, is of singular use and benefit to any Common-wealth; and whereas many Parents and Masters either through an over respect to their own occasions and business, or not duely considering the good of their Children and Servants, have too much neglected their duty in their Education, whilest they are young and capable of Learning; "It is Ordered, That the Deputies and Select men of every Town, shall have a vigilant eye from time to time over their Brethren and Neighbours, to see that all Parents and Masters do duely Endeavour, by themselves or others, to teach their children and servants as they grow capable, so much learning as through the blessing of God they may attain, at least to be able duely to read the Scriptures, and other good profitable Books printed in the English Tongue (being their Native Language) and the knowledge of the Capital Laws and in some competent measure to understand the main Grounds and Principles of Christian Religion, necessary to Salvation, by causing them to learn some short Orthodox Catechisme without Book, or otherwise instructing them as they may be able to give a due answer to such plain and ordinary Questions, as may by them or others be propounded to them concerning the same: And further that all Parents and Masters do breed and bring up their children and apprentices in some honest lawful calling, labour or employment, that may be profitable for themselves, or the Country; and if after warning and admonition given by any of the Deputies, or Select-men, unto such Parents or Masters, they shall still remain negligent in their duty, in any the particulars aforementioned, whereby Children or Servants may be in danger to grow Barberous, Rude or Stubborn, and so prove Pests instead of Blessings to the Country; That then a fine of ten shillings shall be levied on the Goods of such negligent Parent or

Master, to the Towns use, except extreme poverty call for migation of the said fine.

"And if in three months after that, there be no due care taken and continued, for the Education of such children and apprentices as aforesaid, then a fine of twenty shillings to be levied on such Delinquents Goods, to the Towns use, except as aforesaid.

And Lastly, if in three months after that, there be no due Reformation of the said neglect, then the said Select-men with the help of two Magistrates, shall take such children and servants from them, and place them with some Masters for year, (boyes still they come to twenty-one, and girls eighteen years of age) which will more strictly educate and govern them according to the rules of this Order.

This law was based on the Massachusetts acts of 1642 and 1648 and the law of New Haven of 1655. Deputies and selectmen were to see that children and servants were taught and catechized, as already set forth in the New Haven act. Parents and masters were to "breed and bring up their children and apprentices" as directed in the Massachusetts act of 1648, except that the clause "or some other trade" is omitted. After warning and admonition was given by deputies or selectmen to negligent parents and masters, then a fine of ten shillings "shall be levied on the Goods of such negligent Parent or Master, to the Towns use, except extreme poverty call for a mitigation of the fine." For three months more of neglect, the fine was doubled, twenty shillings. For three months more of neglect, the selectmen with the aid of two magistrates could take and apprentice such "Children and Servants" and place them with other masters "which will more strictly educate and govern them." The emphasis is on book and religious education as in New Haven, and there is the same weakness—the failure to provide for a penalty to be levied on negligent officers.

New Hampshire, Maine, and Rhode Island[22] failed to pass acts involving compulsory book or religious education during the seventeenth century. But New Hampshire was under the jurisdiction of Massachusetts from 1641 to 1679, hence the laws of the latter colony applied. Maine also was united to Massachusetts in 1652 and continued under her jurisdiction the remainder of the Colonial period. It thus appears that by 1671 all of the territory of New England, with the exception of Rhode Island, was under a system of compulsory education.

CHAPTER VII

EDUCATIONAL LEGISLATION FOR POOR CHILDREN AND APPRENTICES, 1672–1776

The reasons for passing the extraordinary series of laws on compulsory education, considered in the previous chapter, lie deep in the religious, social, and political history of this section. The forces that determined this legislation also account for a series of laws, of the same period, relating to compulsory schools. Moreover, there were many other laws relating to religion, morals, etc., compulsory in character. There is not space here to analyze the subject in detail, but it may be noted that the laws in question, particularly those of Massachusetts, were largely the work of a religious oligarchy.[1] The leaders may be thought of as occupying a relation to the people somewhat similar to that of the enlightened despots of the eighteenth century. Their purpose was to build up an orthodox paternalistic commonwealth, in which every individual would be compelled to live in an atmosphere charged with religion, with a view to producing a self-conscious attitude which would lead to the performance of religious, moral, and civic duties. Their purpose was to make this ideal practical by seeing that every child was taught to read: first, to understand the principles of the Puritan faith; secondly, to know the capital laws that he might be a law-abiding citizen; and, finally, in order that he might become an intelligent citizen—that is, be able to read "other good and profitable Books printed in the English Tongue."

The method of attaining these ends was through a most rigorous system of laws which regulated, in minute detail, the life of the individual as well as of the community as a whole; secondly, an elaborate system of courts and officials to carry out the laws; and thirdly, a system of penalties and punishments to be imposed by specified officials and courts on anyone neglecting the law, whether a private individual, a public officer, or a whole community as organized into a town or even into a county. It is only through an understanding of this system as a whole that we can appreciate the part that compulsory education and schools were expected to play in a very carefully thought out plan of life for every individual. The success of such a system depended largely on three favorable factors: first, an educated ministry; second, compact population groups—the towns; and, finally, a homogeneous population in blood and religion. The extreme care used in New England to keep out and "warn out" the undesirable citizen was one of the most important, although little appreciated now, of those factors which made this a workable system.[2]

As to the reasons for these particular agencies for education, we may note further that a new country, where people were obliged to live under frontier conditions, demands at the outset material rather than cultural development. Most of the energies of the people were expended in clearing forests, building roads, providing shelter, food and wearing apparel. Parental education and that obtained through apprenticeship were popular agencies, because education could be carried on with little or no expense or loss of the labor of children and youth. With the system of home manufactures prevailing throughout this period, it is clear that compulsory education for all, through organized schools, would interfere seriously with the normal condition of life of large portions of the people in both of these respects. Add to all this the fact that education through apprenticeship helped to solve two more very important problems—namely, idleness or pauperism, and industrial efficiency or a supply of skilled workers—and it is evident that there were excellent reasons in New England for emphasis on these agencies of education.

Let us now follow the legislation of the New England colonies on the subject of compulsory education from 1671 to the Revolution. The period from 1675 to 1689 is one of transition and is marked by two principal events. The first was the breaking out of Indian wars, resulting in severe economic depression due to heavy taxes, destruction of property, and withdrawal of producers from industry.[3] Accompanying, and in part a consequence of, this movement, there was a marked decline in family government, a weakening of the religious bond, a decline in morals, and, in short, a general lowering of the tone and standards of society. This condition was well ex-

pressed by the General Court of Connecticut when reasons were
given for the passing of several laws for the "suppression of some
provoakeing evills." These laws were made necessary because of
"the calamitous time of New England's distresse by the war with the
Indians, in the yeares seventy-five and seventy-six." The legislation
is significant and shows what difficulties towns would be confronted
with in enforcing the laws on compulsory education. The evils to be
remedied were[4] "prophanation of the Sabboth; neglect of cattchise-
ing of children and servants, and famaly prayer; young persons
shakeing of the government of parents or masters; boarders and inmates neglecting the worship of God in the famalyes where they
reside; tipleing and drincking; uncleaness; oppression, in workemen
and traders."

The reaction of the individual New England colonies to these
conditions varied. The principal effect of the Indian wars was to
weaken the enforcement of the laws on compulsory education, to
prevent the passage of new laws, and greatly to increase the number
of poor families unable to provide for the education of their children.
Thus forces were set in motion that influenced the legislation of these
colonies up to the Revolution, especially with respect to compulsory
education of poor children only, through the system of apprenticeship. In this transition period no new law bearing specifically on
compulsory education was enacted by any of these colonies, though
acts were passed by Connecticut in 1676[5] and 1684[6] to enforce the
laws on compulsory religious education; by Massachusetts in 1677,[7]
providing that Indian children bound out to the English should "be
taught and instructed in the Christian Religion"; and by Plymouth
in 1685,[8] giving power to selectmen, acting as a court, to bind out
poor children to service or as apprentices without the delay of six
months called for by the law of 1671, the educational features of
which still remained in force.

The second event of importance was the revocation of the charters
of the New England colonies or the seizure of their governments, and
the organization of all the territory under one government known
as the "Territory and Dominion of New England," 1686–89, with
Sir Edmund Andros[9] as governor. This is known as the Andros
régime. In this period, the laws and courts of the various New

England colonies, as the General Court of Connecticut put it, were, to a considerable extent, "disused."[10] Laws were made by authority of the governor and council for the whole dominion. This régime, following the hard times of the period 1675 to 1686, had a serious effect on educational progress with respect to both compulsory education and schools. One act[11] passed by this government March 17, 1687/8, affected the laws of all the New England colonies on compulsory education. It, in fact, repealed those in force, because of the omission of compulsory religious and educational clauses in previous laws which applied to all children, including apprentices. This was really a poor law and shows no evidence of interest in the mental or religious development of poor children. The law did not, of course, prevent the introduction of an educational clause in the indenture, but it did relieve all the towns of New England of any obligation to require a master to teach his apprentice to read.

With the end of the Andros régime in 1689 the regular governments of the individual colonies were resumed. Let us consider the legislation of the four New England colonies on this subject from 1689 to the Revolution. In 1691 Massachusetts was granted a new charter which changed the government and provided for the annexation of Plymouth colony. In the first session of the new government an act was passed which continued in force to November 10, 1692,[12] all laws which had been made by the "governour and company of Massachusetts Bay and the late government of New Plymouth." At the second session, in October, 1692,[13] a similar act was passed continuing such laws until "the general assembly shall take further order." The evident purpose of this legislation was to re-enact the whole body of law as set forth in the Massachusetts code of 1672 and that of New Plymouth of 1685. It will be remembered that these codes included the laws on compulsory education already discussed. Unfortunately for the progress of compulsory education, both of these continuing acts were disallowed by the Privy Council, August 22, 1695. The reason given was: "It hath been thought fit to repeal both the said acts. It being judged necessary that in any new Law to be enacted for the said purpose the Laws to be continued be therein expressed and particularly specified."[14] It is clear from this evidence that the Massachusetts code of 1672 and that of New

Plymouth in 1685 ceased to be in force at this date (1695), and, therefore, the compulsory education laws for children and apprentices which had appeared in the earlier codes of these colonies. Massachusetts did not issue a real code of laws again during the colonial period. Her laws, printed from time to time, were not codes but rather reprints of the session laws passed between the dates when they were brought together into single volumes for convenience, excluding, however, acts passed from 1692 on, which had been repealed.[15] No law was passed between 1692 and the Revolution involving compulsory education of all children in either religious or book education. Such laws as were passed refer exclusively to poor children apprenticed.

The first act of this character under the new charter was passed at the second session of the General Assembly in 1692.[16] It gave power to the selectmen, or overseers of the poor, with the consent of the justices of the peace, to bind "any poor children" as apprentices. The officers were also to take care that all children should be brought up or employed in some honest calling which would be "profitable unto themselves and to the publick." One misses in this act the compulsory educational and religious features, as well as the mention of special officers and penalties for non-enforcement. But inasmuch as the former law on compulsory education was still in force, the assembly may not have thought it necessary to include these features. With the notice of the disallowance of the continuing laws, however, the foregoing law was the only one in force in Massachusetts, including the former Plymouth colony, relating to the education of children through parents or masters.

The next act, of November 27, 1703,[17] remedied the omissions, in part, by declaring that the act of 1692 had been misconstrued as applying only to "children whose parents were receiving almes." The selectmen, or overseers of the poor, with the consent of two justices of the peace, were accordingly given power to bind out as apprentices all children whose parents the officers specified thought unable "to maintain" them, whether they received alms or were chargeable to the place or not. But an important clause was added, making an exception thus: "so as that they be not sessed to publick taxes or assessments, for the province or town charges." This clause

evidently would prevent the apprenticing of the child of anyone paying a tax, however small, and, therefore, left to chance the question
of his or her education. In the case of children actually apprenticed,
it was required that provision be made in the indenture for their instruction, namely, "to read and write, as they may be capable." This
would include girls as well as boys. Moreover, the officers mentioned
"shall inquire into the usage of children bound out by themselves
or their predecessors and endeavor to defend them from any wrongs
or injuries." Selectmen, overseers of the poor, constables, or "tythingmen" could complain to a justice of the peace or the county
court against a transgressor, who, on conviction, could be committed
to the house of correction. This power, apparently, might be used
to compel a master to abide by an educational clause of an indenture.
It will be noticed that no money penalty was imposed on officials,
parents, or masters, though this is one of the most characteristic
features of the earlier legislation. This act was revised in 1710.[18]
In the new law there was one important change, namely, that indentures should have a clause to the effect that only males were to
be taught to read and write and "females to read, as they respectively may be capable." This law remained in force[19] throughout the
colonial period, and applied to the great majority of children apprenticed. It was supplemented by other acts, but they involved only
special areas and affected relatively few children and, except for one
law, that of 1758, cannot be classed as compulsory acts.

Between 1703 and 1775 three supplementary acts were passed
making changes in the educational requirement of certain boys and
girls apprenticed, but the class of children to be apprenticed, and the
failure to include religious instruction, except in the case of Boston,
and the lack of money penalties for neglect—all these remained unchanged. An act of 1735[20] applied only to the town of Boston. This
is an early example of special legislation for towns or cities where the
conditions demanded special educational laws. This act provided
that in the town of Boston the overseers of the poor should bind out
into good families children who were unable "to distinguish the
alphabet or twenty-four letters, at the age of six years," for a
"decent and Christian education, as when parents are indigent and
rated nothing to the publick taxes, unless the children are judged

incapable, through some inevitable infirmity." Another special act of August 8, 1741,[21] applied to children of parents, unable to maintain them, living without the bounds of any town. Such children could be (not must be) apprenticed with the consent of two justices of the peace by overseers of the poor appointed by the justices of the county courts. The indenture was to contain a clause to the effect that males were to be taught "to read and write and cypher" and females to read only. There was no special provision for enforcement, and no special penalties mentioned for neglect. Moreover, relatively few children were affected by this law, since the great majority lived within the bounds of some town or district. This law was re-enacted[22] in 1749, and then superseded by the act of 1758. A third act[23] was that of July 4, 1771, which amplified that of 1710. It applied to a class of children not mentioned in that act, namely, those coming into a town from another town whose parents were not residents of the town to which the child came. As such children tended to become a burden and expense, either for removal or support, overseers of the poor were given power to bind out such children as apprentices, with the consent of two justices of the peace, in order to provide for their support if they stood in need, and if they were subject to be bound out in their town from which they came by any law of the province. The indentures of males were to contain a clause providing for reading, writing, and ciphering, and those of the females for reading and writing, "if they shall be capable." None of these three special acts can properly be called compulsory, as they lack the mandatory clauses and the provision for penalties.

Though the law of 1758[24] was limited in its application, it introduced for the first time since 1672 two important features of the earlier laws—a money penalty and specific power to remove an apprentice from a master who failed to give him the education specified in the indenture. Unfortunately, however, it applied only to "indented, bought or any way legally bound, servants or apprentice" living outside the bounds of a town or district, thus again, as in the act of 1741, affecting relatively few persons. However, when complaint was made to the county court that such servants or apprentices were neglected by masters or mistresses, "or that the education of such children in reading and writing and cyphering, according to the term of their indentures, had been unreasonably neglected," then such court after inquiry, and being satisfied that the complaint was just, could impose a fine of five pounds on a master or mistress and take such child from master or mistress, and, if the child were under age, the court could bind him or her to another person, males to twenty-one and females to eighteen years of age. If this law had been worded so as to apply to all children apprenticed, those living within towns as well as outside of towns, Massachusetts would have approached the ideals of her earlier legislation with respect to the education of apprentices.

It thus appears that the interest of Massachusetts in the compulsory religious and book education of all children suffered a marked decline from 1695 to the Revolution and that her laws on this subject affected only a relatively few poor children. Moreover, the question whether a child was to be apprenticed or not was left to the judgment of the selectmen, or overseers of the poor. In this sense, all of these acts were permissive and were in great contrast to those of the seventeenth century. Formerly, selectmen were compelled to apprentice poor children who were not taught to read, or suffer a fine of twenty shillings for neglect. None of the later laws provided a penalty on the selectmen or overseers of the poor for failure to apprentice. On the other hand, a penalty was not absolutely necessary to induce selectmen or overseers to bind out poor children as apprentices. The towns were always much worried about the increase of pauperism, and selectmen would feel the pressure to avoid the expense of the support of the poor if opportunity offered. The system of apprenticeship was one sure method of relieving the town of all, or a great portion, of the burden of supporting or of educating a poor child. Once a child was apprenticed, however, he might, under the laws above mentioned, or in case the indenture so provided, be given some book education. Since indentures were enforceable in the courts, and the principal act provided for a penalty—imprisonment for a master who neglected the law—the legislation retained a large measure of compulsion.

When Connecticut resumed her government May 9, 1689,[25] the General Court voted that all laws which were in force when Andros took possession of the government should again be in full force until further alteration. This decision revived the former law on the education of children. In 1690[26] a new act was passed in which the method of enforcement was greatly strengthened. The preamble states that former laws were ineffective and that there were "many persons unable to read the English tongue, and thereby incapable (of) to read the holy word of God or the good laws of the colony." The grand jurymen in each town were ordered once in the year at least "to visit each family they suspect to neglect this order," and see whether all children under age and servants could read "well the English tongue or be in a good procedure to learn the same or not." If they found neglect, they were to return to the next county court the names of the parents and masters of children so untaught, and the guilty parents and masters should then be fined twenty shillings for each child or servant "whose teaching is or shall be neglected." An additional clause, however, declared that the fine might be remitted if it appeared to the satisfaction of the court that the parent or master or neighbors were unable, through "incapacity," as the law reads, to cause them to be taught or the children or servants unable to learn.

In the law appearing in the code of 1702 several important changes occur. The revised law is based principally on those of 1673 and 1690. We may note, first, that the fine of twenty shillings for neglect could be imposed on parents and masters, as well as on selectmen and grand jurymen, "for the use of the poor of the Town." The agency to determine the violation of the law was "any one Assistant or Justice of the Peace to issue and determine the same" instead of the county court. Grand jurymen were particularly warned to be very careful in seeing to the education of children. Secondly, the selectmen, with the advice of the "next assistant or justice of the Peace," could take children and apprentices from parents and masters "negligent of their Duties, in the particulars above mentioned," and place them with others "to the end they may be instructed and forced to submit to Government." Thirdly, questions on the catechism were to be propounded by parents and ministers, the latter instead of the selectmen as formerly. This law relieved the grand jurymen of two duties required by the act of 1690: first, that of visiting, inspecting, and testing children; and, second, that of reporting the names of such as could not read to the county court.

All these changes, however, are less important than one which resulted in the omission of a clause appearing in both of the previous codes of 1650 and 1673. According to the original law, masters of families must catechize their children and servants weekly in the grounds and principles of religion, but if unable to "do so much," they must compel children and apprentices to memorize "a short orthodox catechism." In the code of 1702 and the subsequent codes to the Revolution,[27] the former clause relating to weekly catechizing is omitted, and the latter follows the provisions relating to the requirement for book education. The result was that parents and masters "unable to do so much"—namely, to teach a child "perfectly to read the English tongue" by themselves or others—had only to see that such children and apprentices committed a catechism to memory. Thus as Massachusetts failed to re-enact her general compulsory education act, as found in the code of 1672, so Connecticut, by this revision greatly weakened her law, for illiterate parents or masters could plead that they were "unable" to teach reading. In such a case the officers responsible would have no power to fine a parent or master for such neglect; nor would it be legal for the selectmen to apprentice a child or take an apprentice from a master because of neglect of education, provided the child or apprentice learned an orthodox catechism.

Two acts were passed between 1702 and 1750 as follows: One[28] was an enforcing act of October, 1715, and ordered judges and justices to execute laws, and selectmen to see that every family procured a Bible and in case of neglect to "make return thereof to the next authority"; constables and grand jurymen were to "make diligent search after and presentment of all breaches of the following laws of this colony, 1. An Act entitled Children to be Educated," etc. The second[29] was a special compulsory education act applying to Indians. Complaint was made May 11, 1727, that the English having Indian children "put out" to them to be brought up "do neglect to learn them to read and instruct them in the principles of the Christian faith." It was, therefore, ordered that such do their utmost to teach them to read English and to catechize them. The penalty for neglect by masters and mistresses was severe, namely, a fine of forty shillings; and report was to be made by two grand jury-men or selectmen, and then the negligent persons were to be sum-moned before an assistant or justice of the peace for judgment. The title of the code of 1750 reads, "Acts and Laws of His Majesty's English Colony of Connecticut. etc., New London, 1750." The title of the law on children is "An Act for Educating, and Governing of Children." In this law[30] the wording is simplified, and the substitu-tion of learning a catechism for "Ability to Read the English Tongue well" is even more plainly indicated. The reading is, "That all Parents, and Masters of Children, shall by themselves, or Others, Teach, and Instruct; or cause to be Taught, and Instructed, all such Children as are under their Care, and Government, according to their Ability to Read the *English* Tongue well; and to know the Laws against Capital Offenders: And if unable to do so much, then at least to Learn some short Orthodox Catechism without Book, etc." Another change was that of levying the penalty of twenty shillings only on the parent and master, thereby relieving the selectmen and grand jurymen of liability to a penalty as was the case 1702–50. The method of trial and conviction and the provision for apprenticing remain the same as in the code of 1702. The purpose of apprenticing is made more specific, namely, "to the end they may be suitably Instructed, Imployed and Governed."

It is apparent that there is considerable divergence from 1690 to the Revolution in the legislation of Connecticut as compared with that of Massachusetts. The most notable difference is the fact that in Connecticut, not only is compulsory religious instruction retained, but it is even made a possible substitute for book education. Second-ly, the system of money penalties to be imposed on officers or parents is retained throughout the period, as well as the penalty of removal of the child from a parent or master for neglect. We may note also that the emphasis remains, as formerly, on religious and book educa-tion. We have no series of laws in Connecticut comparable to those of Massachusetts relating specifically to the education of poor children through apprenticeship. Finally, the law applied to all, not merely to poor children. Connecticut did not take for granted, for example, as did Massachusetts, that every parent paying a tax might be depended on to have his child taught to read.

New Hampshire, by a concurrent vote[31] of the Council and Assembly, May 10, 1712, declared that neglect by parents and masters in instructing youth was causing "Ignorance, ill Manners and Irreligion." Therefore, it should be lawful for selectmen with a justice of the peace to examine "all Youth of Tenn Years of Age whether they shall have been taught to Read and All those which cannot Read at Said Age to binde out to good Masters who shall be Obleidged to Learn them to Read and write till they shall be of Age." This is only partially compulsory, since it merely gives power to, does not compel, selectmen to act. If, however, a child was bound out, there was compulsion on the master to teach his apprentice to read and write. No penalty for neglect, however, was provided for either in terms of money or removal of the child. The motive for this vote was primarily educational rather than economic. This vote was not incorporated into a formal law and does not appear in any of the codes giving the laws in force at subsequent dates. A law[32] passed May 2, 1719, for regulating townships gave power to the selectmen, or overseers of the poor, to see that children were brought up to "Some honest Calling which may be profitable to themselves and the publick." They were also ordered, with the assent of two justices of the peace, to bind any poor children belonging to such town to be apprentices "where they shall see convenient," and indentures were made legal. No penalty was provided for neglect, and no book or religious education was specified.

It was not until January 17, 1766,[33] that New Hampshire passed an act involving compulsory book education. The preamble states that poor people "neglect the care and Education of their Children." The selectmen or overseers of the poor, with the assent of two justices of the peace, were, therefore, given power to set to work or "bind out as Apprentices . . . . all Such Children . . . . whose Parents" were thought unable "to maintain" them, whether they received alms or were a charge to the town or parish or not. Overseers of the poor were ordered to insert a clause in the contract or indenture, which must be in writing, to this effect: "for the Benefit of Such Children; at the least that the Master be Instructed to teach Males to read and write, and the Females to read." The officers mentioned "shall inquire into the Usage of Children bound out by themselves or predecessors in said Office, and Endeavor to defend them from wrongs or Injuries." In the case of children not supported by the town, parents were to be directed voluntarily to bind out their children if they could not maintain them, and if they neglected or placed them with persons "Prejudicial to the advantage of the Child," then the officers could remove and bind them out as before. This act lacks the money penalty for neglect by either parent or officers, but a penalty of removal might fall on parents and masters who neglected the education of their children or apprentices, and, when children were bound out, book education was required. The law as a whole is weaker in its compulsory aspect than that of Connecticut, but stronger than those of Massachusetts, particularly because it could be applied even to the children of parents who paid a tax.

Rhode Island alone, of the six New England colonies under consideration, did not pass any compulsory education law, though she enacted laws on apprenticeship.[34] The reasons for the failure of Rhode Island are the same as those which account for her failure to enact laws for compulsory schools. Indeed, Rhode Island's legislation on other matters, such as religion, is in great contrast to that of Massachusetts, New Haven, Connecticut, and Plymouth. The principal cause was the early separation of church and state and the fact that a great variety of religious sects sought Rhode Island as a haven of refuge. The result was a weak central government, lack of unity of religious belief, and the tendency toward individualism—all of which hindered the enactment of general laws on compulsory education.

It is clear that the New England colonies agreed on the main principles of compulsory education where it was introduced.[35] First, all of them, save Rhode Island, finally accepted the responsibility for seeing that a minimum of education was given to all poor children, and in most of the seventeenth century to all children. Secondly, they agreed in making the parent or master the direct agency for teaching, though the option was given of employing others. In the seventeenth century the plan presupposed literate parents or masters, or else ability to pay for instruction—a large assumption, indeed. Such a conception of compulsory education is very different from the present plan of compulsory attendance at organized schools at public expense. Again, these New England colonies were agreed on the principle of adequate machinery for enforcing the laws. Responsible officers were named to locate negligent parents or masters and to test the education of children. The colonies were agreed in having masters and parents, or various responsible officers, presented to some competent court for trial if found negligent. They were agreed in providing for penalties to be imposed on the officials responsible for enforcement or on the parents or masters for proved neglect of the law. In some cases, a money penalty was provided for, in others, the removal of the child, and, finally, even imprisonment of the guilty person. All of the colonies except Rhode Island specified that the agency of apprenticeship for book education of poor children should be used. One cannot but marvel at the high ideals of the framers of these laws, the extraordinary completeness of the acts, especially with respect to the plans for enforcement, and the great superiority of the New England colonies over all others in enacting laws on compulsory education for all children before 1672.

We may also note that parental education and that obtained through the system of apprenticeship was under public control; selectmen, overseers of the poor, justices of the peace, and magistrates being the principal officers, and town and county courts the principal agencies for trial of offenders. Written indentures were the rule, and were recorded in town, county, or colony records. Because they were in the nature of contracts, and because they were in some cases also specifically declared to be legal, these indentures were enforceable in the courts. Practically all of these laws mention that males were to serve to the age of twenty-one and girls to eighteen. Children could be bound out by voluntary action of parents at any time, but this procedure and the enforcement of the indenture were matters of public control. It will be noted that the scope of compulsory education varied in the different colonies. Broadly speaking, in the seventeenth century the general requirement was reading only, plus some form of religious education, for all boys and girls, whether apprenticed or not. New Haven was the exception in requiring both reading and writing for boys from 1660 to 1665. In most of the eighteenth century only Connecticut required either instruction in reading or religion for all children. Massachusetts required instruction in reading and writing only for boys apprenticed, and reading only for girls apprenticed, except in the case of the latter for the brief period 1703–10. The addition of "cyphering" for boys apprenticed, from 1741 on, was only for those living outside of towns and districts, or those entering a town from 1771 on, from some other town. The addition of writing for girls was only for those corresponding to this last case mentioned for boys. The requirement in New Hampshire, from 1766 on, was reading and writing for boys, and reading for girls, apprenticed, as in Massachusetts. Neither of these last-mentioned colonies required religious instruction in the eighteenth century, and Rhode Island required neither book nor religious education at any time in the colonial period, though a requirement for reading or writing usually is included in indentures.

As a whole, the eighteenth century marks a decline in the efforts toward compulsory education. In Massachusetts the emphasis is placed on vocational training and the maintenance of poor children rather than on the mental and religious education of all children, whether apprenticed or not. Secondly, there is a failure to make the apprenticing of poor children certain because of the omission of money or other penalties levied on officers responsible for neglect, though certain towns like Boston made this compulsory. There are good reasons for this difference of attitude toward compulsory education, but these same reasons also account for other changes in the educational development of the New England colonies in the eighteenth century. We may note the following: first, a weakening of the religious motive and in particular a decline in the influence of the clergy, quite apparent by 1676; second, the spread of population toward the outer boundaries of the towns and to the interior and frontier areas of the colonies, thus making enforcement of laws affecting all children very difficult; third, the effect on the second and third generations of a frontier environment, that is, a decline in educational, religious, and moral ideals; fourth, the decentralizing tendencies of democracy which weakened the power of the central government and produced individualism—namely, opposition to minute regulation of private life; fifth, the great demand for industrial efficiency as the tendency toward manufactures, trade, and commerce developed, and as population increased, so that division of labor became more necessary, especially in the larger towns. It should also be noted that laws establishing compulsory town schools were enacted by most of the New England colonies, that the practice

TABLE I

FOR ALL CHILDREN

Massachusetts	1642–1695
Including New Hampshire	1641–1679
Including Maine	1652–1695
Including New Plymouth	1691–1695
New Haven	1655–1665
New Plymouth	1671–1691
Connecticut	1650–1702
Including New Haven	1665–1702
Optional book or religious education (including New Haven)	1702–1776

FOR CHILDREN APPRENTICED ONLY

Massachusetts (including Maine and New Plymouth)	1703–1776
New Hampshire	1766–1776

developed of providing free education at these schools for poor children, and that support by a general property tax, making schools free for all, was common from the second quarter of the eighteenth century. There was, therefore, less pressure to emphasize parental education. It was, perhaps, assumed that, as a result, only poor children would fail to gain a knowledge of reading and that this class was theoretically provided for by the acts for education through apprenticeship.[36] Table I will show those portions of New England which were under compulsory education laws requiring some book education, during the colonial period.

CHAPTER VIII

COMPULSORY AND FREE EDUCATION FOR POOR CHILDREN AND APPRENTICES[1]

Compulsory education in the home, by parents or others, or by masters through the system of apprenticeship, with appropriate penalties for neglect, preceded by two centuries the modern idea of compelling pupils to attend organized schools for free education at public expense. This system, as developed in New England, was of great importance for three classes of children: for apprentices, for those "put out" to service for their maintenance only by selectmen or overseers of the poor, and for the children of illiterate parents or those too poor to pay tuition fees commonly exacted in many town schools in the seventeenth and even in the eighteenth century. In this last case the law virtually forced towns to pay the cost of educating poor children.

The educational legislation of the New England colonies was of two general types. There were laws, like that of Massachusetts (1647), which made the establishment of schools compulsory for all towns of a certain population; viz., in the case of elementary education, for towns of fifty householders; those having a population of about two hundred and fifty people. It should be understood that this law and other similar laws provided only for schools. It did not compel parents or others to send a child to school. Not a clause is found in a single educational act of any New England colony up to the Revolution which made attendance at school compulsory.

Paralleling this legislation on schools there were acts requiring parents, masters, or others to see that children should have the ability to read. Such laws however varied considerably with respect to the length of time they were in operation and the class of children involved. In Massachusetts education was compulsory for all children to 1695 and after that only for certain classes of poor children bound out. In Connecticut a general law was in operation throughout the colonial period. This chapter is intended to show how these laws worked in practice; what efforts various officers, parents or masters, towns and county courts, made to enforce the law in question. The relation of the system of compulsory schools to that of compulsory education is also considered.

The germ of a system of education through agencies other than organized schools is found in English laws and practice, particularly from about the middle of the sixteenth century.[2] The English Statute of Apprentices of 1562 and the Poor Law Act of 1601 provided, the former, for industrial or trade education, and the latter, for the maintenance of poor children through the system of apprenticeship or by "binding out." The indenture or contract between the master and the apprentice or the master and the overseers of the poor sets forth the duties and obligations of each party. In general the master agreed to teach the apprentice a trade and support him for a period of years in return for his labor. In binding out a poor child for maintenance the master need provide only support, unless otherwise specified in the indenture. The purpose of the first act was to provide skilled workers and that of the second to help solve the problem of pauperism. In both cases the indenture of apprenticeship was publicly recorded by town authorities, and if either master or apprentice violated his agreement an appeal could be made to a justice of the peace.[3] While neither the Statute of Apprentices nor the Poor Law Act provided that masters were under any obligation to teach the rudiments of education, the use of the system of apprenticeship as a means of education was not unknown, since indentures have survived that contain an educational clause. One for Leicester reads: "A glover, for 20s., agrees to take an orphan boy and keep him as his own child, without further cost to the town, till he is of years of discretion and then take him as an apprentice, or keep him at school as well as if he were his own child, if he will take learning."[4]

It is also true that no English law provided for three types of education, as did that of Massachusetts in 1642; namely, industrial training, ability to read, and religious education (catechizing). The act complains of "the great neglect in many parents and masters in training up their children in learning and labor and other employments which may be profitable to the Commonwealth . . . . especially of their ability to read and understand the principles of religion

and the capital lawes of the country." The penalty on such parents
was the loss of their children—"to put forth apprentice the children
of such as shall not be able and fitt to employ and bring them up."
As education was sometimes provided for in English indentures, so
there are examples of compulsory religious training by town ordinance. Interestingly enough, this same town, Leicester, provides an
example.

> FOR CHILDREN: Also it was then (anno Eliz. XXII°) further agreed that
> every childe from the age of viii yeres upwards shalbe toughte the Lords Prayer,
> the Articles of there beleefe, and also to answere to certen poynts of the Cate-
> chisme, upon a peynaltie to the parents and masters, of everyone to the con-
> trarye, beinge no nedyates,* as followeth:—viz. the XXXIIII[ti] xii[d]., the
> XLVIII[ti] vi[d]—and other commonners iii[d]. a pece, or iii dayes ymprisonment at
> Mr. Mayors pleysure. And to begyn att Christomas next comynge.[5]

> * viz: idiots.

The imposition of a penalty upon those who failed to give their
children religious instruction is of great interest, as it is in principle
one of the important ideas back of the Massachusetts law of 1642.
It does not appear, however, that in the foregoing case children were
to be taught to read but rather to repeat from memory the subject
matter mentioned. The colonists, then, inherited the idea of binding
out children for the purpose of industrial education; that of including in indentures a clause providing for the rudiments of education,
that of publicly recording indentures and enforcing them through
court action, and that of imposing penalties on parents and masters
for neglect of duty.

Before the passage of this first Massachusetts act there are examples of the practice of including an educational clause in an indenture of apprenticeship. Thus Thomas Lechford, a lawyer in Boston, records in his notebook the substance of an indenture of date
1639 to this effect: "Dermondt Matthew did bind Teg Mathew his
sonne a child of 9 yeares old apprentice to the Said George Strange
for ten years from the said 9th day of May [1639] with Covenant to
keepe him two yeares at School."[6] Similarly, in New Haven in the
same year Charles Higginson was apprenticed to Thomas Fugill,
"and to keep him att schoole one yeare, or else to advantage him as
much in his education as a years learning comes to."[7] In the first

case because Strange refused to show the indenture to the father of the boy, the former requested the court that "they [the indentures] may be recorded." In the second case Higginson's indenture was recorded in the *New Haven Colony Records*.

The examples given show the process of the transfer of institutions and ideas from the Old to the New World. But besides the reproduction of current practices the colonial assemblies often modified old or invented, so to speak, new social institutions and practices. A most significant contribution was made by Massachusetts, when by the act of 1642 the idea of industrial and religious education was combined with that of providing for the rudiments of education by making all three compulsory with provision for penalties to be imposed on those responsible for neglect.

The responsibility for the enforcement of the various laws providing for the education of children through parents or masters of apprentices or through those to whom poor children were "bound out," fell for the most part on the selectmen and overseers of the poor of the various towns and on the county courts, though some other officials were involved, such as constables, tithingmen and grand jurors. The indentures or agreements were recorded both in town and county-court records where also are found examples of the methods of enforcing the laws.

A common practice was that of apprenticing a child for the purpose of teaching him a particular trade and also of instructing him in reading and religion. Watertown, Massachusetts, voted (1656):

These are to show, that Elizabeth Brailbrook widow of Watertown, hath put her daughter (with the consent of the selectmen) into the hands of Simont Tomson & his wife of Ipswich ropemaker to be as an apprentice, untill she comes to the age of eighteen years, in which time the said Sarah is to serve them in all lawful Comands, and the said Simont is to teach her to reade the English Tongue, and to instruct her in the knowledge of God and his Ways.[8]

A typical indenture[9] reads as follows:

This indenture witnesseth that Jonathan Stoughton, son of Thomas Stoughton of Windsor in the county of hartford and Coloney of Connecticut in new england, with his father's consent hath put him selfe an apprentice to Nathan day of the aboue said windsor county and coloney: blacksmith and white smith to Learn his art, trade or mystery after the manner of an Apprentice to serve him until the said Jonathan Stoughton attaines the age of twenty-one years, during all which time the said apprentice his master faithfully shall serve, his secrets keep, his Lawful commands gladly obaye he shall not do any damage to his said master nor see it don by others without giveing notice thereof to his said master. He shall not waste his said master's goods or Lend them unLawfully to aney, he shall not commit fornication nor contract matrimony within the said terme, at cards, dice or any other unlawfull game he shall not play whereby his said master may suffer damage. he shall not absent himself day or night from his master's service without his leave. nor haunt ale houses, Taverns or playhouses butt in all things behave himselfe as a faithfull apprentice ought to do during the said terme, and the said master shall do his utmost to teach and Instruct the said apprentice in the above mentioned blacksmith and white smiths trade and mistery and to teach or caus the said apprentice to be Taught the art of Arithmatick to such a degree that he may be able to keep a book well, and provide for him meat, drink, apparel, washing and lodging and phisick in sickness and health suitable for such an apprentice during the said terms, and att the end of said terme the said master shall furnish the said apprentice with two good new suits of apparel boath wooling and lining for all parts of his body suitable for such an apprentice beside that apparel he carrieth with him and for the performance of all and every the said covenants and agreement either of the said parties bind themselves unto the other by these presents in witness whereof they have interchangeably put their hands and seals this first day of September in the year of our Lord god, 1727.

And I the said Daniel Cook do promise and Ingage for myself my Executors and administrators to Learn and Instruct my said Apprentis William Potter In the trade mistry or art of a Joyner in the best manner that I Can within the said term, and also Instruct him in the trade of a House Carpenter as I have oppertunity; and not put him to any other servis dureing the said term without his Concent; and also Learn or Cause him to be Learned to or taught to Reade English and wright and Cypher so far as to keep a Booke.

In the Watertown case the cost of education was borne by the master. There are other cases, however, where the town paid a part of the cost. For example, the selectmen of Dorchester, Massachusetts, made the following agreement (1651):

It is agreed between the Selectmen and br Tolman that hee shall take Henry lakes child to keepe it untill it com to 21 years of age etc. and therefore to haue 26 pounds and to give security to the towne and to teach it to reade and wright and when it is capable if he lives the said br Tolman to teach it his trade.[10]

The money paid for the education of this child was a charge on the taxable property of the town and hence illustrates partial town support of education for a poor child. There are many other examples of this practice.[11]

When indentures were made under the direction of the county court the cost of education usually fell on the master. Thus a boy, Hugh March of Newbury, of his own will and with the consent of his parents was apprenticed to Benjamin Lowle, of Newbury, blacksmith, for six years, "to learn the trade of a blacksmith, and said Lowle to perfect him in writing and casting accounts, in reading English and in the trade of making or mending locks."[12]

In some cases poor children were bound out with the express provision that masters must not only teach the child a trade but provide for their education by sending them to school for a specified period.[13]

Besides the method of providing for the education of children through masters of apprentices the New England assemblies also provided for parental responsibility; viz., teaching children to read, regardless of whether the child was bound out or not.[14] Selectmen or others were instructed by a vote in town meeting to visit homes of parents and masters and see that the laws on education were enforced. The first town to recognize the importance of a general education for all children was, as we might expect, Cambridge, the location of Harvard College. On November 9, 1642, five months after the passage of the law mentioned, the town meeting voted as follows: "According to an order by Courte made the last generall courte for the townesmen to see to the educating children."[15] It was ordered that six men named should be responsible for all the families living within specified boundaries; that is, each must see that children within his district could read, etc. So Billerica (1661) appointed two men "to examine the severall families in our town whether the children and servants are taught in the precepts of religion in reading and learning their cathechism."[16] In 1675 this duty was delegated to a minister, thus:

The selectmen do order that all children and youth, single persons from eight years old and upward, their parents and masters shall send such children and servants to the Rev. Mr. Samuel Whiting, at such times as shall afterwards be appointed by him, to be examined of both [catechizing and reading], as hoping this might be a good expedient for the encouragement of all superiors and youth.[17]

The Watertown selectmen were also anxious to obey the law and to prevent illiteracy in their town.

January the 3d 1670.—At a meeting of the select men at the house of Isaake Sterns: It was further agreed that the select men should goe thrugh the town in their ceueral quarters to make tryall whether children and servants be educated in Learneing to read the English tongue and in the Knowledg of the capitall Laws according to the Law of the Country also that they may be educated in sum orthadox Catacise.[18]

Later in the year the town became anxious about the education of particular children.

At a generall towne meeteing Nov. 7, 1670. Ordered that John Edy seir shall goe to John Fisk his house and to George Lorance and Willyam preist houseis to inquir a bought their Children wither they be Lerned to read the english tong and in case they be defective to warne in the said John George and Willyam to the next meeting of the selectmen.[19]

The result of this inquiry was somewhat discouraging.

Willyam priest John Fisk and George Lorance being warned to a meeting of the select men at John Bigulah his house they makeing their a peerance: and being found defecttive weer admonished for not Learning their Children to read the english toung; weer convinced did acknowledg their neglect and did promise a mendment.[2]

Two years later there was another still more saddening report.

Nathan fisk John whitney and Isaak mickstur meaking return of thear inquiry aftur childrens edduccation finde that John fisks chilldren ear naythur taught to read nor yet thear caticise.[21]

The Dorchester selectmen found (1671) one parent who did not take kindly to the duty of educating his son. Timothy Wales replied in "words and answers [which] were very offensive and contemptuous unto the Selectmen." Summoned again he appeared with his sons

and upon examination of the boys they weer found to be very Ignorant and not able to read, and being admonished was dismissed at that time only he made some acknowledgment of his offensive words and carriage the last day of meeting and that in wrighting which remains on file.[22]

When the selectmen were unable to comply with the law because of the resistance of parents they sometimes appealed to the county court. The selectmen of Lancaster wrote a letter (1673) to the court complaining that they had labored with a certain Edmund Parker "in Reference to his son to get him sum learning and to bring him up to som employment according as the law provides or suffer them to doe it, but nothing would prevail with him." The court replied that unless Mr. Parker reformed the selectmen should "dispose of the sonne to service where he may be better taught and Governed."[23]

There are cases of the presentment of individuals to a county court for neglecting to teach their children to read as required by the law. Thus in September, 1677, Goodman Lancelot Granger of Suffield was presented to the Hampshire County Court "for the neglect of learning his Children to read." In March, 1678, he appeared and said he was "using the means to learn them to read, and promised to do his best and was discharged."[24]

The selectmen of towns were also presented to the county courts for breach of the laws on education, catechizing, and unemployment. An early case is that of the selectmen of Charlestown. It reads as follows:

Charlestowne Selectmen being presented for not observing the Law conc'ning the Katechiseing of Children, and Keeping them to imployment. The Court comended it to ye selectmen, that they attend their duty there in as the law directed, and make returne thereof to the next Court, and to pay costs—2s. 6d.[25]

Topsfield was also presented. The selectmen were ordered to cease their "former neglect" and to bring to the next court a list of the names of all "yong persons." Attention was called to the law (1648) which required that the selectmen see that all youth be taught "to read perfectly the English tongue, have knowledge of the capital laws, and be taught some orthodox catechism."[26] York County Court, in Maine, 1675, presented the selectmen of several towns for neglect of the law. That for Kittery reads: "We present the Selectmen of the town of Kittery, for not taking care that their children and youth be taught their catechism and education according to Law."[27]

In July, 1674, the selectmen of Salem, Beverley, and Manchester were presented for failure to see that the children of their towns were properly educated. The presentment of Salem and the reply of Beverley follow:

The Selectmen of Salem being presented for breach of that law Instituted, children and youth in page 26 they not making of it to appeare, the said law have beene fully observed, they are admonished to take care to see that wholesom and profitable law to the comon wealth be duly executed and this court shall give you all due incouragement, advice and assistants therin. And further doe order that upon the penalty of £10 they bring into the next court at Salem, an acct. of what youth from the age of 9 yeares and upward that canot read or are not profitably employed to the benefitt of the Comonwealth and to pay costs.[28]

The return[29] made by Beverley in November, 1674, follows:

This Present writing may humbly Informe the honoured Court now sitting at Salem that whereas the honourable court was pleased at the last Sessions to stirr and Admonish the selectmen of Beverly to take Care not only to see that good and wholesome Law Intituled Children and youth might be duly observed but Likewise to Lay it as an Injunction upon the aforesaid selectmen that Return Bee made to this honoured court of what youth there are within the town from the age of nine years and upwards that cannot Read or are not proffitably Imployed to the benefitt of the Comonwealth. Now the above said selectmen have in obeidience not only to that good and wholesome Law but likewise to this honoured Courts particular Order and injunction whose fatherly care wee desire to so acknowledge with all thankfulness given warning in a general way that the severall masters of families doe Instruct their Children and servants in the particulars required in the said law before mentioned and likewise have more lately taken a more particular acount of the State of the youth within our limitts in that Respect and doe not find any youth of the age of nine yeares or exceeding it that canot read: or that are not Induvouring as those under whose tuition those are, being very few doe say who have likewise promised to use their farther Indeavour to perfect them in reading: neither doe not find any that are not Imployed in some honest and Lawful calling as those under whose charge they are doe find caus to apoint.

Per order of the Select Men
PAUL SHORIDIK

Dat. 24th. 9th: 1674

The selectmen of the town of Manchester certified to the court that they had performed their duty and the law was observed,[30] and the court at this session accepted the returns of all three towns.[31]

These reports concerning the state of education are decidedly optimistic, but they are quite common. When towns were indicted the selectmen were compelled to satisfy the county court of the ability of children within their town to read. If found guilty of negligence they might be fined. In answer to an inquiry of the Middlesex County Court (1680), five towns reported on the state of their schools. All asserted that their educational facilities were satisfactory. Concord, for example, replied: "As for Schools, we have in every quarter of the Town both men and women that teach to read and write English, when parents can spare their children or others go to them."³² This proves, however, that education was available rather than actually given to all children. A more detailed report is that of the town of Wayland (1680) which reads as follows:

> And as for Schools, tho' there be no stated school in this town, for that the inhabitants are so scattered in their dwellings that it cannot well be, yet such is the case that, by having two school dames on each side of the river, that teacheth small children to spell and read, which is so managed by the parents and governors at home, and prosecuted after such sort as that the selectmen who distributed themselves did within three months last past so examine families, children, and youth, both as to good manners, orderly living, catechizing, and reading, as that they returned from all parts a comfortable good account of all these matters, and render them growing in several families beyond expectation, rarely reprovable anywhere, encouraging in most places, and in others very commendable, so as that the end is accomplished hitherto. And for teaching to write or cypher, here is Mr. Thomas Walker, and two or three others about this town, that do teach therein, and are ready to teach all others that need, if people will come or send them.³³

It is difficult to believe that in all these towns most children were able to read at this date, but such is the evidence given by the select-men. It is evident that they were motivated by the desire to avoid a penalty.

Connecticut does not seem to have made as much effort as Massachusetts to enforce her laws on education, although her act of 1690 complains that there were "many persons unable to read the English tongue, and thereby incapable [of] to read the holy word of God or the good laws of the colony."³⁴ A school act of 1678 had provided that every town of thirty families should maintain a school to teach children to read and write. A vote of the town of Norwich (1680) indicates that this town was willing to bear the whole expense of educating poor children:

> 1st, that parents send their children; 2d, that they pay their proportion, according to what is judged just; 3d, that they take care parents be not oppressed, espeshally such who are disabled; 4th, that whatever is additionally necessary for the perfecting the maintenance of a school-master, is a charge and expense belonging to all the inhabitants of the town, and to be gathered as other rates; 5th, whatever else is necessary to a prudent carrying through this occation is comitted to the discretion of the said selectmen.³⁵

The quality and quantity of instruction of course depended on the ability of both teacher and child. The case of Samuel Hadley apprenticed to Joseph Pike who was to be taught the trade of a weaver ("Said Pike was to teach him to read and write well") is an example. The case came before the county court. One deponent swore[36] that while Hadley had lived at his house "he and his sisters took a great deal of care and diligently instructed him in reading and he was put to school, but he did not gain much of what might have been expected." The deponent further stated, "In his ordinary employment he was incapastious that I never saw one of that age soe unfit for larning and any work in which was needfull to have discresion used."

The New England colonies passed important acts establishing a system of compulsory schools, as well as a system of compulsory education. The famous Act of Massachusetts (1647) provided that when towns attained a population of fifty families, someone must be appointed to teach children who came to him to read and write. Advantage was taken of this and similar acts by parents and by masters of apprentices in order to comply with the requirement that all children must be taught to read. That is, a choice could be made whether a child should be taught at home or sent to a school. Since in many towns tuition fees were charged, the problem of the education of children by illiterate or poor parents and masters was a common one.

Salem voted,[37] September 30, 1644, "Also that if any poore body hath children or a childe, to be put to school and not able to pay for their schooling, that the Towne will pay by rate." Plymouth voted (1705) that "children of such as through poverty are rendered oncapable to pay, theire Children to goe to school free."[38]

In the eighteenth century the idea of a free school for all children made rapid progress. This was a great advantage to those to whom poor children were bound out, for by the terms of the indenture they were required to see that the child received the rudiments of education. If parents or masters could afford to pay a tuition fee they were often required to do so in towns where such fees were demanded. Thus, "at a Town Meeting held at plimouth July 31, 1699 voted that the selectmen should take care to provide A scoole

Master . . . . and that Every Schollar that Coms to *wrigh or syfer* or to learn latten shall pay 3 pence per weke if to Read only then to pay 3 half pence per weke to be paid by their Masters or parents."[39]

On the other hand, Northampton voted (1693) £40 to the school-master "and the Scholars to go free."[40] So Malden (1701) declared[41] that "the School is to be free for all the inhabitants." Another method is illustrated by a vote[42] of Charlestown in 1712.

Then voted five pound to be raised for the payment for some poor Children at such Womens Schools as Shall be allowed of by the Selectmen being for such Children . . . . as those parents are not able to bring them to School which Shall be determined by Capt Samuel Phipps and Capt Jonathan Dowe.

During the eighteenth century the indentures apprenticing poor children continued to include clauses requiring instruction in the rudiments of education as required by the laws. Where in 1642 only reading was required, the poor law of 1710 (Mass.) provided[43] that when male children whose parents did not pay taxes were bound out, such children must be taught both reading and writing (females reading only), and that officers must inquire into the "usage" of children bound out. Malden "voted [1745] that Edward Wayte shall have John Ramsdell who is about five years old till he come of age and said Wayt shall have thirty pounds old tenor with him in case said Waitt wil be obliged to learne said child to read, wright and cypher and also to learne him the Shoemakers trade."[44]

The practice of inspecting the status of apprentices according to the act of 1710 (Mass.) is illustrated by a vote of the selectmen of Charlestown:

In observance of a Province Law the Selectmen as overseers of the Poor being accompanied with the Rev. Mr. Hull Abbot and Mr. Seth Sweetser school-master have taken their Journeys to visit the Children put out by Indenture under their care (as they did last year) and find them well provided for, viz., at Watertown Ephraim Mallit with Nathan Fisk, and Josiah Dyer with Samuel Bowman, etc.[45]

The names of seven boys and six girls are given.

It appears, then, that the acts providing for instruction by parents in the home, by masters of apprentices, and by others, such as schoolmasters or schoolmistresses, were enforced by towns and county courts; that a system of visitation and scrutiny by selectmen and grand jurors existed; and that poor children were taken from their parents and bound out as apprentices and given the rudiments of education as required by law. Since apprenticeship was compulsory for children of those parents who could not bring them up properly and since indentures generally included clauses providing that the child should be taught to read and were publicly recorded, we may conclude that many children profited from this system, especially in the seventeenth century. After the development of the idea of a free public school for all children, in such towns as took this action, there was free education for poor children and apprentices; viz., masters of apprentices, if they chose, might conform to the requirement for education as set forth in the indenture by sending an apprentice to a free school. The laws providing for parental responsibility and those for making the master of an apprentice directly responsible for education, as administered by selectmen, grand jurors, and county courts, are important in estimating the facilities and extent of free elementary education for poor children. Taken in connection with the laws compelling towns to set up elementary schools and the tendency to support these schools by a general tax on all property holders for the benefit of all children, one can better appreciate the basis of New England's right to claim great credit for establishing the American idea of universal elementary education for all children.

PART III

FREE EDUCATION FOR POOR CHILDREN
AND APPRENTICES IN THE SOUTH

CHAPTER IX

INFLUENCES AFFECTING EDUCATION
IN THE SOUTH

From the founding of the American colonies until the present time, education has not been in the hands of the central government. During the colonial period of our history each colony acted independently in this matter, and when our constitution was formed the states retained the power to regulate education. Moreover, during the colonial period and until the second quarter of the nineteenth century, with few exceptions, both colonies and states left the subject almost wholly in the power of the local units of government—the town, district, county, or parish—or intrusted education to private or other agencies. This led to extreme variation in educational ideals, institutions, and practices, many of which have persisted to this day.

It has not been sufficiently emphasized that the same great underlying forces which have, to a large extent, determined the origin and development of American institutions of a political, social, and religious character have also determined those relating to education. These forces have had their basis in specific geographical areas, or sections, such as New England, the South, and the West. In these sections the people enacted legislation to establish and control types of institutions, the form and development of which tended to become closely adjusted to the needs and desires of the people. These were determined by inherited ideals and institutions, by environment, and by other factors, previously discussed with respect to New England.[1]

Perhaps even more strikingly than was the case in New England, the southern group of colonies reflected in their educational legislation and institutions their conditions of life and environment and their unique political, social, and economic system. Some of these original factors have continued to influence the educational progress of the South even to the present time. These facts well illustrate the reason why the American public-school system is an ideal rather than a fact; why we have forty-eight systems rather than one national system; why such important variations in the state systems persist, and why they continue to be the despair of those who wish to remodel our whole educational system in order that educational practices discovered and proved to be desirable in the more progressive may replace those which are inefficient in the less progressive states. One who is seeking specific and easily accessible information respecting the more important forces that controlled the development of education in the sections mentioned will find little to enlighten him in our general or special histories of education. And yet this is a kind of information greatly needed for an accurate knowledge of how the present developed out of the past.

What were some of the forces and influences which determined the educational development of the southern colonies? One of the striking facts of American colonial history is the contrast in the institutional development of the southern as compared with the New England colonies. This was due to the varying influence of those factors which account for the origin and development of all our institutions. Habits of mind, and the political, social, and religious practices and institutions of the Old World, which the colonist inherited and largely reproduced in the New World, were of most importance. Educational development was determined directly by the inheritance of the classical culture of the ancient world, the influence of religion as a motive for education, and the belief that the church should have a large part in establishing, controlling, and operating the agencies of education. It was also determined by those inherited theories, forms, practices, and machinery connected with the various agencies and processes of education. These influences were an inheritance of the upper class who emigrated to Virginia not less than of many who emigrated to New England, and constitute the background of the educational development of the South. But they did not produce the same results as in New England with respect to the kind, quality, distribution, and effectiveness of the schools and other agencies established to promote education. A study of some of the factors which account for the variation will enable us better to understand educational development in this section. The factors considered relate specifically to Virginia, though the account of the general characteristics of this colony will serve for a description of the general characteristics of all the colonies in this. group.

As in New England, one group of factors centers around the personality and motives of the settlers. There was a marked contrast between the migration from England to Virginia in the period 1607–40 and that to New England. Whether we consider the remark of the Rev. William Stoughton of Dorchester, Massachusetts, concerning the character of the immigrants to New England as an exaggeration or not, namely, "God sifted a whole Nation that he might send choice Grain over into this Wilderness,"[2] one could hardly maintain that such a description could be applied with equal truth to the early settlers of Virginia. Whatever else may be said with respect to the general character of the two groups of settlers, it is certain that the Virginia group was very different in one important respect. Its members were not actuated by as strong religious motives as the New England settlers. But the religious motive was the most important factor in the early colonial period both in perpetuating the inherited connection between religion and education and in providing a stimulus to establish and maintain schools. More important still, Virginia lacked educated leaders who might promote education. In the first fifteen years of Virginia's history we have record of only two or three men with university training who had settled within her borders. But in the first fifteen years of the history of Massachusetts at least fifty religious leaders with university training became pastors of her churches. Most of these men were graduates of Cambridge and Oxford. One can see from this comparison that Virginia was seriously handicapped by the absence of two important factors that promoted educational progress at this time.[3] The general plan of the Virginia Company for the establishment and development of the colony, the method of colonization, the relation between the settlers and the company, all affected the progress of education. The early settlement of Virginia was not by families, neighborhood groups, or congregations, so characteristic of Massachusetts. On the contrary, for a considerable period the settlers were adult males originally, for the most part,

unknown to each other. Up to 1619 most of the settlers were servants of the Company.⁴ While Massachusetts, in 1643, after fifteen
years of settlement, had a population of at least 12,000, Virginia, in
1628, after nearly twenty years of settlement, had only about 3,000,
and even as late as 1635 only 5,119.⁵ Not only was the settlement a
feeble one in the early years, but the absence for a long period of any
considerable number of women and children affected the progress of
education adversely.

If we consider the general development of Virginia after 1625,
through the seventeenth and on into the eighteenth century, we may
note that the population became stratified, three main groups developing. The classes referred to are the planters, the white servants, and the negro slaves. The first class was divided into two
groups: "the higher planter class," owning a considerable quantity
of land and slaves, and the lesser planters and small farmers, those
with much less land, perhaps only a few acres, holding a few slaves
or, as in many cases, none at all. It was that comparatively small
group, the higher planter class, that controlled the political, economic, and social development in Virginia in this early period and, hence,
was largely responsible for whatever educational legislation was
passed.⁶

The white servant class⁷ was called into being principally because
of the economic conditions in England in the seventeenth century.
There was first the theory of the economic relations between a colony
and the mother country, involving the need of a large labor supply
to clear the land and develop the agricultural resources of the
colonies. England had a surplus of poor laborers, due to various
causes, too poor to pay their passage to the New World and with
little hope of bettering their economic condition in England. A large
population was needed in the colonies in order that trade and commerce might develop rapidly; the greater the population and labor
supply, the more raw materials could be shipped to England, made
into finished products, and sold to the colonists. Thus, settlers must
be attracted to the new lands and an adequate labor supply provided.
The economic basis of the system of white servitude was a grant
of a tract of land, about fifty acres, a "head right" to anyone who
would import a laborer or servant to the colonies, and a similar

allotment to the servant after he had served his master a period of
about five years. Thus the custom arose for men and women and
even children, in order to secure transportation to Virginia, to bind
themselves by contract, called an indenture, to serve some person, a
planter perhaps, for a term of years. The latter would advance the
passage money and accept the labor of the servant for the terms of
years specified in satisfaction. Thus an important element was
introduced in the population of Virginia and other southern colonies.
In fact, in the latter colony, it constituted in 1671 nearly one-sixth of
the white population.[8]

With the opening of the eighteenth century the negro slave became more important than the white servant in the labor system
of Virginia, though both continued to the Revolution and after.
By 1754 negro slaves constituted about two-fifths of the total population.[9] The presence of these two elements in the southern colonies
directly affected educational progress. They made possible the
planter class, encouraged the concentration of large tracts of the
best lands in a few hands, and led to a society with aristocratic
institutions and tendencies. These were reflected in the agencies
provided for education. Moreover, the presence of large groups with
relatively low religious and moral standards reacted on the standards
of the ruling classes in these respects, and was another adverse
factor in educational development.[10] So much for those personal
elements which were to influence the progress of education in this
section.

Another group of factors hindered the development of public
education even more, perhaps, than the personality and character
of the settlers—namely, environment, economic organization and
conditions, and distribution of the population. Nature has divided
the Atlantic seaboard into sections which differ materially in area,
configuration, climate, character of soil, and natural resources.
These basic conditions in the southern colonies foreshadowed an
agricultural land and labor system differing much from that of New
England, particularly with respect to the distribution of the population, forms of local government, and, in short, the whole social
system; all this could not fail to influence educational development.

It must also be remembered that the physiography of Virginia, and the South as a whole, was such that in the colonial period it was divided into two distinct sections: the low country or tidewater region, a comparatively narrow strip of one hundred miles in width, more or less, and the back country or "up country," so called. The former region was settled by the great planters, who monopolized most of the political power and wealth, the best lands, and the slaves. The latter region was peopled largely by the poorer class, in part by indented servants who had served their time, and, in the eighteenth century, by many Germans and Scotch-Irish. Much of the back country was unsuited to the slavery system and to the growing of the great staple crop of tobacco and, farther south, of rice and indigo. Moreover, the people inhabiting the back country were principally of a religious persuasion different from that of those in the tidewater region. Though, by the time of the Revolution, this region had a larger population than the tidewater area, the political power was retained by the coast group.[11] This fact had a bearing on the character of the educational laws which were enacted.

More in detail we may note the following contrasts: One of the chief motives of the Puritan migration was a religious one. Thus England had no need to stimulate settlement, for this motive was so strong that nearly 20,000 people emigrated to New England in the course of about twenty years, 1620-43.[12] But the situation in the southern colonies was quite different. Though people migrated to this section from different motives, that most predominant was economic rather than religious. The chief end in life of large numbers was material well-being. But if England expected a rapid settlement and development of the southern colonies, some stimulus other than the religious would be necessary. To develop the resources of the South on a large scale there was need of both capital and labor. Fortunately, nature had provided a substitute for religious motive in the large amount of rich land which England might offer gratis to settlers and laborers. The "head right" system, already explained, enabled an individual to secure large grants of land suitable for an extensive system of agriculture—the growing of the great staple crops and the use of a labor system based on low-priced unskilled labor. This had two important effects: First, it produced a tendency for the best lands to become concentrated in comparatively few hands and encouraged the development of the plantation system. The immediate effect was the creation of a landed aristocracy. Secondly, and perhaps more important still, from the standpoint of educational development, large land grants in connection with the extensive system of agriculture dispersed the population over a large area. The plantation with a single family became the unit of the social and economic life rather than the town—a community group made up of twenty, fifty, a hundred, or more families. Plantations might include from a few hundred to many thousands of acres. Moreover, since they were not necessarily contiguous—that is, large tracts of vacant lands might, and usually did, intervene—they were commonly several miles distant from each other. Thus a few plantations with intervening unoccupied land might cover an area equal to that of a township in New England. But, whereas the township, perhaps thirty square miles in area on an average, would contain from twenty up to several hundred families, one hundred to one thousand people or more, the corresponding area in the South might have perhaps only ten families, seldom more, and these scattered over a large area.

This sparseness of population and lack of centers corresponding to towns or villages was one of the important factors which helped to prevent the growth of the notion of public education. How sparse was the population of the southern colonies about 1724 may be realized by an examination of certain data available for this date. In this year the Bishop of London sent a list of queries to rectors of parishes in several colonies, including Virginia,[13] Maryland, and South Carolina. One of the questions was: "Of what extent is your parish and how many families are there in it?" In Virginia the replies show that the average area of twelve typical parishes was 545 square miles. Comparing the area of a parish, the smallest governmental unit, with the New England town, we note that it was nearly twenty times as large at this date. The average number of families (white) per parish was 372, considerably less than one family per square mile. It is clear that an act like that of Massachusetts in 1647 was impossible in Virginia, because within the area of land involved by the act, and the number of families mentioned, there were relatively few areas where a sufficient number of children lived within a reasonable distance of any place that might be chosen for the location of a school corresponding to a town school. Moreover, in comparing the town with the parish, we must remember that the bulk of the population in the former, during the seventeenth and the early eighteenth century, ordinarily lived in a compact village, within a mile or so of the church. It was in this area, near the church, that the school was located. In the parish, on the contrary, not only was there no village center in most cases, but even the best located parish churches were so situated that the majority of the people often had to travel from five to ten, or even more, miles to attend service.

The form of local government in New England—township government—promoted public schools. But in the South the system of local government harmonized with the land system and the distribution of population. The county was the unit for both political and judicial purposes; but the justices, the governing body of the county, were appointed by the governor. The vestry, the governing body of the parish, with power over church affairs, the poor, and other matters, became a close corporation and self-perpetuating. Thus the people lacked the forms of democratic, direct, local self-government. The plantation system made the planter live a more or less isolated life, with less opportunity and inclination for uniting with his neighbors to promote the common good than was the case in a New England town. Neither the county nor the parish form of government allowed him to meet to express his will even for electing local officials, much less for voting on the multitudinous details of community life so characteristic of the town meeting. But the promotion of public education demanded just such opportunities. It demanded a social consciousness, an altruistic sentiment, a spirit of sacrifice for the common good which the economic, political, and social system of the South made difficult. Such a society was foredoomed to adopt private agencies as the principal method of promoting education.

We may note further that the plantation system did not effectively promote either widespread religious or secular culture. The main energies and thoughts of the planters were centered on material gains. Even where religion might have acted as an intellectual stimulus, the formalism of the established church, the character of many of the clergy, the influence of the slavery system, all tended to produce a low religious tension.[14] Even widespread secular culture was inhibited by such an environment. The intellectual development of a people as a whole depends, among other things, on the cultivation of certain habits, and the presence of the means whereby those habits may be easily continued. Among these means are educated leaders, a supply of books, private and public libraries, the reading and writing habit, interchange of thought through frequent and regular meetings of a social, political, or religious nature, and, particularly, the presence of public schools and institutions of higher learning for the training of leaders and teachers; but it is well known that the southern colonies were backward in these respects. Hugh Jones, a professor in William and Mary College, wrote a book in 1724 called *The Present State of Virginia*.[15] In this book he has an interesting passage commenting on the character of his countrymen, and throwing considerable light on the effect of the plantation system on the intellectual side of life. He says:

> Thus they have good natural Notions, and will soon learn Arts and Sciences; but are generally diverted by Business or Inclination from profound Study, and prying into the Depth of Things; being ripe for Management of their Affairs, before they have laid so good a Foundation of Learning, and had Such Instructions, and acquired such Accomplishments, as might be instilled into such good natural Capacities. Nevertheless thro' their quick Apprehension, they have a Sufficiency of Knowledge, and Fluency of Tongue, tho' their Learning for the most Part be but superficial.

> They are more inclined to read Men by Business and Conversation, than dive into Books, and are for the most Part only desirous of learning what is absolutely necessary, in the shortest and best Method.

It is apparent from this survey that adverse factors hindered educational development in the southern colonies, especially with respect to the maintenance of public schools, and even hindered in no small way private education. What was accomplished, therefore, was in spite of unfavorable factors and without the influence of many of the favoring factors which aided New England in solving her educational problems.

An examination of the educational legislation of the southern colonies shows that it was concerned with three main problems:

First, the passing of laws which would safeguard the educational rights of certain classes of children, such as orphans. Another problem was that of protecting the parishes from the burden of maintaining certain classes, such as the children of poor, idle, dissolute, or vagrant parents, or those of illegitimate birth. Of the latter there were, apparently, more in the South than in other sections. This was due to the presence of large numbers of white servants, negro slaves, mulatto servants, and free negroes, many having very low moral standards. Out of this situation there arose the demand, in part at least, for a system of education through apprenticeship. A third problem was that of providing facilities for a more advanced type of education, mainly for a limited number of boys drawn from the poor or middle classes, who could not afford to bear the cost of an entirely private education.

CHAPTER X

VIRGINIA'S EDUCATIONAL LEGISLATION
FOR POOR CHILDREN

If one turns to the existing accounts of the history of American colonial education, he will observe that many writers assume that most children who were given the rudiments of education attended organized schools. That such an inference is entirely erroneous is easily realized by the performance of a simple arithmetical problem —namely, that of dividing the population at any given date by the number of schools known to have been in existence at that date. The percentage of persons receiving a part of their education in such institutions would be highest in the New England colonies, but even in this section it would surprise most students if they were aware of how many learned how to read or write through some other agency than organized schools.[1]

In the middle and southern colonies a still smaller percentage of the total number who secured the rudiments of an education received it in an organized school. It is doubtless true that there were many private schools whose existence we shall never be able to prove, but, even allowing for this possibility, it is not believed that the statement made need be greatly modified. It is, therefore, important to stress the agencies for education other than organized schools if we are to gain a proper perspective of the evolution of American education. The well-known tendency to read into the past the ideals, and even the institutions, of the present is responsible for a very common fallacy—that of mistaking the special for the general fact. Contemporary conditions, not later theories, govern and explain the development of institutions; and the general fact, the typical institution, cannot vary widely from the general conditions, which must in the long run determine what is general and what exceptional.

During the colonial period much the larger proportion of the people at any one time were living under frontier conditions. Wherever such conditions were the controlling factor, organized institutions, such as the church and school, were not general, except perhaps in portions of New England, notwithstanding the assertions of our enthusiastic and imaginative racial, sectarian, and other types of historians, who often assert the contrary but fail to produce the evidence.[2] When a given area ceased to be governed by frontier conditions, then organized institutions gradually became the general rather than the special fact. Frontier conditions imply, among other things, a sparse population; absorption of energies, time, and thought in satisfying material needs—shelter, subsistence, and protection; occupations largely connected with agriculture or extractive industries; lack of easy means of communication, and hence isolation, particularly in the late fall, winter, and early spring months; and, finally, conservation of labor, even of children, during those months of the year in which the farming operations are pressing. If we realize, also, the weak cultural ideals, inevitable and inherent in frontier groups, and the impossibility of locating organized schools so that any large proportion of those of school age could be reached, under such conditions, even supposing the desire to exist, we can easily see that a great many persons who learned how to read and write must have taken advantage of other agencies than schools. Two were of the greatest importance—namely, home instruction given by the parents, and the apprenticeship system, instruction given by the master or his agent.

Both of these agencies were the subjects of legislation and voluntary use in every colony. Voluntary education through apprenticeship occurred when, through custom or agreement, an indenture was drawn so as to secure for the apprentice book or religious instruction, with or without instruction in a trade, and his maintenance, the latter being one of the main purposes of the system in its historical development. No special law concerning the enforcement of the indenture was needed in such cases, for indentures were almost universally looked upon as contracts, became a matter of public record, and hence were enforceable in the courts. In some of the colonies parental education was made compulsory through laws passed to this effect—as in New England.[3] In this study we are concerned with the system of compulsory education in Virginia as a type of southern colony where it was instituted by law through the agencies of parents, guardians, and overseers, and particularly through masters and mistresses in connection with the system of apprenticeship.

Having discussed the general factors[4] which influenced the development of education in the southern colonies, we will now note how far Virginia enacted laws involving the principle of compulsory education. In view of the factors mentioned, it is not surprising that laws of this character referred to special rather than to all classes of children, as was generally the case at first in New England. The classes provided for were orphans, poor children, and those of illegitimate birth, in the last case with respect to three classes: first, those born of free white women and white servants; second, those born of convict servant women; and, third, mulatto children born of a free, or white servant, mother. The conception that the state was in part responsible for the education of the classes mentioned was expressed in compulsory laws, specifying the machinery for enforcement, similar to those in New England.

ORPHANS

The first class provided for was orphans. The legislation respecting these unfortunates is relatively large in the southern and middle colonies as compared with New England, where there is hardly a reference to such children. No less than seventeen acts were passed by Virginia alone relating to this class, most of them involving the principle of compulsory education. The principal reason for the increase of orphans was the presence of the white servant, and to some extent the negro slave.[5] A little less than one year after Massachusetts passed her first act on compulsory education, that of June 14, 1642, Virginia enacted one in March, 1642/3,[6] relating to orphans the first of many laws relating to this class. Because guardians and overseers had neglected and "very much abused" orphans' estates, they were ordered to report annually an account of the estate and their service to the commissioners of the county court. They were also ordered "to educate and instruct them according to their best endeavours in Christian religion and in rudiments of learning." If they were found delinquent in their duties in these respects, the commissioners were ordered to see that the said orphans were provided for "according to their estates and qualities."

The act of 1656[7] provided that orphans must be educated on the interest of their estates according to its proportion, but if "so meane and inconsiderable that it will not reach to a free education," then such orphans must be bound out as apprentices until twenty-one years of age, to learn some manual trade, unless friends or relatives agreed to keep them for the interest of their estate. The court was ordered to take sufficient security for orphans' estates, inquire yearly of the security, whether orphans were "educated according as their estates will beare," remove them to other guardians if notorious defects were found, and change the master of orphans bound as apprentices if he used them "rigourously" or neglected to teach them his trade.

It will be noticed that the degree of education varied with the estate and quality of the orphan, and that in case of orphans apprenticed no book education is specified, though the law seems to imply that the court should provide for such education in the indenture. It was not until 1705, however, that specific instructions were given to this effect. The act of 1656 is clearly compulsory in character, as it is mandatory and provides for education and for a penalty for neglect by the guardian or master, that is, removal of the child. An order of the assembly of 1659[8] required sheriffs to summon all persons to bring in their accounts of orphans' estates, and clerks of county courts to register these accounts. An "Orphans' Court,"[9] to consider cases concerning orphans, was held in one county as early as 1648.[10] A general act of 1645/6 had already provided that commissioners of county courts, neglecting to punish offenders "according to the merit of the cause," upon complaint could be fined at the discretion of the governor and council.[11]

An act of 1705[12] again repeated most of the provisions of the two earlier acts, but added for the first time a specific requirement respecting the education of apprenticed orphans; namely, that "the master of every such orphan shall be obliged to teach him to read and write." That of 1730[13] also reiterated the powers conferred in previous acts, declared that "great abuses" had been committed by guardians of orphans and justices of county courts, who had been negligent, and called again for annual reports by guardians, gave them custody of their "tuition," and gave power to the county court to make additional rules "for the better education and usage of orphans," when complaint was made that guardians were "neglecting the care of their education," with power to appoint another guardian if the former did not "take due care of the educating and maintaining of any orphan, according to his degree and circumstances." The act of 1740,[14] for enforcing the execution of laws for better managing of orphans' estates, because of neglect by the justice of many county courts, recapitulated the previous orders and provided for an annual return to the August court of accounts of guardians, ordered the justices to direct process to issue against all guardians failing to appear, and provided for a penalty to be imposed on justices of county courts who neglected their duty, a forfeit of five thousand pounds of tobacco, one half to the use of the county and the other half to the informer.

The act of 1705 was the first to provide definitely for book education, and apparently made it compulsory only for boys. A failure to carry out the educational terms of the indenture, as in the case of those referring to trade education, might lead to the removal of an orphan apprenticed, as is proved by cases on record. The neglect by justices, mentioned in the act of 1730, doubtless continued and led to that of 1740, providing for a severe penalty to be levied upon negligent justices. By this date then, the imposing of penalties was highly developed, as guardians, masters, and justices could all be penalized for neglect of orphans.

The last act passed before the Revolution was that of 1748,[15] in effect June 10, 1751. It was a codification of previous laws, and, in fact, repealed all former acts. Nearly all the former orders mentioned were repeated, and there was added this clause referring to orphans apprenticed: "Every male [to be apprenticed] to some tradesman, merchant, mariner, or other person approved by the court," to twenty-one years of age, and "every female to some suitable trade or employment" to eighteen years of age, and the master or mistress of such servant "shall find and provide for him or her, diet, cloathes, lodgings and accommodations fit and necessary, and shall teach, or cause him or her to be taught to read and write."

This was the most comprehensive law enacted in the colonies on the education of orphans, and shows unexpected concern by Virginia for the education of girls, as well as boys, of this class.

POOR CHILDREN

It has already been shown[16] that the nature of the population of Virginia, and of the South in general, was made up of several groups, such as the higher planter class; the smaller planter with a few slaves; the independent farmer; the white servant, who after his term of service of four or five years usually became a small farmer, a laborer, or an artisan, and the negro slave. Out of the last class there developed two more, the free negro and the mulatto servant; the latter, born of a free white mother or white servant, after a long period of service becoming a free man or woman. There was, therefore, a large element of the population from which poor children might arise. Moreover, many of the white servants were of poor stock, ignorant, lazy, and with low moral standards. Some were convict servants, those liberated from the English jails and sold as servants, or given a sentence by English judges of servitude in the colonies in lieu of a jail sentence in England.[17] The moral standards of this last class were very low, and, of course, there is no need to comment on the lack of moral standards of the negro slaves. There was complaint from an early date of "vagrant idle, and dissolute persons," largely recruited from the white servants. They frequently became the fathers of illegitimate children, by both free white and white servant women. They ran away, with the result that their children were often thrown on the parish for support. White men servants, after their term of service, might become vagabonds or dissolute persons, or, if married, desert their wives and children, who would then be thrown on the parish. Some white servant women also gave birth to illegitimate mulatto children, which by the law[18] of Virginia were free after their term of service.

The problem then for Virginia, and for other colonies, was much the same as that which had confronted Old and New England, only it was a more serious and pressing one. That problem was first economic—how to protect the parish from the burden of maintaining poor children; how to provide for an artisan class skilled in trades

and needed in the colony; how to reduce idleness and unemployment, and how to add rapidly to the wealth and property of all the
people. The second aspect of the problem was educational. The
natural conception of the relation of the state to education was
largely laissez faire, on the theory that this was a matter to be intrusted to private initiative or the church. But the pressure of a
rapidly growing class of poor children, and the consequent expense
to the parish, coupled with the difficulty of obtaining the much-
needed supply of artisans, forced the state to modify this conception.
Poor parents could not educate their children, and some degree of
book education was desirable for artisans in order that they might be
efficient in their trades. Two influences also promoted this conception. The period from the Reformation to the great Civil War is
marked, in England, by the stimulating effect of religion on education, especially the efforts of competing religious denominations
and their anxiety to increase their power through instruction in the
peculiar tenets of their creed and in their catechism. In states where
there was union of church and state—the established church in
Virginia—this influence was strong. A second influence was the
beginnings of the humanitarian movement, as exhibited in philanthropy—the desire to give poor children some opportunity for education—best illustrated in the work of the Society for the Propagation
of the Gospel in Foreign Parts.[19]

All these forces led to the conception that the state was responsible, to some extent at least, for the education of certain classes of
children. From an economic, religious, and humanitarian standpoint, it was undesirable that a large body of illiterate laborers,
tradesmen, or farmers should be allowed to develop. From a purely
selfish standpoint, the money cost, the state was compelled to take
some action. As in the New England colonies, and perhaps influenced by their legislation, the system of apprenticeship seemed to
be the most effective agency to gain the ends desired, with the least
expense, loss of time from labor, and, in the case of the southern
colonies, the least interference with their general attitude toward the
relation of the state to education.[20]

An examination of the legislation of Virginia reveals the fact that
at least eight important laws were passed from 1646 to 1769 having

for their purpose religious, industrial, or book education of poor children of various classes; that five of these acts contemplated some form of book education, and that four of them can be properly classed as compulsory laws. There were, in addition, general laws applying to all children and providing for compulsory religious education. An act of February, 1631/2,[21] provided that all churchwardens should take an oath, administered before the commissioner of the monthly court, to the effect that they "present such maysters and mistresses as shall be delinquents in the catechisinge the youth and ignorant persons." Another act[22] of the same session provided that the minister should upon every Sunday "examine, catechise, and instruct the youth and ignorant persons of his parrish, in the ten commandments the articles of the beliefe and in the Lord's prayer. . . . . And all fathers, mothers, maysters and mistresses shall cause theire children, servants or apprentizes which have not learned the catachisme to come to the church" to learn the same, and if any of the above neglected their duties they should be "censured by the corts in those places holden." By the act of 1644/5,[23] ministers failing to catechise every Sunday were to forfeit five hundred pounds of tobacco for the use of the parish. Finally, the act of 1645/6[24] provided that all masters and families failing to send their children and servants to be catechized, upon warning given by the minister where they would officiate, were to be subject to a penalty of five hundred pounds of tobacco for the use of the parish "unless sufficient cause be shewn to the contrary."

The increase of children in Virginia was slow for the first thirty years of the settlement, but by 1646[25] "God Almighty, among many his other blessings, hath vouchsafed increase of children to this colony, who now are multiplied to a considerable number, who if instructed in good and lawful trades, may much improve the honor and reputation of the country, and noe lesse their owne good and their parents comfort." This refers, of course, not to children of wealthy planters and well-to-do farmers, but to poor children. The first three acts relating to this class were those of 1646, 1668, and 1672. They did not, strictly speaking, involve compulsory education, since the laws are permissive rather than mandatory, but they require comment in order to show the conditions accounting for the passage of later compulsory laws.

The act of 1646[26] refers to sundry laws and statutes of parliament established "for the better educateing of youth in honest and profitable trades and manufactures, as also to avoyde sloath and idlenesse wherewith such young children are easily corrupted, as also for the reliefe of such parents whose poverty extends not to give them good breeding." Accordingly, justices of the peace were given power to bind out poor children to tradesmen or husbandmen "to be brought up in some good and lawful calling." The remainder of the act outlines an ambitious plan for industrial education. Two children from each county, chosen by the commissioners of the counties, were to be sent to public flax houses to be taught in "cording knitting and spinning." Such children were to be taken only from those parents who "by reason of their poverty are disabled to maintaine and educate them." State and county were to provide the funds to defray the cost of buildings, food, clothing, shelter, etc., including "a sow shote of six months old, two laying hens," etc. The act of 1668[27] was somewhat similar. It contemplated the promotion of manufactures —wool, flax, and hemp—and the increase of artificers. It gave power to the commissioners of each county court, with the assistance of the vestries of the parishes, to build houses for "educating and instructing poore children in the knowledge of spinning, weaving and other useful occupations and trades," with power to take poor children from indigent parents to place them to work in such houses. In 1672,[28] because of the increase of "vagabonds idle and desolute persons," justices of the peace and county courts were impowered to place out all children, whose parents were not able to bring them up, apprentices to tradesmen, males to twenty-one and females, "to other necessary employments," to eighteen, and churchwardens of every parish were to be ordered by the county courts to give an account annually at the orphans' court "of all such children within their parish, as they judge to be within the said capacity."

None of these three acts specifies book education, and there is no evidence that the workhouses provided for were ever built. There was no reason, of course, why the justices could not introduce a clause into the indenture providing for book education, if they wished to, and such a practice was not uncommon from 1646 on, but we are here concerned principally with the laws which made this practice compulsory. With these permissive acts as a foundation, Virginia opened the eighteenth century with a law providing for compulsory book education of orphan boys, as already stated, and in 1727 this act was made applicable to poor boys apprenticed.

The act of 1727[29] complains that idle and disorderly persons able to work "strole from one county to another, neglecting to labour," and vagabonds "run from their habitations and leave either wives or children, without suitable means for their subsistance." When such parents, because of "idle disolute and disorderly course of life," were judged by the county court to be incapable of supporting and bringing up such children, or when they neglected to "take due care of the education and instruction of such child or children, in christian principles," the churchwardens, on certificate from the county court, were given power "to bind out or put out to service or apprentice" the children of such parents, for such time and "under such covenants as hath been usual and customary, or the law directs in the case of orphan children." This last clause refers to the act of 1705 which required that in the case of orphan boys apprenticed, "the master of every such orphan shall be obliged to teach him to read and write."[30]

The act of 1748,[31] in force June 10, 1751, was a revision of that of 1727, with important changes respecting the education of poor children. When county courts judged that any person or persons were incapable of supporting and bringing up their children "in honest courses," or when it appears to the court "that he, she, or they, neglect to take due care of the education of his, her, or their child or children, and their instruction in the principles of christianity," then, on order of the county court, churchwardens of parishes could bind such children apprentices "in the same manner, and under such covenants and conditions as the law directs for poor orphan children." This refers to another act of 1748, passed at the same session, providing that the master of an apprenticed orphan should "teach, or cause him or her to be taught to read and write." It will be noticed that this act specifies for the first time as a reason why the court should take a child from a parent the "neglect to take due care of his education." Previous acts had mentioned lack of support, lack of ability to bring up to trades, or lack of instruction in Christian religion. This approaches the ideals of New England in the seventeenth century, and, as we shall see, there is not wanting evidence to show that parents were called to account merely for neglecting the education of their children.

ILLEGITIMATE CHILDREN

Virginia also passed laws for the education of another class of children, those of illegitimate birth. By the end of the seventeenth century there was a large number of indented servants, causing serious problems to arise respecting the maintenance and education of children of this class. Laws were passed as early as 1642/3[32] against the marriage of servants without the consent of their masters, against fornication between servants, and against fornication between freemen and servants. The number of illegitimate children seems to have been considerable, judging from the laws and the recorded cases in the parish records. The first act bearing on the subject was that of 1657/8,[33] requiring the father of an illegitimate child to give security to indemnify the parish against the expense of keeping the child. If the father were an indented servant, he would be unable to obey the act; hence, in 1662, another act[34] provided that the parish should "take care to keepe the child during the time of the reputed father's service by *indenture* or custome, and that after he is free the said reputed father shall make satisfaction to the parish." Thus in the indenture there might be provision for teaching the child to read. If the child were not indentured and the father died or ran away, it became a permanent charge on the parish. The only method of relieving the parish of this expense was to bind out the child as an apprentice, as was provided for in the act. The act of 1769[35] complains that the laws in force are insufficient to provide for indemnifying parishes "from the great charges frequently arising from children begotten out of lawful matrimony." It provides specifically for binding out by the churchwardens the illegitimate child of a single free white woman, in language similar to that of 1748, including this phrase: "and the master or mistress of every such apprentice shall find and provide for him or her diet, cloathes, lodging, and accommodations fit and necessary, and shall teach or cause *him* or *her* to be taught to read and write." If the illegitimate child were born of a convict servant woman during the time of her service, because such a servant could not legally give testimony, and hence the reputed father could not be discovered, the master of such servant was obliged to maintain the child until it was twenty-one or eighteen years of age, and was entitled to its service, provided he "find or provide for such child, the like accommodations, education and freedom dues, and shall be compelled to answer his or her complaint, made to the county court, for default therein, or for ill usage, in like manner, as is before directed in the case of other apprentices."[36]

MULATTO CHILDREN

The act of 1691[37] complained that there was need of preventing "that abominable mixture and spurious issue which hereafter may increase in this dominion as well by negroes, mulattoes, and Indians intermarrying with English, or other white women, as by their unlawful accompanying with one another." A free English white woman having an illegitimate child by a negro or mulatto was subject to a fine or was sold for five years. If the woman were a servant, she was sold for the same number of years after her time as a servant had expired, and in each case the child was to be bound out until he or she should be thirty years of age. By the act of 1705[38] this was increased to thirty-one. The law of Virginia had provided as early as 1662[39] that all children "born in this country shall be held bond or free only according to the condition of their mother." A mulatto, then, born of a free white or white servant mother, was not a slave, but, after the time of service expired, was a free man or woman. The act of 1753[40] continued these provisions for binding out such children, but up to this date no specific provision had been made for their education unless we consider the laws relating to poor children as applicable. The act of 1765[41] reduced the time of service, males to twenty-one and females to eighteen years of age, because the former age was "of unreasonable severity towards such children." Moreover, because mulattoes had been sold as slaves, a penalty of fifty pounds was imposed on the seller to be paid to the purchaser, and an additional penalty of twenty pounds to the informer. For a second offense the service of the servant was forfeited, and the latter was to be bound out to serve to twenty-one years of age "in the same manner as is by law directed for the binding out of orphan children." This would seem to indicate that provision for teaching such a boy or girl to read and write was contemplated. There were actual indentures, to be cited later, which so provided.

CONCLUSION

It is apparent that Virginia considered the education of these unfortunate classes—orphans, poor, illegitimate, and even mulatto children—to be a matter of importance, for no less than ten important laws[42] were passed involving these classes which mention specifically that the guardian or master is responsible for some book education. They provide for direct education by guardians or others for orphans with estates and for poor orphans and children through the system of apprenticeship; and those acts which do not directly mention education, or such subjects as reading or writing, do not prevent the inclusion of educational clauses in the indenture, as is proved by cases to be cited.[43] The attitude of Virginia toward education was evidently one which recognized that the state was responsible for the education of only those children whose parents were not likely to attend to the matter themselves. There is only one law which would allow the justices to interfere with other children than the poor, for the act of 1748 may be so interpreted. The assumption was that education was a private affair and that capable parents would voluntarily attend to the education of their own children. It will be noticed that during most of the seventeenth century Massachusetts and Connecticut made no such assumption.

It will be observed that the acts concerning orphans provide: first, for education through payment of tuition fees, in the case of those orphans whose estates produced interest on the principal sufficient for the purpose; secondly, for education through the system of apprenticeship, where orphans had a very small estate or none whatever. Although the first law mentioning book education for orphans apprenticed was that of 1705, yet the general acts of 1646 and 1672, giving power to justices of the peace to bind out poor children, would permit them to include a clause in an indenture providing for book education for an orphan bound out. A case of an apprenticed orphan with such a clause included in the indenture is recorded as early as 1648.[44] The fact that a session of the county court was called an "Orphans' Court" at this early date is evidence that the class was of some importance.

It will be noted that there is a progressive increase of orders respecting the administrative features of these laws. The purpose was to provide better methods of discovering whether an orphan was being educated to protect his estate for this purpose, to increase the degree of education, and to provide penalties for negligence. Thus guardians were to make annual reports, provide security, and see that orphans were instructed according to the proportion of their estates. Judges at first merely saw that orphans were provided for; then they were to make yearly inquiry; then they must apprentice the orphan if the estate was small, remove him from the master or guardian in case of neglect, and appoint new masters or guardians. Sheriffs also summoned guardians, and clerks of courts made public record of their accounts. Judges were obliged to see that an educational clause was inserted in the indenture, after 1705 for boys and after 1751 for girls, and could make additional rules for education in 1730. In 1679 they were chargeable for losses for their failure to take sufficient security from guardians, while, in 1740, they were subject to a severe penalty for neglect of the laws respecting orphans.

A comparison of the legislation of Virginia with that of the New England colonies with respect to the compulsory education of poor children shows similarities as well as differences. The economic motives appear to be much the same; namely, the effort to avoid pauperism and idleness, and a desire to develop an artisan class. The religious and educational motives are also similar. The laws apply mainly to special, not to all, classes of children, as was the case in New England during most of the seventeenth century, and the purpose of book education is not so specifically stated. There is a failure to mention a specific money penalty to be imposed on parents or masters or the churchwardens for negligence of the law. The classes of children involved, however, were poor and illegitimate children, and since the desire to relieve the parish of the burden of supporting such children was very strong, a money penalty was perhaps not needed in order to make it certain that they would be apprenticed. It will be remembered that not even Massachusetts imposed a money penalty on officers, except in one instance, after the laws on compulsory education were framed so as to apply only to poor children apprenticed—that is, after the act of 1703. The plan for workhouses for poor children contemplated state, county, and parish support by taxation, though the acts are not compulsory, and only that of 1755 mentioned education directly.

It is apparent that Virginia not only recognized her responsibility for the compulsory education of the classes of children mentioned but passed a series of notable acts designed to accomplish the purpose. While they are not so elaborate as those of the New England colonies for the seventeenth century, they are in the eighteenth century quite up to the New England standard and in some respects above it. For example, the law required that after 1751 all orphan and poor girls apprenticed should be taught to read and also to write. No New England colony, after 1710, required all girls apprenticed to be taught to read and write. The acts cited show that we may fairly assert that Virginia established a compulsory system of education for these special classes of children. The laws are mandatory, indicate the machinery for enforcement, name the responsible officers, provide penalties for negligence of parents, guardians, and masters— namely, removal of the child—and, in the case of negligent justices, provided a money penalty, or its equivalent in tobacco. The central feature of the system was the county court, composed of the justices of the peace. It was entirely responsible for the workings of the laws respecting orphans. In the case of poor and illegitimate children the churchwardens were about equally responsible with the justices. There is thus the same tendency as in New England, that of making special officers of local units the responsible persons for carrying out the law. There is also the same tendency to increase the amount of education required for boys and girls apprenticed, and to place less emphasis on religious instruction in the eighteenth as compared with the seventeenth century. We shall see from the evidence in court and parish records that these acts were enforced, to some extent at least, but how effectually or universally it is difficult to say. But

this observation can be made quite as truly of the legislation of the
New England colonies. A tabular view of the compulsory laws
passed by Virginia involving book education is given in Table II.
This may be compared with the table given for New England in
chapter vii, p. 115.

TABLE II

Date	Class of Children	Education Required
1642/3–1776....	Orphans with estates	According to the proportion of their estates and circumstances
1705–76........	Poor orphan boys and girls apprenticed because of little or no estate:	
	1705–76, boys	To be taught to read and write
	1751–76, girls	To be taught to read and write
1727–76........	Poor boys and girls apprenticed; children of parents unable to support, or who neglected to instruct, them in Christian principles:	
	1727–76, boys	To be taught to read and write
	1751–76, girls	To be taught to read and write
1751–76........	Any child apprenticed, because parents neglected his or her education or instruction in the principles of Christianity	To be taught to read and write
1765–76........	Mulatto boy or girl born of a free white or servant woman and apprenticed, because sold as a slave by a master, being his second offense	To be taught to read and write
1769–76........	Illegitimate child apprenticed, born of a single free white woman	To be taught to read and write

CHAPTER XI

EDUCATION FOR POOR CHILDREN IN VIRGINIA THROUGH THE APPRENTICESHIP SYSTEM

The laws enacted by colonial assemblies for the regulation of society, such as the criminal codes, slave codes, laws involving public and private morals, religion, education, and, in fact, most other subjects, represent an ideal or a theory. In most cases the actual practice did not coincide with the laws, either because they were contrary to public sentiment, or because they could not be enforced, owing to inefficient machinery or officials whose duty it was to put them into operation. On the other hand, customs or practices sometimes became so regular and certain that laws were enacted to register this condition and to give added force to what was recognized as desirable. In such cases the practice often coincided to a remarkable degree with the laws. In either case, general laws or practice seldom operated in the same way over a large area. Indeed, important variations might occur in adjoining counties or even in parishes. The account[1] which follows is intended to show that the laws on compulsory education were put into operation in the cases cited, leaving open for further study the question how far the counties and parishes from which illustrations are given were typical of all the counties and parishes in Virginia.

ORPHAN CHILDREN

The chief agency provided by law for the enforcement of the legislation concerning orphans was the county court. This body was made up of justices of the peace appointed by the governor, and met quarterly to attend to the business of the court. The powers of county courts were derived not only from statutes conferring direct powers but also from custom and common law. They were quite independent bodies and often paid but slight attention to the laws passed fixing their powers. In fact, many of the laws appear merely to confirm existing practices of the county courts. The general practice under the acts relating to orphans tended to bring them under the jurisdiction of the county court in various ways. The first act, passed in 1642, required guardians and overseers to report annually to the court an account of their service; the second, in 1656, required the court to inquire yearly whether orphans were educated; if not, they were to be bound out as apprentices. The law of 1659 required sheriffs to summon all persons to bring in their accounts of orphans' estates, and that of 1740 ordered the justices to summon all guardians failing to appear, under a penalty of five thousand pounds of tobacco. It was customary, also, for a person to make application to the justices for appointment as guardian. Such petitions might be presented at any court, but some counties, from an early date, had one term of the court called "Orphans' Court," for the purpose of attending to all business relating to orphans.

While no law was enacted until 1705 specifying the exact character of education to be given to apprenticed orphans, yet the first act passed, that of 1642–43, had specified that guardians were to educate orphans "in Christian religion and in rudiments of learning," and that of 1656, in proportion to the interest of their estate. The following cases illustrate early seventeenth-century practice. There was a session of the York County Court, called "Orphants Cort," held as early as August 24, 1648. Stephen Gill, godfather to John Foster, an orphan child without maintenance or estate, petitioned the court that he might have "tuition and bringing upp" of the orphan, whom he had already provided for and kept for about one year. The court ordered that the orphan should "live and remaine under tuition" for nine years, during which Stephen Gill was ordered to provide sufficiently for him and "take care that he bee brought upp in the feare of God and taught to Reade."[2] Two years before, in 1646, a record of the same court shows that the fathers-in-law of three families of orphans, involving six children, filed their accounts. The court ordered that the increase of their estates should belong wholly to the orphans, without further charges for their subsistence or education as long as they remained under the tuition of their guardians.³ The cases of two orphan girls are interesting. An orphans' court of Isle of Wight County, on May 1, 1694, received the petition of Charles Edwards for Grace Griswood, an orphan girl, to live with him till eighteen years old or until she was married. The petition was granted on condition that the said Charles "doth hereby oblige himselfe to mainteyn her decently and see that she be taught to read, sew, spinn and knitt," etc.⁴ So the Elizabeth City County Court, on July 18, 1698, bound Ann Chandler, an orphan girl, apprentice, "to be taught to read a chapter in the Bible, the Lord's prayer, and ten commandments, and Sempstress work."⁵ The Essex County Court bound out an orphan boy, James Evans, January 10, 1697, to John Williams, who agreed to give the boy "two years schooling," with orders to take care of what estate belonged to the orphan.⁶ After the act of 1705, which required a clause in the indenture of an apprenticed orphan boy providing that he be taught to read and write, indentures containing the clause in question are common in the county court and parish records.⁷

The number of orphans in Virginia was apparently quite unusual. There are in the Surry County Records, 1679–84, fifty bonds in which guardians bound themselves to educate orphans in their care, viz., to have them taught in school according to their estate or quality.⁸ In Spottsylvania County, will book "B" contains a list of forty-five guardians' bonds between 1749 and 1761, involving seventy children. Will book "D" contains thirty-eight guardians' bonds, 1762–72, involving seventy-two children.⁹ There is evidence that the proportion in other counties was even larger.

Compulsory education of orphans did not depend solely upon the law or upon the order of the county court setting forth the conditions under which a person might be appointed guardian. The orphan, his friend, or the grand jurors could bring the case to the attention of the court if there was negligence on the part of guardians, or failure to carry out the terms of the indenture. For example, an orphan complained on July 2, 1685, that he was held in a severe and hard servitude illegally and that he was taken by one Major Hawkins "under pretense of giving him learning." The case came before the court again on August 2, but the justices decided that he must continue in the service of his present master.[10]

Under the act of 1656 the county court was given power to apprentice orphans whose estate was too small to give them a free education. This act called only for a change of master if he neglected to teach him the trade agreed upon. Nevertheless, under the general powers granted to vestries by the act of 1657–58,[11] they had control over parish matters, including the care of the parish poor. An interesting method of enforcing the educational provisions in indentures of orphan children by one parish is that adopted by the vestry of Petsworth Parish, Gloucester County, October 8, 1724; viz., "It is also ordered by this present vestry thatt all Orphant children, bound out by the Parish hereafter, that if they cannot Read at thirteen years old that they shall be sett free from theire said masters and mistresses or be taken from them."[12] This seems to be an isolated case, but it illustrates the fact that educational practice in Virginia did not depend solely on general laws any more than it did in Massachusetts. County courts as well as parishes imposed penalties of their own making for the purpose of enforcing the terms of an indenture. Thus the Elizabeth City County Court bound out an orphan boy on July 18, 1694, till he became twenty-one years of age, on condition that the master teach him "to Read a Chapter in the Bible, the Lord's Prayer and Ten Commandments," or in case of delinquency pay the apprentice, when free, five hundred pounds of "Legall Tobacco in Casque."[13]

Since guardians were obliged by law to report annually to the county court (act of 1642), and the justices were likewise obliged to inquire annually whether orphans were educated (act of 1656), we find that county court records contain data (other than court orders) which illustrate the enforcement of the laws on education of orphans. These data consist of the records of guardians' bonds and accounts, sometimes kept in separate volumes. The record for Louisa County, covering the period from 1767 to 1819, has a dozen or more such accounts from 1767 to 1777. For example, the account of Thomas Paullet respecting the education of two orphan girls, 1766–70, is interesting, for it shows the amount and expense of their education during this period.[14]

The Estate of Ann Sanders and Mary Sanders to the Estate of Thomas Paullet, Dec^d. Dr.

1766—Oct. 22

To 8 months schoolling....................................	13s. 4d.
To Boarding for 1 Year....................................	£8
1768	
To 3 Months Schoolling....................................	10s.
To the Dancing Master....................................	£2
To Seven Months Schoolling...............................	£1 3s. 4d.
1770	
To half Year's Schoolling for Ann........................	10s.
To 1 years Ditto for Mary................................	£1

The account for William Lipscomb, guardian of two orphan girls, Elizabeth and Sarah Hall, shows expenditures of 10s. 10d. February 10, 1775, "For Schooling" and £2 on December 24, "To Schooling" the two children. There is also a total charge of 2s. $1\frac{1}{2}$d., consisting of "To one Battledor 3d., To one Primer $7\frac{1}{2}$d., To one Spelling Book 1/3."[15]

POOR CHILDREN

By the act of 1646 justices of the peace were given power to bind out children of parents "whose poverty extends not to give them good breeding"; the act of 1672 gave power to county courts to bind out children whose parents were not able to bring them up apprentices; that of 1727 gave power to the church wardens, on order of the county court, to bind out children of idle and dissolute parents who could not support, or did not take due care of, their children or their instruction in "Christian principles," and provided for a clause in their indenture to teach boys to read and write; the act of 1748 gave power to the county court to bind out the children of any person who was judged incapable of bringing up his children or who failed to take due care of their education. Apprenticed boys and girls were to be taught reading and writing.[16]

There are numerous examples, dating from the seventeenth century, of the education of poor children through the system of apprenticeship. These cases occurred before there was any law requiring book instruction of the apprentices. For example, a boy, William Rogers, was bound out by the Surrey County Court. June 15, 1681, "his master to teach him his trade of blacksmith

and to read and wright."[17] Another boy was bound out by the
church wardens of Petsworth Parish, Gloucester County, April 4,
1700; the master promising and obliging himself by the indenture
"to give unto the above Richard Allen three years' Schooling and
he to be sent to school at the years of twelfe or thereabouts."[18] An
indenture recorded September 24, 1690, provided that Rebeccah
Ffrancis serve as an apprentice till twenty-one years old, to be
"virtuously brought up" and given a 'Compleat yeares schooling
to be Educated in Reading the Vulgar tongue, to bee taught as
aforesaid within the aforesaid term of Apprenticeship."[19] There
are six cases of boys bound out by the Essex County Court in the
month of July, 1698. One was to be taught to read and write, one
to read and have a year's schooling, two to be put to school at
nine years of age and kept there until twelve, and two others to be
given two years' schooling.[20] Even free negro boys bound out as
apprentices were sometimes given the benefit of an educational
clause in the indenture. Two such cases occur in the Princess
Anne County Records; one, in 1719, to learn the trade of tanner,
the master to "teach him to read," and the other, in 1727, to learn
the trade of gunsmith, the master to teach him "to read the Bible
distinctly."[21]

The enforcement of the terms of the indenture, as in the case of
orphans, depended on the success of the apprentice in getting his
case brought to the attention of the court through friends or grand
jurymen. To make the enforcement more certain, the court might
fix heavy penalties for neglect of the terms of the indenture. Thus
a boy was bound out on July 18, 1694, on condition that the master
"Teach him to Read a chapter in the Bible the Lords Prayer and
Ten Commandments and in case of delinquency in any of the prem-
ises the said Mr. Lowry his Executor or Administrator Shall fforfeit
and pay unto the said apentis when ffree the sume of five hundred
pds of Legall Tobacco in Casque."[22] Direct complaints to the county
courts were not infrequent. Thus two men declared under oath
on April 1, 1685, that Thomas Pell had been bound for nine years as
an apprentice on condition that his master, William Gemovel, teach
him the trade of carpenter and "give him Convenient Learning."
The court ordered that the apprentice "be taught to Write and

Read."[23] On May 26, 1690, the parents of a boy apprenticed for nine years brought suit against the master, Robert Green, because he employed his apprentice "to labor daily in the ground contrary to the Indenture." This law provided that he be taught the "Arts and Mistery of a taylor and to teach or cause him to be taught to reade and write a Leagable hand." It was complained, also, that the master had omitted to give him "Learning or teach him his trade which is to ye said Apprentice utter Rewing and undoing." It was therefore ordered that the master enter into a bond of four thousand pounds of tobacco and give good and sufficient security to fulfil every clause of the indenture.[24] Another case is that of the failure of a master (apparently) to give the instruction promised. The Surrey County Court, May 4, 1697, ordered "that unless Jn° Clements do put John High to School to learne to reade and write, he do appeare at the next court, and bring the said John with him, that the Court may then do therein as shall be found fitt."[25] Another example is the complaint of William Creek and wife that "Steephen Howard" and wife had not performed an order of the Elizabeth City County Court of September 16, 1688, respecting Thomas Powell, an apprentice bound to Howard's wife. The court ordered that the master enter into bond, with security, to put the "Apprentice to Schoole and learne him to Reade a Chapter in the Bible," or forfeit to the apprentice, when free, one hundred pounds of tobacco.[26] The interest of a county court in education is shown by the case of one Sarah Oulton who was neglecting her son. She was ordered to give bond and good security for maintaining and "Educating of her Son," and if she failed, the sheriff was ordered to take the son into custody and place him under the care of one "Allexander Marshall under whose care and charge the said Lodowick hath been formerly maintained and educated."[27] The Princess Anne County Court ordered the Sheriff on May 1, 1717, to summon George Smyth to the next court to answer the complaint of his apprentice and "Shew the court reasons why he does not Teach him to read as by Indenture he is obliged." On June 5, Smyth appeared and promised "to put his apprentice forthwith to Schoole."[28]

Under the acts of 1727 and 1748 the apprenticed poor boys and girls were to be taught to read and write. The laws declared that a failure to instruct children in "Christian principles" or to take "due care of their education" was sufficient reason for taking them from their parents and binding them out as apprentices. Complaint was made to the Charles City County Court in March, 1737, by Benjamin Harrison, that Richard Bragby and Elizabeth his wife, and Mary Evans, did not bring up their children to "an honest way of Liveing as well as in the fear of God." It was ordered that the parents mentioned be summoned to the next court to show cause why their children should not be bound out as the law directs. They appeared as ordered but failed to give satisfaction to the judges. The children were accordingly bound out.[29] So on October 1, 1760, it appeared to this same court that John Warren, father of Matthew Warren, "is not able to bring up and educate him in a Christian like manner." Accordingly, the church wardens were ordered to bind the boy out "agreeable to Law."[30] Similarly the Elizabeth City County Court, on March 2, 1763, ordered "that the church wardens of this parish bind out the children of Joseph Bonshell and John Lewis according to law, it appearing to the court that they have neglected their education."[31] The following case is one in which the terms of the indenture were not observed. On complaint of Eleanor Dunn, June 21, 1769, James Steward was summoned to court to explain why he did not teach his apprentice, Walter Dunn, his trade and "cloathe and provide for him according to law."[32] Another case is that of the petition of the mother of an apprentice, May 19, 1773, to the effect that her thirteen-year-old son, who had been bound out to James Sallas, "could be better educated if bound to Adam Wall." The court so ordered.[33] The law only required that indentures should provide for reading and writing, but this did not prevent the inclusion of other requirements. For example, the Augusta County Court ordered a boy to be bound out "to have the trade of a Weaver, and to read, write and cypher as far as the rule of three."[34]

ILLEGITIMATE CHILDREN

Illegitimate children as a class could be considered as falling under the general heading of poor children. There was no special law involving the education of this class until 1769, but they were recognized as having a right to educational advantages. Lancaster

County Court on January 6, 1655, ordered that such a boy "bee kept" by Roger Harris and wife till eighteen years of age, provided the "child be taught to write and reade."[35] Another case is that of a girl of this class bound out November 10, 1696, the master promising in court and "obligeing himselfe to learn the said [Jane] Holding to Read."[36] The vestry books of Virginia parishes contain numerous examples of binding out this class of children, especially from 1727 on, when complaint was made of the large number of such children.[37] The indentures, however, did not contain educational requirements so frequently as was the case with orphan and poor children.[38]

MULATTO CHILDREN

The mulatto class of children presented an early educational problem. Though no special law was passed until 1765, involving their education, instances of educational clauses in the indentures of such children occur long before this date. The vestry book of Petsworth Parish, Gloucester County, contains an indenture dated October 30, 1716, stating that Ralph Beves agrees to give "A Molattoe boy of the age of 2 years, 3 years' schooling, and carefully instruct him afterwards that he may read well in any part of the Bible."[39]

Occasional cases of the action of the county courts or vestries respecting the inclusion of educational requirements in indentures are less valuable as an indication of average practice than a series of cases covering a period of years, for the records give evidence that some indentures were made with no educational requirement, despite the law. It was the practice in some parishes for the church wardens to keep a separate record of indentures, especially after the acts of 1672 and 1727, the former providing that they must bring to the county court lists of children in their parish whose parents were not able to bring them up apprentices, and the latter giving them power to apprentice poor children on order of the county court. Two such record books are those of Fredericksville Parish, Louisa County, 1742–85, and Dettingen Parish, Prince William County, 1745–82. In the former, sixty-three indentures are recorded, and in the latter, ninety-eight. A study of these indentures is of great interest because of the light they throw on the education of the various classes of children provided for by apprenticeship laws.[40]

These indentures are analyzed in Tables III–V according to the distribution of the children described—orphans, poor, illegitimate, mulatto; the sex, the character of the book education, or the period of time in school prescribed; and the industrial training mentioned, trade or occupation.[41]

Other trades mentioned were: bricklayer (2), saddle-maker (1), tailor (3), millwright (2), silversmith (1), barber (1). In the remaining cases the description is general, such as "apprentice," "servant,"

TABLE III

CLASSES OF CHILDREN	DETTINGEN PARISH		FREDERICKSVILLE PARISH		BOTH PARISHES		TOTAL
	Boys	Girls	Boys	Girls	Boys	Girls	
Orphans........	26	11	19	6	45	17	62
Poor............	30	5	22	7	52	12	64
Illegitimate......	9	4	2	2	11	6	17
Mulatto........	8	5	4	3	12	8	20
Total.......	73	25	47	18	120	43	163

"suitable trade or employment," or merely "bind out" with no trade specified. No trade is mentioned for girls unless we may call "spinster" a trade, mentioned once.

Attention may be called to certain details concerning these tables. The orphans constituted 38.01 per cent of all the children apprenticed and were, with one or two exceptions, bound out by the church wardens of their own parish on an order from their county court. The boys were most often apprenticed to learn the trade of carpenter, shoemaker, blacksmith, and planter or farmer. The reason for the predominance of artisans over farmers is explained by the fact that the various acts passed from 1656 on were designed to meet the shortage of skilled tradesmen, a condition always present in Virginia in the colonial period. Girls were usually apprenticed as domestic servants with no particular trade mentioned. However, in nine of the cases where reading is required in the indenture of girls, there is an additional requirement that they be taught to knit, spin, and sew. The educational requirement, it will be seen, is sharply differentiated as between boys and girls. The minimum for every boy was reading and writing, when the degree of education was specified. We may assume that one or two years' schooling and the phrase "as the law allows" or "learning," the

TABLE IV

Classes of Children	Reading and Writing	Reading	Reading Writing Cyphering	One Year	Eighteen Months	Two Years	"As Law Allows" or "Learning"	No Education Required	Total
Orphans									
Boys..........	27	......	......	4	......	3	4	7	45
Girls..........	3	12	......	......	......	......	1	1	17
Poor									
Boys..........	22	......	2	6	1	4	6	11	52
Girls..........	2	4	......	......	......	......	5	1	12
Illegitimate									
Boys..........	3	......	1	2	......	......	......	5*	11
Girls..........	2	......	......	1	......	......	......	3*	6
Mulatto									
Boys..........	1	......	......	......	......	......	2	9	12
Girls..........	1	2	......	......	......	......	......	5	8
Total........	61	18	3	13	1	7	18	42	163

*Three boys and one girl were illegitimate children of a free negro woman.

TABLE V

Trade	Dettingen Parish	Fredericksville Parish
Blacksmith.....................	3	3
Cooper........................	3	2
Carpenter and joiner............	10	10
Cordwainer and twiner..........	8	....
Shoemaker.....................	18	....
Weaver........................	4	2
Planting and farming............	5	9

latter description occurring only once, contemplated or required reading and writing. Girls, on the other hand, were to be taught both to read and write in only three cases, and no provision was made for sending any orphan girl to school. Reading and writing for girls were required by the act of 1748, but there were some indentures after this date in which such a requirement is lacking, showing that the law was not strictly observed. Since orphans apprenticed were supposed to be without an estate, the fact that seven boys were to have from one to two years' schooling is interesting. This may be due to the endeavor to give certain orphans greater advantages because of their "quality." The percentage of indentures of orphan boys which did have an educational clause is 84.5, while that of girls is 94.1, a somewhat surprising figure considering the oft-repeated assertion that the education of girls, especially of the poorer class, was almost totally neglected in Virginia. It will be noted that a high percentage of poor girls apprenticed also had an educational clause in their indenture.

The table shows that there were fifty-two boys and twelve girls apprenticed, described as poor children or undescribed. In the latter case, we have considered that they should be placed in this class. These children constitute 39.3 per cent of all those apprenticed. About the same trades are conspicuous as in the case of orphans, and for the same reasons. The percentage of boys to be sent to school from one to two years, 21.1, indicates the use of organized schools as an agency the master must employ for the education of his apprentice. The inclusion of the requirement of "cyphering" in only two cases (1763 and 1769) indicates the comparatively late development of the notion that arithmetic should be included in the indentures of this class of children. One of the two indentures of this class, that of 1769, uses the phrase "to read the Bible and write and cypher as far as the rule of three." The percentage of poor boys to be given book education was 78.8. As in the case of orphan girls, it was specified in only two indentures that they were to be taught both to read and to write, and these indentures were dated 1752 and 1779, after the act of 1748 which required both subjects in the indentures of girls. Besides reading, three indentures for girls called for instruction in spinning, knitting, and sewing. The fact that only one indenture of an apprenticed girl failed to provide some book education shows about the same interest, 91.6 per cent, in the education of poor girls as was shown in the case of orphan girls.

The number of cases of illegitimate children is rather small for the determination of general practice with respect to this class. They were apparently treated as poor children and considered as falling under the same laws. No act specifically providing for the education of these children was passed until 1769, and all of the indentures are dated before the passage of this act. It is noteworthy that in four out of seven indentures for boys and two out of three for girls, where the degree of education is specified, both reading and writing are included, and in the case of one boy, cyphering in addition; also, that two of the boys and one of the girls should be sent to school. The percentage of indentures not having an educational qualification is larger than in the two previous classes, but three of the boys and one of the girls not having such requirements were the illegitimate children of a free negro woman, a class that was not looked upon with favor. On the whole, the educational requirements were high for this class, for, considering the white children only, out of a total of thirteen indentures, nine had an educational clause, or 69.2 per cent.

The mulatto class was not provided for until the act of 1765, and then only partly, when a mulatto servant sold as a slave a second time must be taken from the master and apprenticed and be taught to read and write. Nevertheless, six out of twenty indentures have an educational clause, three for boys and three for girls. One of the boys was to be taught to read and write. Two boys were to have education "as the law allows." One of the girls was to be taught to read and write. One other girl not included in the above was to be brought up in a "Christian-like manner." Only two of all of these indentures were dated after 1765—one, that of a boy, having an educational clause, and the other, that of a girl, making no such provision.

Considering the forty-two cases where no educational clause occurs, we note that fourteen were for mulatto children and four for children of free negroes, twelve boys and six girls. This leaves a total of only twenty-four white children, out of one hundred and forty-five apprenticed, for whose benefit no educational clause is found in the indenture, twenty boys and four girls. The percentage of indentures in which such a clause is found is thus 83.4. It may be noted further that it was possible, at least in some of the cases, that a boy or girl already knew how to read or write before being indentured, and if so, there would be no reason for including such a requirement. This is certainly an exceedingly good record for Virginia, so far as observing the intent of the law is concerned, and shows that in the parishes mentioned, at least, elementary education was an important characteristic of the apprenticeship system. The figures given, however, prove rather a sentiment for the education of these classes than the fact, for it is impossible to say how faithfully masters of apprentices lived up to the educational requirements of the indentures. Occasional cases in the county records have been cited to show the possibility and actuality of enforcement, but we have no method of determining the percentage of cases in which the apprentice received the education provided for. It must be confessed that this depended largely on the individual master or mistress. It was not all certain that the master who neglected to have his apprentice educated according to the terms of the indenture would actually be called into court. We cannot assume that the apprentice was always anxious for the book education to which he might be entitled, or that he or his friends, if he had any, would bring the case to the attention of the court. Moreover, it is likely that justices of the county courts and the church wardens were more interested in relieving the parishes of the burden of supporting poor children and in providing skilled workers in the trades than they were in the book education of these children. When the children were once indentured, these two main purposes of the apprenticeship system had been accomplished. Except in the case of orphans, no penalties were provided by law for officials who neglected their duty. On the other hand, both the parish and the county court could and did impose penalties on masters for failing to carry out the terms of the indenture.

We may conclude that Virginia did establish and develop a real system of compulsory education for the classes of children mentioned; that the legal requirement for a clause in the indenture requiring book education was actually included in a large percentage of the indentures examined; that the motives expressed in the laws reappear in the indentures—first, economic, the desire to increase the number of artisans for the production of manufactured goods and to encourage industrial efficiency, to provide industrial or vocational education, and to relieve the parish of the support of poor children; secondly, humanitarian, a desire to alleviate the condition of the unfortunate children whose parents were poor, idle, or dissolute, including those of illegitimate birth; thirdly, religious, to promote the teaching of the Christian religion and the practice of reading the Bible; fourthly, educational, to give these children a minimum of education—reading and writing for boys and girls. We may also conclude that the county court records give evidence of the actual enforcement of the law and the terms of the indentures where the master failed to give the education required; that this system did provide many children with the rudiments of an education and an opportunity to obtain industrial skill—children who otherwise would probably not have received any, or as much, education had this compulsory system not been in force; that the percentage of children who were actually taught to read or write under the terms of the indenture cannot now be determined any more than it can be in Massachusetts or any other colony; and, finally, that the system of apprenticeship was an important agency in colonial Virginia for the elementary education of poor children.

PART IV

TYPES OF PUBLIC POOR RELIEF SYSTEMS

CHAPTER XII

THE DEVELOPMENT OF PUBLIC POOR
RELIEF IN VIRGINIA

It is well known that the humanitarian movement in the second quarter of the nineteenth century was one of the important social effects of the industrial revolution. That great outpouring of human sympathy for the unfortunate elements of society—the poor, defectives, sick, and other unfortunates—continues to bear fruit on an ever increasing scale. Never in the world's history have such unprecedented amounts of money been granted by private and public agencies to alleviate human suffering. While the modern historical development of this movement is well known, the colonial background of one phase, poor relief in America, is not so familiar. It is, therefore, proposed in this chapter to discuss some of the conditions that confronted colonial Virginia,[1] and the public agencies devised to solve problems of this character.

For the historical background of poor relief in Virginia one needs to call to mind important English economic and social changes in the sixteenth century.[2] With the expansion of England's foreign trade and increased demand abroad for woolen cloth, sheep-raising was stimulated. This was the important reason for the enclosure movement,[3] the fencing in of open fields for grazing, and, in consequence, the decline of an agricultural economy to pasture farming. There followed a surplus of unemployed agricultural laborers, for a few herders took the place of many farm laborers. Thus the number of unemployed and poor persons had been on the increase for a long period before American colonization began. In fact, at this date, 1607, relief of the poor was one of the most pressing questions of the day. Not only the unemployed but also the vagabonds, rogues, beggars, paupers, and the criminal classes increased rapidly.[4] Wages of farm laborers fell as low as a shilling a day, while rents and prices rose several fold.[5]

Previous to the confiscation of the church property by Henry

VIII there had been little legislation with respect to the poor, for the guilds and monasteries had been active in poor relief.[6] With the confiscation of the main sources of supply, poor-relief legislation increased. Thus an act of Edward VI instructs collectors "to gently ask and demand of every man and woman what they of their charity will give weekly towards relief of the poor."[7]

The important act of 1562,[8] the Statute of Artificers, attempted to solve many of the problems mentioned above and others such as the wages and hours of labor, the checking of enclosures, the fixing of prices, unemployment, pauperism, and apprenticeship as a system for national welfare. Migrations from the rural districts to the towns, due to the conversion of arable to grazing land, led a contemporary preacher to lament thus.[9] "O, Merciful Lord! What a number of poor, feeble, halt, blind, lame, sickly, yea with idle vagabonds, and dissembling catiffs mixed among them, lie and creep begging in the miry streets of London and Westminster." This movement was not to the liking of the craft guilds and town artisans, who wished to protect their calling from an oversupply of labor. In the country districts conditions were almost as bad. Sir Thomas More in his *Utopia*[10] (written in 1515) complains that sheep from being meek and tame now "consume, destroy, and devour whole fields, houses and cities"; that the husbandmen were forced out of their homes, or compelled to sell all for almost nothing and to

depart away, poor, seyle [innocent], wretched fools, men, women, husbands, wives, fatherless children, widows, woeful mothers, with their young babes . . . . out of their known and accustomed houses, finding no place to rest in. . . . . And when they have wandered abroad . . . . what can they else do but steal, ... or else go about a begging. And yet then also they be cast in prison as vagabonds, because they go and work not: whom no man will set to work, though they never so willingly profer themselves thereto.

The Statute of Artificers attempted to fix wages and hours of labor and, through the system of apprenticeship, raise the standard of skill in the industrial arts. But more than this it tried to solve the problem of pauperism and vagabondage by placing the worker of the nation in the occupation for which he was best suited. It dealt with the able-bodied poor not by giving alms but by forcing them to work, and through the apprenticeship clauses provided for children. Persons not otherwise employed between twelve and sixty were ordered to be servants in husbandry. Youths who refused to serve as apprentices might be imprisoned. Another clause forbade anyone below the rank of a yeoman to withdraw from an agricultural pursuit in order to be apprenticed to a trade. This doomed the farm laborer to his calling notwithstanding the scarcity of work.

The poor, however, increased, and in 1601 was passed the great Poor Law Act, which emphasized the system of apprenticing poor children. It attempted to "provide work for those who could work, relief for those who could not, and punishment for those who would not."[11] The Act of 1601 provided that overseers of the poor should be nominated for each parish by the justices, with the addition of the church wardens and several householders. Their duty was to set children to work whose parents were unable to maintain them, to raise by taxation sums necessary, and to place out poor children as apprentices. The desire to find someone to maintain the child rather than to teach him a trade was the important feature of this act.[12]

With this English background in mind, let us now turn to colonial Virginia. It will be found that those elements of society needing poor relief, as well as the agencies devised to support and administer funds for this purpose, were closely related to the conditions in England. As early as 1574 Sir Humphrey Gilbert declared:

We might inhabite some part of those Countreyes (America) and settle there such needy people of our countrey which now trouble the commonwealth and through want here at home are enforced to commit outrageous offences, whereby they are dayly consumed with the gallows.[13]

Richard Hakluyt in his *Discourse on Western Planting* (1584) declared that many thousands of idle persons in England were without work,

very burdensome to the commonwealthe, and often fall to pilferinge and thevinge and other lewdness, whereby all the prisons of the lande are daily stuffed full of them . . . . these pety thieves might be condempned for certen yeres in the westerne partes, especially in Newfounde lande, and set to work.[14]

So Velasco, the Spanish minister to England, wrote in 1611, "Their principal reason for colonizing these parts is to give an outlet to so many idle, wretched people as they have in England, and thus to prevent the dangers that might be feared of them.[15]

Those elements of Virginia society that made a system of poor relief necessary may be described as follows. The chief dependence for a supply of labor in the seventeenth century was this large body of unemployed in England—the poor, paupers, vagabonds, and convicts, who were transported to Virginia mainly through the agency of the indentured servant system. In the eighteenth century the chief dependence was the negro slave, though many indentured servants continued to arrive.[16] The children of the servant class and the freed servant, legitimate and illegitimate, were one important element of society calling for poor relief. Besides the presence of these two classes, many of the free whites who had descended from the poorer elements of the white servant class became objects of charity. There were complaints from an early date of "vagrant, idle, and dissolute persons."[17] Such persons often became the fathers of illegitimate children by both free white and white servant women. If they ran away, as frequently happened, their children were thrown on the parish for support. Such persons also often deserted their wives and children.[18]

Another class was made up of free negroes and mulatto servants.[19] The latter, born of a free white mother or white servant, were indentured as servants and after a long period of service became free negroes. Of course, there were other unfortunates, such as the defectives, the sick, idiots, etc. All these classes of society called for poor relief. In general, then, Virginia was confronted with a great problem, as in England, namely, how to protect the parish from a large number of paupers, and how to provide work in order to reduce idleness and unemployment on the one hand and on the other to train workers for the needs of a growing colony.

The machinery for administering poor relief was ready at hand —the English parish system, reproduced in Virginia.[20] The counties were laid off in Virginia in 1634 and in 1641 divided into parishes.[21] The governing body of the parish was the vestry, a group of twelve men,[22] after 1676 chosen by the freeholders,[23] whose duty it was to levy and collect parish tithes; appoint clergymen; investigate cases of immorality and disorder; administer the poor laws; and, in general, care for the religious, moral, and charitable affairs of the parish. The executive arm of the vestry was the church wardens, whose duty it was to administer the business of the parish, and present cases needing the attention of the vestry.[24]

While George Washington was for years a vestryman of Truro Parish, and while as a rule it was expected that the vestrymen should be "the most able and discreet persons of their Parish,"[25] not all vestrymen measured up to this high standard. The Assembly dissolved the vestry of Suffolk in Nansemond County because of "several unwarrantable practices in the misapplication of divers charitable donations given for the use of the poor of the said parish known by the name of the Lower Parish."[26]

Owing to the organization of new counties and parishes, due to the westward movement of population, and to the division of counties and parishes because of the increase of population, the number of parishes increased throughout the colonial period. In 1722, there were 29 counties and 54 parishes.[27] In 1774 there were 62 counties and 95 parishes.[28]

The vestries of these parishes acted under general and special laws governing the care of the poor. Those having to do with the system of apprenticeship were designed to protect the parish from maintaining a large number of poor and illegitimate children; to reduce idleness and unemployment, and to stimulate the development of an artisan class skilled in the trades. In these acts there was also the notion of improving the religious, moral, and educational status of poor children.

A brief sketch of the legislation[29] affecting poor, illegitimate, and orphan children will help in understanding the practice. At least eight important acts affecting poor children of various classes were passed between 1646 and 1769. That of 1646[30] gives as one motive for the act of necessity of avoiding "sloath and idlenesse wherewith such young children are easily corrupted, as also for the reliefe of such parents whose poverty extends not to give them breeding." It provided that justices of the peace should, at their discretion, bind out children, and establish public flax-houses to which two children from each county might be sent and taught to spin. Again, in 1672,[31] because of the increase of "vagabonds, idle and dissolute persons," justices of the peace were empowered "to place out *all* children whose parents were not able to bring them up apprentices." Again in 1727,[32]

the act of that year complains of "divers idle and disorderly persons"
able to work who "stroll from one county to another, neglecting to
labour"; and vagabonds, "run from their habitations and leave
either wives or children, without suitable means for their subsistence, whereby they are likely to become burthensome to the parish
wherein they inhabit." Children of such parents, because of their
"idle, dissolute and disorderly course of life," could be bound out
by church wardens on certificate from the county court.

Besides the acts relating to poor children, several were passed
affecting illegitimate children.[33] The number of illegitimate children
increased with the increase of indentured servants. As early as 1642–
43[34] laws were passed against fornication between servants and free
men and servants. In 1657–58, the father of an illegitimate child
was obliged to give security to indemnify the parish against keeping
the child.[35] If the father were an indentured servant, he could not, of
course, indemnify the parish. So, in 1662,[36] it was provided that the
parish should "take care to keepe the child during the time of the
reputed father's service by indenture or custome, and that after he
is free the said reputed father shall make satisfaction to the parish."
Finally, in 1769,[37] because the laws in force were insufficient, and because of the "great charges frequently arising from children begotten
out of lawful matrimony," the church wardens were instructed to
bind out illegitimate children of free single white women. If the illegitimate child were born of a convict[38] servant woman during the
time of her service, the master of such servant was obliged to maintain the child until twenty-one or eighteen years of age, and was entitled to its service.

Still another problem for the parish was the increase of mulatto
children. The act of 1691[39] complained that there was need of preventing "that abominable mixture and spurious issue which hereafter may increase in this dominion as well by negroes, mulattoes,
and Indians intermarrying with English, or other white women, as
by their unlawful accompanying with one another."[40]

Another problem was the care of orphans. No less than seventeen acts were passed by Virginia relating to this class, most of them
having to do with the management of orphans' estates, but some
providing for the binding out of poor orphans.[41]

It is, of course, true that the laws enacted by the assembly represent an ideal rather than actual practice. The administration of poor relief was, indeed, largely regulated by law, but, on the other hand, the vestries often acted from custom rather than law. This is clearly shown in the minutes of the vestries, several of which have been published.[42] It is from these records that we can learn the actual practice and methods of poor relief in Virginia.

The most important function of the vestries was their duties as financial managers of the parish. Each year, in meeting assembled, they made up their budget and divided the amount by the total number of tithables in the parish. The tithe was generally paid in kind, usually tobacco, but might in some cases be levied and paid in wheat or maize.[43] This method of payment made it necessary to appoint a collector, who worked on a percentage basis. He had power "to make, distress for the same," viz., to compel payment by selling the property in case of a refusal to pay the tithe.

It appears that in the period from 1720 to 1730, the vestry of Bristol Parish levied 370,982 pounds of tobacco, of which 34,415 were for poor relief.[44] The ratio was thus about 9 per cent. In St. Peter's Parish, for the year 1722, the percentage for poor relief was 22, or nearly one-third of the total levy.[45] A typical year (1726) in the case of Bristol Parish shows a levy of 66,789 pounds of tobacco, the number of tithables being 1,236, or 54 pounds per poll. Of this total, 6,124 pounds were for poor relief, and the number aided was eight.[46]

Parishes also received bequests from time to time. Thus, in 1674, James Bennett of Nansemond gave the parish two hundred acres of land. The rents were to be received yearly by the church wardens and applied to the relief of poor, aged, and impotent persons forever.[47] Again, in 1707, a Mrs. Hill bequeathed by will 350 acres for the benefit of the poor of the parish.[48] Besides land, cattle, tobacco, and slaves were left for the support of the poor. Thus Mathew Godfrey of Norfolk County left by will, 1715–16, 1,000 acres and slaves, to be let out each year, the income to be used for the support of the poor of the county, and to be divided equally among three parishes.[49] In view of both public and private aid for the poor, Beverley's assertion (1722) that the poor of Virginia were well cared for seems fair. He says that some countries gave but just sufficient to preserve the poor from perishing, but in Virginia "the unhappy creature was recéived into some charitable planter's house where he was at the public charge boarded plentifully."[50]

The administration of poor relief for children rested largely on the apprenticeship laws, already discussed, and for adults on general laws. A petition[51] of 1641 complained that "Divers poore men have longe inhabited heere and nowe are growne decrepped and impotent." In 1642–43, a general law,[52] defining the duties of vestries, states that the poor had been of long continuance in the colony, and that many were prevented from laboring because of sickness, lameness, or old age. On complaint to the vestry, such could be certified to the commissioners of the county court as to their poverty and freed from all public charges "except the ministers' and parish duties." Under their general powers, then, the vestries could apprentice poor children, administer bequests for the poor, make levies, and allot aid according to the needs of individual cases. The vestry, however, was under the supervision of the county court, and, in case of neglect of duty, could be called to account. It was also of course subject to the general assembly.[53]

Plans for "farming out" all the poor to the lowest bidder were sometimes proposed but seldom carried out in practice. Thus, in 1719, in St. Peter's parish, it was voted that

Whereas, Capt. John Scott has made an offer to take all the Poor People of this Parish: It is ordered That he shall Receive all the poor people which shall be sent him by the Church Wardens. And to provide for them all such necessaries as Shall be Convenient (Except Apparrell) As the Church Wardens and he can agree.[54]

This plan, however, was not carried out, nor were similar votes of Bristol parish "That the Church wardens at the most Convenient place put up the Poor of this Parish to the lowest Bidder."[55] An elaborate plan for a poorhouse, to be supported by three parishes, Bristol, Martin's Brandon, and Bath was also proposed, but this likewise failed to mature.[56]

The common method of administering poor relief was to have the poor cared for in different homes, by paying a sum agreed upon for each person. This involved either total support for those entirely disabled, or partial support for persons needing temporary relief, or for those not wholly without resources. This called for a grant of a specific sum for the time kept for service rendered. Thus the persons receiving aid and the kind of aid given were extremely varied. A typical budget,[57] made up by the vestry of St. Peter's Parish, New Kent County, for the year 1744, reads as follows:

At a Vestry held for St. Peter's Parish September the 29th, 1744.

Present:

The Rev'd David Mossom, Min'r; Maj'r John Dandridgge, Capt. Rich'd Littlepage, Capt. Wm. Massie, Mr. Walter Clopton, Mr. Thomas Butts, Mr. Chas. Massie, Coll. Dan'll Parke Custis, Maj'r Jos. Foster, Mr. Ambrose Dudley, Vestrymen; Coll. Wm. Macon, Mr. Jos. Marston, Church Wardens.

St. Peter's Parish,	Dr.	
To the Rev'd Mr. Mossom his Salary to September the 29th		16000
To Cask to Do. a 4 P. ct.		640
To the Rev'd Mr. Mossom for the Deficiency of Glebe		1600
To Cask to Do. a 4 P. ct.		64
To James Holmes his Salary to September the 29th		1800
To Stephen Broker, Sexton, his Salary		630
To Sarah Broker for washing the Surplice these 2 years		100
To James Ashcroft for keeping his Father		600
To Hugh Grindley for keeping Charles Goodwin		450
To David Patteson for keeping Mary Hazard		800
To Israel Asutin for keeping his Brother		250
To John Phillips for his Support		600
To Cornelius Matthews for the Support of his Mother		500
To Samuel Bailey for keeping Mary Major		450
To Henry Strange for keeping Marg't Grumbal		700
To Phillis Moon for keeping her Son		967
To George Heath for keeping John Vincent, an orphan child		600
To Sarah Broker for keeping Christ'r Bendall in his Sickness		300
To Maj. John Dandridge his acco't.		380
To Mr. Ben. Waller for a copy of the List of Tithables		18
To Capt. Wm. Massie his L3, 3, 10, in Tobo. at 10 P. ct		638
To Rich'd Crump, Sen'r, his Acco't, L4, 2s., o, in Tobo, at Do.		419
To Coll. Macon his acco't, L8, 17, 4, in Tobo, at Do		1744
		30280
To George Taylor for keeping Catherine Taylor in Child bed		400
To Hannah Morgan for keeping Marg't Foster 4 weeks		400
To Sarah Broker as part of her Fee for Bring Cath. Taylor to Bed		30
		31110

(Budget continued on next page)

Ord'd that the Sume of 12750 lb. of Tobo. be Levyed for the use of the
Parish... 12756
                                                                        43866
To the Coll'n at 6 P. Ct... 2632
                                                                        46498
To a Rem'r due from the Coll'r.. 54
                                                                        46552

Per Contra,   Cr.

By 1058 Tithables at 44 lb. Tobo. Pr. Poll........................ 46552

It will be noted that out of a total levy of 46,552 pounds of tobacco
no less than 7,040 pounds were for poor relief, involving thirteen
different persons; also, that a father, brother, mother, and son were
"kept" by immediate relatives; also, that aid was granted for the
care of an orphan, for women "in child bed," and for poor persons
in general.

The problem of total support may be illustrated by the following
cases:

Upon the petition of James Turner Setting forth that he has been visited
with Lameness and sickness severall years in So much that he hath spent all
his substance upon Phesitians and nessicaries, therefore, ordered that Samuell
Waddy keep the same James Turner during Life and to find him sufficient Clothing, meate, drink, washing and Lodging, and all nessicaries, and to be paid
twelve hundred pounds of Tobacco and Cask p annum. and soe proportionable
for a longer or a shorter time the said Wadde assuring to this vestry to keep the
said Turner for the Sume of 1200 lbs. of Tobacco, and bring noe Claime against
the parish for the same.[58]

This is a case where the vestry burdened itself with the maintenance of one person for his whole life, at a fixed sum per year, with
no further claim against the parish.

A widow, Elizabeth Faulkner, was a source of great expense to
St. Peter's parish for a number of years, 1690–1710. Let us follow
the history of the Widow Faulkner. First, in May 1690, five hundred pounds of tobacco were granted toward her maintenance for
one year.[59] In November, Lyonell Morriss agreed "to find her sufficient accomodations" at the rate of one thousand pounds of tobacco
a year.[60] In 1696, Thomas Minns was paid 1,040 pounds of tobacco
for "keeping" the widow Faulkner one year and "providing her a
pr. of shoes."[61] The next year he was paid 1,080 pounds for keeping
her and 30 pounds for another pair of shoes.[62] Two hundred and
ninety-two pounds were also paid Mr. Wyatt for her "Cloathes."[63]

This same amount, 1,080 pounds, was paid for the next few years, 1699–1706.[64] On May 8, 1707, however, Mr. Minns made a complaint. Perhaps the widow was either eating too much, or the cost of living was rising. The record reads "Whereas Tho. Minns complains that his allowance for keeping Wid. Faulkner is too little, the vestry have ordered it increased for ye future 1100 lbs. tobo. . . . . if she lives."[65] The Widow Faulkner was thus supported by the parish, in three different houses, for twenty years, at a cost of 20,619 pounds of tobacco.

In general, the old, impotent, and lame were charges on the parish, as well as those who were temporarily or permanently disabled by sickness or other causes.[66] The dreaded modern scourge of cancer is reported in 1728.

Robt. Glidewell Being afficted With a Cancur in his face which hath made him unable to labour for his livelihood it is ord'red that the Church Warthen find him necessary Cloathin and likewise that John Browder find him necessary board and he to be allow'd one hundred pounds of tobo pr. month.[67]

These cases illustrate the method of total support. Persons not wholly without resources also received either permanent or temporary aid. Take the case of Anthony Burrass, "stricken blind," November, 1696.

Whereas Anthony Burrass of this parish is stricken blind and his wife is very ancient by what means they are incapable of getting their living and that the said Anthony addressing himself to this vestry for a maintanence.

It is therefore ordered that the Church wardens forthwith cause the said Anthony Burros to convey over unto them for the use of this parish forever his plantation, Cattle, horses and hoggs and that there be allowed to each of them five hundred pounds of Tob. and Casq's for their maintanence during their or either of their natural lives or till he may be recovered of his eye sight.[68]

Later he accepted 1,600 pounds of tobacco yearly for the maintenance of himself and his wife, and this agreement was carried out for some years.[69]

The parish helped the able-bodied poor by enabling them to help themselves. Robert Magrime could work, but apparently was in danger of becoming a parish charge. So

Mr. Gideon Macon offering to this vestry to take the said Magrime and keep him as long as he can work and pay levys and keep him from being a parish charge During his natural life, therefore ordered that the Sheriff sumon the said Magrine to appear at the next Court to answer what the Court shall therein order.[70]

Another type of poor relief was the provision for the partial support of, or aid to, the poor for a limited period, viz., occasional temporary relief. Margaret Butler, having petitioned that she "being disabled by Sickness is not Able to help herselfe," the vestry ordered that she live with Richard Butler "untill the vestry can Agree with A Doctor to cure her if possible he can." Mr. Butler was allowed eight pounds of tobacco a month for the time she lived with him, he "to find her diet, lodging and washing for the time."[71] The vestry also agreed with "Doctor Thompson for the Cure of Jacob Butler and to Bring in their accm't at the laying of the nex parrish leavy."[72]

In case of accident, relief was often given. Thus "Peter plantin being Much Burnt by acsident and he being poor and aged Not Able to pay for his Cure Mary hall is ord'red to take Care of the Sd plantine and to Do her Endeavour to Cure him and she to bring in her account at the laying the Next parrish leavy."[73] The practice of making a contract with a doctor to cure the sick was very common. Thus "Ordered that ye Church wardens Agree with Some Doctor to Cure Mary Wilde of her Ailement, and if she think herself able to undergo a Course of Phisic. The Church wardens are to agree w'th ye Doctor for ye same."[74] Parishes might even provide for the expense of taking a person to a health resort. Thus "Ordered that the Church Wardens Agree with some Person on the best terms they can to carry Richd Sentale to the Spring on New River for the Recovery of his health."[75] Another type of aid occurred when the church wardens were "impowered to give Thomas Ashcraft Credit in a Store for forty Shillings towards finding him in Cloathes for the ensuing year."[76] Still another method of aiding the poor was the distribution of fines. Thus the church wardens were ordered to distribute fines in their hands "among the Poor of the Parish."[77]

Another form of temporary aid was that of freeing persons from parish dues. Persons unable to pay might secure relief by petitioning the county court or they could apply directly to the vestry for relief.[78] Thus "Tho. Andrews being Anciant and Crasey and not Able to Work is Acquitted from paying P'ish Levies."[79] Robert Glascock being upwards of 60 years old and lame is Acquitted from paying P'ish Levies."[80] "Upon the petition of Phillis Moore for to gett her Son John Moore levy free, Setting forth in her petition that her

S'd Son is troubled with Convultion fitts and much burnt. It is ordered that the Said Jno. Moore be exempted from paying of parish Levy During his Infirmity."[81]

Generally speaking, charity seems to have been given with some regard for the feelings of the recipient. In Bristol Parish, however, the church wardens ordered the pews numbered, and after four had been reserved "for the use of the Poor," ordered that they "lett the Same, to the highest Bidders."[82]

The binding out of poor, illegitimate, and orphan children, as provided for by law, was one of the important duties of the vestry, and their minutes contain numerous examples of the practice. Thus, at one meeting of the vestry of Bristol parish, it was ordered that eight poor children, five from one family, should be bound out to various persons.[83] A specific case is that of "Agnes Tudora, poor Infirm Girl, being put upon this parish for a Charge and Rich'd and Sarah Brookes being willing to take the said Girl, Ordered that the Church wardens bind the Said Agnes Tudor to the Said Rich'd and Sarah Brookes for Seven Years."[84]

The vestry was, broadly speaking, the moral sponsor for the parish. Accordingly, the vestry books abound with records of illegitimate children whose maintenance might result in added burdens to the parish, and the prosecution of which cases was intrusted to the vestry. There are orders to support or bind out all types of illegitimate children, white and mulatto, born of free white women, and white servant women.[85] Thus "It is ordered that a thousand pounds of tobacco and cask be paid unto Mary Wilkinson for nursing a bastard child belonging to a servant woman of Capt. Joseph Forster this ensuing year."[86] The process of binding out such a child is illustrated by the following entry:

Margaret Micabin servant to Mr. David Crawley having a bastard Child Mr. Crawley prays the Gentlemen of this Vestry to bind out the said Child as they think fitt. It is ordered by the Vestry that the Church-Wardens bind out the s'd Child named John Sadler born the 26th July last 1720. The fores'd Child is by indenture bound unto Mr. David Crawley to serve according to Law.[87]

There was a great increase of illegitimate mulatto children in the eighteenth century, born of free white women or white servant women. In either case the child was not a slave, but, according to law, must be bound out to service till of age. Thus in October, 1724, "Hen. Royall pettitioneth that he hath two Moll. children born in his house by Name Wm. and hannah may be bound to him and his heirs according to Law his pett. is granted."[88] At the meeting of June 28, 1725, three petitions were received to have two mulatto girls and one boy, born probably of white servant women, in three different houses, bound to the masters and mistresses of the servants.[89]

Orphan children also were bound out to relieve the parish of keeping them. The number of orphans is surprising. In Spottsylvania County, will book "B" contains a list of forty-five guardians' bonds between 1749 and 1761, involving seventy children.[90]

The system of poor relief became more and more unsatisfactory in the latter half of the eighteenth century. Changes in Virginia society, the inefficiency of the Anglican church, the westward movement of population, the formation of large back country parishes, and the delay in the formation of parishes were some of the new factors. One complaint was made that, because of the want of a vestry in Botentourt Parish, the poor were likely to suffer "for want of proper support and maintenance."[91] From 1780 to 1785, the assembly by a series of acts dissolved the vestries and provided for overseers of the poor in each county. The preamble of the act of 1780 reads, "Whereas great inconveniences have arisen from the mode prescribed for making provisions for the poor" in seven western counties named, the vestries of such were dissolved, and the sheriffs were ordered to elect five freeholders as "Overseers of the Poor," with the powers and duties of vestries and church wardens.[92] In 1782, another act dissolved the vestries of five more western counties, because the former act "hath greatly removed the inconveniences for making provision for the poor."[93] Finally, in 1785, a general act was passed to provide for the poor in all the counties of the state, by appointment of overseers of the poor who also were given the same powers over bastards and vagrants, formerly exercised by the vestries.[94] Thus the care of the poor passed out of the control of the Anglican church to that of the counties. This was one of the consequences of the American Revolution and the separation of church and state in Virginia.

CHAPTER XIII

THE DEVELOPMENT OF PUBLIC POOR RELIEF IN NEW ENGLAND

Those aspects of the historical background of poor relief previously considered apply likewise to the New England colonies. The important facts to remember are those English economic and social changes of the sixteenth century which led to the excessive number of unemployed persons and in consequence the rapid increase of the idle, pauper, and criminal classes. England's efforts to solve this problem through legislation, particularly by the Statute of Artificers (1562) and the Poor Law Act (1601), have been discussed.[1] A brief account of other features of England's poor relief policies will enable us to understand better the historical background of the development of thought and practice on this subject in the New England colonies.

As early as 1349 England began to seek remedies for unemployment, vagrancy, and pauperism. By the Statute of Laborers of this date she endeavored to prevent the agricultural laborer from wandering from place to place for the purpose of seeking work and to compel him to work at fixed wages for those who needed his services. This act also forbade "valiant beggars" to ask alms and persons solicited to give alms.[2] During the next century unemployment continued to increase. Though thousands were willing to work, jobs were not available and so beggars and paupers multiplied. Instead of seeking a remedy for these evils at their source England merely labeled such persons criminals. In harmony with the prevailing theory of punishment for crime it was naïvely believed that severe penalties were cure-alls for every species of wrongdoing. The act[3] of 1531, for example, declared that not money but vagrancy and idleness were

the mother and root of all vices, whereby . . . . daily insurgeth and springeth continual thefts, murders, and other heinous offences and great enormities, to the high displeasure of God, the iniquitation and damage of the king's people, and to the marvellous disturbence of the commonwealth.

By this act, impotent persons who begged without a license were to be whipped or set in the stocks for three days with nothing to eat but bread and water. If able-bodied they were to be tied to a cart's tail and whipped through the town. Scholars and students begging without a license were to be whipped on two successive days and for a second offense put in the pillory and have an ear cut off.[4] The idea that vagrants and beggars, both impotent and able-bodied, were criminals persisted for nearly a century[5] and reappeared in New England colonial legislation. No provision was made for the support of the impotent nor were agencies devised to find work for the unemployed.

The act[6] of 1536 provided that "sturdy vagabonds and valiant beggars" should be "set and kept to continual labour in such wise as they may get their own living with the continued labour of their own hands." But with a large surplus of labor this worthy idea was impossible of execution. Moreover, as in the previous act, no agencies were provided for finding jobs for those out of work. How the legislators expected to reduce the number of "valiant" beggars by this law is a mystery. They were evidently thinking more of protecting society from certain evils than in discovering a remedy to remove the causes of such evils. In both of these acts the impotent poor were not differentiated from the able-bodied so far as the theory of punishment was concerned.

It was just at this time, at the beginning of the English reformation, that Henry VIII began to confiscate the property of religious foundations and to dissolve the monasteries. Thus the important agencies heretofore depended on to care for the poor were largely swept away. The monasteries, hospitals, and guilds, together with private donations, had, up to this time, been the chief reliance for the support of the poor. This system, however, tended to stimulate rather than to decrease begging. For it was human nature for idle persons and beggars to avoid work when it was so easy to obtain food from kind-hearted religious persons. Gradually it dawned on England that a new system of poor relief was absolutely necessary.

From 1536 to 1601 there was gradually developed the policy of a general tax for the support of the poor. Voluntary contributions had for a long time been asked for by church and civil authorities.

In 1563 a weekly contribution was demanded and one who "obstinately" refused might be brought before the justice of the peace who could assess such a person on penalty of imprisonment.[7] By act of 1572 the justices were empowered to levy a general tax to be administered by overseers of the poor.[8] Complaint was made that

all parts of this realm of England and Wales be presently with rogues, vagabonds and sturdy beggars exceedingly pestered, by means whereof daily happeneth horrible murders, thefts, and other great outrages, to the high displeasure of Almighty God, and to theyre great annoyance of the Commonwealth.[9]

Three years later (1576) houses of correction or workhouses were provided for, and idle youth and other needy poor persons might be committed to these institutions and set to work with materials provided. A penalty of twenty shillings was imposed on those who aided or harbored a beggar.[10]

Finally, the act of 1601 (elaborating one of 1597) incorporated the experience of a century and more of legislation and thought respecting poor relief. By this act[11] the poor were divided into three classes. First, the lame, impotent, old, blind, and others unable to work were to be relieved through general taxation. Secondly, the able-bodied poor, "sturdy vagabonds," and "valiant beggars" must work. Vagrants must be returned to the place where they had last dwelt for a year. Materials for work must be provided for in each parish by the justices, church wardens, and appointed householders. This "stock" included flax, hemp, wool, thread, iron, and other materials. Thirdly, poor children must be bound out as apprentices.

The New England colonists were of course familiar with English experience. Their first care was to prevent persons from entering the colony or towns; those who were objectionable for either political, religious, or economic reasons; that is, in the latter case, because they might become "chargeable."[12] Thus developed the practice of scrutinizing the economic status of immigrants, strangers, and visitors with a view to preventing them from gaining a settlement, or the right of inhabitancy.

Plymouth colony made masters of vessels responsible for bringing in persons liable for charges which might arise and required them to return such persons to the place of their origin.[13] Massachusetts provided that shipmasters must deliver to the "receiver" a perfect list of passengers with their names and circumstances, and give security for those likely to become chargeable or transport them out of the province.[14] In 1722, town treasurers and selectmen were authorized to receive the lists in ports where there were no receivers. The intent of this act was stated two years later: "to prevent the importation of poor, vicious and infirm persons."[15] Masters of vessels were required to give bond so that no passenger would become chargeable for five years.[16] The Boston seleotmen's records (1736–42) give numerous instances of shipmasters giving bonds for landing Irish passengers "to save the town harmless from all charges."[17]

Besides shipmasters, others responsible for receiving or bringing into a colony those likely to become paupers must "discharge the town." Those coming from England or elsewhere, who were likely to be chargeable, "by reason of impotency, disease, or otherwise," or who brought a servant, "which by God's providence shall fall diseased, lame, or impotent by the way or after they come here," must free the town or maintain such person at their own expense.[18]

A person who succeeded in entering a New England town did not immediately become an inhabitant. Rather he was put on probation for three months to a year, during which period he was a non-inhabitant. If he became chargeable before gaining a residence, then the burden of support fell upon the person responsible for his entrance.[19] Under the Massachusetts act of 1655, towns were granted the right to determine what persons should come into the town, and votes in town meeting show that they acted accordingly.[20] In case of dispute between towns respecting the responsibility for the support of poor persons, the matter was decided in Massachusetts by the general court or two magistrates with "power to determine all differences about the lawfull settling of poor persons (and) to dispose of unsettled persons into such towns . . . . most fitt for their maintenance."[21]

The problem of "entertaining" persons, even for a short visit, led to the enacting of stringent laws designed to compel the entertainer to bear the burden of support if the visitor became chargeable.[22] Fines were provided varying from twenty to forty shillings a week, and even more,[23] and towns were not slow to take advantage of this method of lessening the burden of the support of the poor.[24]

The very rigid system of scrutinizing strangers who came into a town made it desirable for a person to have a letter from the selectmen of his own town stating that he was an inhabitant and that the town would provide for his support if necessary.[25] A Dorchester father who entertained his own daughter, resident of Milton, a neighboring town, had to "gitt a note" from the selectmen of that town promising that they would receive her back again as an inhabitant; viz., that they would assume responsibility for her support if necessary.[26]

The interesting old English custom of "warning out" was widely practiced in New England from 1656 on, often for the purpose of avoiding the responsibility of supporting prospective paupers. It was the duty of householders to inform the selectmen if strangers came to reside with them, to enable the former to warn them out if they saw fit. The following is an order[27] sent to the selectmen with the indorsement "Ezra Putnam's Letter—Warned out Isaac Peabody and wife, 1763."

To the Selectmen of Danvers

GENTLEMEN: these are to inform you that I have taken into my House Isaac Peabody and Sarah Peabody, his Wife, Molley, Sarah, Isaac, Huldah and Rachel, their Children; they came from Middleton the 22d of December, 1768; their Surcumstances very Low in the World.

EZRA PUTNAM

In Connecticut, the constable or selectmen had the opportunity, for three months, to warn out those who by sickness, lameness, "or the like," needed relief.[28] If security was given the person was usually allowed to remain. From 1679 to 1700, 252 bonds were signed in Boston by persons who agreed that they would free the town of any charge of supporting intending settlers. Samuel Sewall, for example, became surety to the town for Samuel Greene, printer, and his family. A typical bond reads:

I, John Williams of Boston, Butcher, doe binde myself, to Tho. Bratle, Treasurer of Said towne, in the Some of forty pounds, That Richard Deven Shall not be Chargeable to the Towne. 29th Sept. 1679.

His

RICHARD DEVEN   JOHN X WILLIAMS
                                                             Marke

One Henry Allen signed a bond for a Mr. Armstrong and his wife but had the misfortune to be sued by the town because "the wife of the said Armstrong was a charge to the town 8 months before that time," viz., October 1, 1695.[29] Persons remaining in a town after being warned out might be fined.[30] Massachusetts provided that towns might petition the county court "by way of complaint" if poor persons remained as inhabitants after being warned out.[31] The two petitions which follow well illustrate this method of dealing with poor people. The first is from the selectmen of Marblehead (1676) to the Essex County court. It reads:[32]

Whereas the lawes of this common wealth ordereth that every Towne shall provide for their owne poore; phillip welch of Topsfeild being reputed A very poor man and of late com with his Family into our Towne of Marble Head without Leave obtained from either Towne or selectmen, also, beeing ackcording To our towne order warned either to depart or give bond for the Townes secuitie hee refusing to doe either, wee doubte not but this honnoured court will give releeffe against this iniust intrusion.

The second is from the selectmen of Manchester (1679) complaining that Thomas Chick with his wife and three children had come into the town to settle. It reads:

But wee findeing him to be in a poare condision not haveing wherewith to suply the present nesesity of himselfe and his family neither for food nor Raiment and therefore wee canot see but in al probabillity if the said Chick shood setell in our town he will quickly be chargable to us and wee our selvs being unable to contribut to such a condision in regard of our own inabiliti and the smallnes of our town and acomadations wee therefore according to law for the prevention of such charge coming upon us have indeavered to remove the said Chick by giveing him due notic and leagall warning to remove out of our town and other wise to provide for himselfe but the said Chick have refused to take any notic of such warning saying he will not troble himselfe to remove out of the said town. He had often affirmed that he had three acres of land at Netchuwauick or thereabouts besides some other considerable estate in his father-in-law's hands.[33]

The court ordered that Chick be sent to New Chewauake, and that this place receive him.

The general practice of deporting undesirables was practiced from an early date in the New England colonies. The purpose was at first to rid the colony of political and religious malcontents,[34] "persons unmete to inhabit here." In the eighteenth century many deportations occurred for the purpose of expelling paupers. An act of 1701 provided that towns might deport persons and be reimbursed out of the province treasury in the case of unsettled dependents ill with infectious or contagious diseases.[35] There are records of deportation of Irish paupers explained by a memorial (1755) from the frugal Boston selectmen.[36] "The sending them out was to prevent a greater (evil), which must necessarily have arisen to the Province had they been permitted to tarry in it, they being extreamly poor, and unable to maintain themselves." On various occasions sums were appropriated by the province for deportation of dependents. Thus, in 1755, £14 were allowed for the passage of a man to Ireland who was being maintained at the cost of the province. In 1765, £8 were allowed for the passage of an Irish pauper who petitioned to be returned to Ireland. And in 1769 a poor "distracted old man was returned."[37]

The legislation on the actual care and support of poor persons already in the town or those admitted as inhabitants was extensive. It dealt with such topics as the nature, agencies, and methods of support and the various classes involved: such as, on the one hand, the impotent poor—the aged, diseased, lame, sick, wounded, widows, and children. On the other hand, effort was made to develop the principle of self-support; to compel the able-bodied poor—the idle, vagrant, and vagabond classes and others capable of self-support— to work. In general, the towns and county courts were made responsible for the support of the poor and the administration of the laws.

There were first general laws providing for relief of the impotent poor. Thus, Plymouth colony (1642) declared that every town should maintain their poor "according as they shall fynd most convenyent and suitable for themselves by an order and genall agreement in a publike town meeting."[38] So Connecticut in 1673 ordered every town to maintain its own poor. This act is the first important general poor law in New England. It provided that after three months' residence any person who "by sickness, lameness or the like comes to want," relief should be provided for by that town.[39] In 1702 the selectmen or overseers of the poor must attend to the relief of the poor so far as "*five pounds* will extend," or more, with the advice of the assistants or justices of the peace, for the supplying of their poor with "victuals, clothing, firewood, or any other thing necessary for their support or subsistence."[40] Massachusetts provided (1692) that towns must relieve those unable to work.[41]

Under these laws each case involving the impotent poor was dealt with separately in town meeting or by the selectmen. It was common to place a poor or sick person with some family, or to provide food, clothing, or money. Thus, upon complaint made to the selectmen of Cambridge that John Johnson was in a "low and pore condishon," it was ordered that he be supplied out of the town rate not exceeding forty shillings until further "order be taken."[42] In Watertown (1680) the selectmen inspected the town to see who might need help "both concerning there soules" and "there bodies." They reported that twenty-two people needed relief.[43] Ten pounds a year were allowed "Widow Bartlet to diet ould Bright and to carry in his diet or send it for his necessary supply" and the selectmen sent Deacon Thatcher and "Corporall" Hamon to make an agreement "to Diet Henry Thorp as they should se fiting and best for his releife" and they were also to "nottis" what need of clothing he had.[44] In Hadley (Massachusetts) it was voted in town meeting (1687) that Widow Baldwin should be sent from house to house two weeks in each family "able to receive her" and so "round the town."[45] Braintree voted (1701) £5 to Nathaniel Owen to help build a room for the keeping of his father and mother.[46]

In Connecticut, 1680, the Committee for Trade and Plantations made one of its queries read, "What provision is there made . . . . for relieving poor, decayed and impotent persons?" Governor Leete wrote[47] this somewhat optimistic account of the poor:

> For the poore, it is ordered that they be relieved by the townes where they live, every towne providing for theire own poor; and so for impotent persons. There is seldom any want releif; because labor is deare, viz., 2s., and sometimes 2s. 6d. a day for a day labourer, and provision cheap.

Large seaport towns like Boston, Philadelphia, and New York were in a peculiar and unfortunate situation both with respect to poor immigrants and because of the policy of the smaller inland towns, by warning out, to force their poor to move to the larger towns. The situation in Boston in 1679 is set forth in a petition[48] to the general court:

Because the Constitution of the Towne of Bostone is such in respect of the continuall resort of all sorts of persons from all partes, both by sea and land, more than any other towne in the Collony, there is a necessitie of some peculiar power or priviledge whereby to defend themselves from that pphanesse and charge two much growinge upon us. . . . . The towne is fild with poore idle and profane persons which are greatlie prejuditiall to the inhabitants.

Boston provided for visiting families by justices, selectmen, overseers of the poor, constables, and tithingmen. In 1715 the purpose was stated: "to Inspect disorderly persons, New-comers And the circumstances of the poor and education of their children."[49]

There were various methods of giving the poor temporary relief. Abatement of taxes was common. After Boston's great fire of 1683, because many homes had been destroyed and "many impoverished," the selectmen reduced the taxes of the poor.[50] A list of abatements in Boston for 1700,[51] because of poverty, illness, or unemployment, etc., affected twelve persons at a cost of £7 7s. 8d. Efforts were made to provide the poor with food and clothing at low prices. In 1740 Boston converted an old church into a granary where twelve thousand bushels of grain could be stored at a time, and sold to the poor in small quantities on an advance of 10 per cent on the cost to cover the expense and waste.[52] Town cows have an interesting history. Legacies were made for the purchase of cows for the use of the poor. Concord thus purchased a town cow and pastured it on the common land.[53] Many fines or breaches of the poor laws were employed for the relief of the poor, such as fines on those refusing to work at harvest time; selling bread and butter at short weight; not attending public worship or making shingles contrary to the required dimensions of length, breadth, and thickness, etc.[54]

The number of poor persons increased rapidly in the eighteenth century, especially in Boston. By 1735 a petition to the governor complained that the expense of maintaining the poor had increased from £940 in 1728 to £2000 in 1734. At this date there were eighty-eight persons in the almshouse, about one-third of whom were born in Boston. The petition requested aid from the province and as-

serted that two-thirds of the poor were not born in Boston. The
increase in population was asserted to be mostly due to the number
of poor coming in and that the town was powerless to prevent it.
Probably this increase was due partly to the efforts of the smaller
towns to evade the responsibility for their own poor and partly to
the increase of poor immigrants. Similar petitions were presented
in 1737, 1752, and 1753.[55] By 1770 out of a total expenditure of some
£245 by the town of Braintree £90, or 36 per cent, were spent for
poor relief.[56]

This increase in the cost of poor relief led to laxness, negligence,
and even to evasion of responsibility by towns, selectmen, and overseers of the poor. Consequently, the general court of Massachusetts
(1742) complained of the neglect of these officers in caring for the
poor. Disputes as to which town was legally responsible for relief
were common, and there was often a "pretense" that the condition
and circumstances of poor persons were not so "necessitous" as to
require support or render them a proper town charge. The law provided that the county court should determine the responsibility of
towns and fine selectmen forty shillings on proof of neglect of duty.
This sum was to be applied for support of the poor. Towns also
might be assessed by the justices if they failed to provide for the
poor and the sums obtained were to be disposed of as the justices
saw fit.[57]

Besides the impotent poor there was another source of pauperism,
namely, the able-bodied poor who were not self-supporting. Idlers,
vagrants, and vagabonds had plagued England for centuries and
these classes appear in the New England colonies in surprising numbers. Disinclination to work rather than lack of employment was
the primary cause. For shortage of labor was one of the most common complaints throughout the colonial period.

England had discovered that idleness was a source of crime and
costly to the state in terms of taxes, courts, and jails. She, therefore,
encouraged the emigration of convicts, felons, paupers, vagrants,
and vagabonds. Indeed, she forced such emigration through her
transportation laws which made the penalty for crimes transportation to the colonies through the indentured servant system.[58] An
English act of 1662 provided that judges in quarter sessions should

report to the Privy Council the names of rogues, vagabonds, and sturdy beggars whom they considered fit to be transported and indentured as servants for a term not exceeding seven years.[59] An act of 1717 provided for the transportation of idle persons under twenty-one years of age.[60] These laws are one source of the idle and vagrant classes in the colonies.

The New England colonists were well aware of England's discovery that idleness bred crime, was costly, and led to pauperism. The Puritans, however, had a special horror of idleness and its consequences because they interpreted the Bible, "God's word," to mean that it was a sin. Then hostility to idleness developed because of environmental influences. With a relatively poor soil, hard work was essential to secure a decent living; hence, the emphasis on industry, thrift, and frugality. The Puritans were anxious to avoid the heavy burden of taxes, common enough in England, where some parishes expended nearly a third of their income for the support of the poor. Considering these powerful economic and religious motives it is not surprising to find that the New England colonies were extremely hostile to idlers, vagrants, and vagabonds and passed numerous laws to compel them to work.

The first instructions of the Massachusetts Bay Company to Governor John Endicott, May 28, 1629, provided that:[61]

Noe idle drone bee permitted to live amongst us, which if you take care now at the first to establish, wil be an undoubted meanes, through God's Assistance, to prevent a world of disorders and many grievous sins and sinners.

Massachusetts provided in 1646 that towns might "present" to the quarterly court all idle and unprofitable persons in order that the court might dispose of them "for their owne welfare and improvement of the common good."[62] In Connecticut idle persons might be punished as the court should "think meet," and later the selectmen were given power to put out to service those who lived an "idle and riotous life." So in 1717 they were required "to diligently inspect into the affairs of poor or idle persons and if likely to be reduced to want" to dispose of them to service.[63]

Idleness seemed to increase, however, for, in 1682, a Massachusetts act declared that in the several towns there were many idle persons who did not follow any employment for a livelihood "but mispend their time and that little which they earne to the impoverishing, if not utter undoing of themselves and families."[64] The tithingmen of each town were ordered to inspect all families and persons and return the names of idle persons to the selectmen and the constables, who were required to see that they worked if capable. Otherwise they were required to send them to the house of correction and set them to work. .

A particular case well illustrates the problem of merely punishing an idle person instead of providing work for him. The early houses of correction, or common jails, were not equipped, like the later workhouses, with facilities to put those able to work. It appears that Boston got tired of supporting one of these jailbirds and appealed to the Suffolk County court for relief with the following result:[65]

William Batt, haveing lyen some yeares in prison, being committed to the house of correction as an idle person, and there continuing at charge to the Town of Boston without doing any labour for his maintenance; the Court impower the Selectmen of Boston to take any further order relating to said William Batt, and to dispose of him for improvement as they shall see meet.

Vagrants and vagabonds, "wanderers," usually able-bodied, were one class of idlers and hence prospective paupers. Massachusetts provided (1662) that vagrants should be whipped;[66] and, in 1692, selectmen and overseers of the poor must see that those who wandered from place to place "fit and able to work" should be sent to the house of correction, whipped, and made to work.[67] Rhode Island declared that vagrant persons who came into towns became a burden, lived idle and vicious lives, and had a corrupting influence.[68] Governor Leete of Connecticut wrote[69] in 1680 that:

Beggars and vagabond persons are not suffered, but when discovered bound out to service; yet sometimes a vagabond person will pass up and down the country, and abuse the people with false news, and cheat and steal; but when they are discovered they are punished, according to the offense.

Connecticut did not differentiate between paupers and vagrants until 1713. At that date it was asserted[70] that "wanderers" and others were of pernicious consequence and might be sent to jail, made to labor, and, on order of the court, whipped. In 1718 it was reported[71] that "idle persons, vagabonds and sturdy beggars" had greatly increased and "likely more to increase." Those found wandering up and down in any parish were to be adjudged rogues and were to "be stripped naked from the middle upward, and be openly whipt on his or her naked body, not exceeding the number of fifteen stripes" and ordered to "depart the town or parish."

How far the laws on vagrancy were enforced is difficult to say. But in one case at least a certain John Smith suffered the extreme penalty. His case came before the Suffolk County court and the record reads as follows:[72]

John Smith a Vagrant idle Person who hath formerly been whipt out of Town for a Vagabond; but is since returned and imposeth himself upon the Town of Boston without approbation of the Selectman and contrary to former order of this Court and is very Suspitious both in words and carriages of being an evill-minded person, having lyen a considerable time upon charge and refuseing to worke for the discharge thereof for his own maintenance: The Court orders that the said John Smith bee disposed of by Sale out of the County for Satisfaction of his charges by advice of the Honorable Governor.

The early history of poor relief is largely that of care of the poor in private homes. Idlers and vagrants were at first confined in houses of correction, "bridewells," or common jails. There was little or no classification of the poor on the basis of age or sex, worthy or vicious, sane or insane; nor was opportunity provided for the able-bodied to work. In the eighteenth century, institutional care of the poor developed slowly through almshouses and workhouses where more effort was made to segregate the various classes of poor. In a few large towns the impotent poor and decrepit were put in an almshouse, vicious persons and criminals in houses of correction or jails, and the able-bodied poor in workhouses.

Plymouth colony authorized the erection of a workhouse or house of correction (1658) controlled by the governor and assistants. The inmates were to:

have noe other supply for theire sustainance than what they shall earne by theire labour all the while that they shall continue there.[73]

No information of the workings of this institution is available. Boston had an almshouse in 1660 but up to 1712 it was little more than a house of correction where all classes of poor and vicious persons were herded together. Complaint was made in town meeting that the almshouse ought to be restored to

its Primitive and Pious design, even for the releife of the necessitous, that they might lead a quiet Peaceable and Godly life there, whereas tis now made a Bridewell and House of Correction which Obstructs many Honest Poor Peoples going there for the designed Releife and Support.[74]

The next year the town ordered that only persons "proper objects of the charity of the town" should be admitted to the almshouse.[75] Because the idle and poor had so increased in Boston the general court passed a special act which provided for twelve overseers of the poor, with power to erect a workhouse and commit idle and indigent persons. They also had power to bind out children and concurrent power with the selectmen to warn undesirable newcomers out of town.[76] It was not until 1739, however, that the workhouse was opened. Only the able-bodied poor were admitted and set to work picking oakum, carding and spinning, etc. Children were also admitted but were put out to service when they arrived at a suitable age. The earnings of the inmates were used in part to support their families, if in need.[77] By a later act the smaller towns could unite. two or more, erect workhouses and appoint overseers of the poor.[78] Apparently few such towns established workhouses before the revolution. Braintree proposed building a house for the poor as early as 1747,[79] but the proposition was defeated in town meeting.[80]

In 1699, Massachusetts provided for the suppressing and punishing of "Rogues, Vagabonds, Common Beggars and other Lewd Idle and Disorderly Persons" by ordering the establishment of houses of correction, really workhouses. Towns must levy taxes to provide materials, tools, implements, and "stock" for work (parents or masters in the case of children and servants). The inmates were paid 8d. out of every shilling they earned, part of which might be used for the support of their families. Expenses above earnings were charged to the town. If the inmates became stubborn, disorderly, or idle, they could be punished by whipping and the master might "abridge them and their food." Besides rogues, vagabonds, and idlers the law names others who might be committed to the workhouse:

Common pipers, fidlers, runaways, stubborn servants or children, common drunkards, common night-walkers, pilferers, wanton and lassivious persons either in speech or behaviour, common railers or brawlers such as neglect their callings, misspend what they earn, and do not provide for themselves or the support of their families.[81]

Connecticut also turned from private care to public institutions. In 1713, for the first time, vagrants or "sturdy beggars" were differentiated from paupers. County jails were made houses of correction for "wanderers" and the keeper was instructed to set inmates to work "at such labor as such offender is capable of."[82] A colony workhouse was provided by the act of 1727. The method of overcoming the evils of vagabondage and idleness by whipping was at last seen to be not a "timely remedy."[83] A suitable means and place to restrain and employ such classes was now thought of as the best remedy. This colony workhouse was finally established but did not prove successful and was helped by the assembly (1734) with a grant to be used to procure materials for setting the inmates to work. For this colony workhouse there were later substituted county workhouses, supported by taxes assessed by the county court.[84]

Most of the smaller towns continued to care for the poor in private houses up to the Revolution. The records[85] of the overseers of the poor for the town of Danvers, Massachusetts, for the years 1767–68, give an interesting picture of the method of caring for the poor and their character. Several practices were followed. Thus notice was given that the overseers would meet April 13, 1767, and "put out the poor to such persons as will take and keep them Cheapest, or as the Overseers and they Can agree." This is the system of auctioning off the poor. The account for this date shows that ten persons were "put out at sums ranging from £5 to £8 per year." The form signed provided that a person should be supplied with "all the necessaries of Life if he Live so Long, except Clothing and Extraordinary Sickness, or the want of a Doctor, which the Town will Provide if timely Notifyed." At a meeting April 20 it was "agreed to do something to Thomas Nelson's Clothes—And git an under Jacket and aporn and a pare of Stockings for Isaac Pelas." The following bill of Doctor Amos Putnam was allowed for his services to the poor.

1767—The town of Danvers to A. Putnam, Feb. 1st to December 4th,

For 1 visit to John Cromwell, Jun., and for			Dr.
medicines adminis'd 4s.,.................	£0	4	0
to medicines adminis'd to Jos. Very,..........	0	4	0
to sundry medicines for Mrs. Coes 3s. 6d., Cath.			
Rhei, &c., for Margaret Royal 1s.,..........	0	4	6
Adminis'd to Caleb Wallis's wife sundry medi-			
cines and six visits......................	1	1	0
	£1	13	6

Error Except.

AMOS PUTNAM

The overseers also paid bills brought in for the support of persons according to agreement. Thus John Shelton presented an account of "what he has Done for his Mother Magery, a widow, from the first of March to the eleventh of April, 1767." It will be seen that the overseers were not worried by the Eighteenth Amendment nor the Volstead Act and that the widow Magery was well provided for.

John Shelton's account of what he has Done for his Mother Magery, from the first of March to the 11th of April, 1767:

To 2 galons New Eng. Rum.............	32 shil.
and 1 galon West Eng. Rum at..........	28 shil.
1 quart of West inde...................	7 shil. 6d.
and 2 quarts of New Rum..............	7 shil. 6d.

to bisket 5 shil.—to plums 2 shil. 5d.—to 2 ounces of tea 4 shil. 9d.—for bisket agin 1 shil. 6d.— to 6 ounces of tea 14 shil. 3d.—to 7 pounds of Shugar more 22 shil. 6d.—to oatmeat 5 shil.—to Bisket again 2 shil. 6d.—to 9 pounds of Beef 16 shil. 6d.—to 7½ lbs. Beef 15 shil.

Moreover this bibulous widow continued to consume a great quantity of liquor, as appears from another account presented to the overseers. She seemed to be more fond of West Indian than New England rum. She drank altogether during the year 9 gallons, 1½ pints of rum and 1 quart and 3 gills of brandy, at a cost of £9, 13 shillings, and 7 pence, old tenor. This thirsty widow had nothing to complain of even if she was short on other supplies.

A general account of orders drawn on the town treasurer for one year for support of those not "put out" follows:

Orders Drawn on the Treasurer Exclucief of the poor that is put out By the year:

	£	s	d
An order to Caleb Walles for his and his wife's Suport 4 weeks,.....................................	£0	10	9½
An order For the French Nuterls,..................	9	00	0
Do to Curnelius Tarbel for ceeping M'gt Royall,.....	0	06	0
Do Caleb Walles and his wife agin,.................	0	18	0
James Upton to mending shoes,....................	0	02	0
Do Caleb Walles for his Suport,...................	0	12	0
Do Caleb Walles for his Suport 5 weeks,...........	0	15	0
Do Caleb Walles for his _____,..................	0	12	0
Do Caleb Walles his _____,.....................	0	12	0
Joseph Brown to wood	1	01	4
Do Caleb Walles for his and his wife's Suport,.......	0	14	0
Gideon Putnam for clothing for ye poor,...........	13	02	10
Do Caleb Walles for his and his wife's Suport agin,...	1	14	0
Lydia Nurse for Supporting Sara Very,.............	0	16	0
James Prince, jun., for wood,.....................	1	06	8
Doctr Sam'l Holten for medesons for ye poor,........	0	02	0
Gideon Putnam for other Nesesaries,..............	2	19	11
Elisha Flint for clothing,........................	5	12	11
Do Caleb Walles for his and his wife's Suport,.......	0	15	0
Caleb Nurse to wood,............................	0	06	8
Jacob Goodell to ceeping John Croell,..............	0	11	0
Doct. Amos Putnam for doctering the poor,.........	1	13	6
Wido Abigail Cutler for what she provided for Abigail Marsh in her last sickness and tord her funeral,....	2	2	10
Tarrant Putnam's bill for Suplies,.................	2	11	8
Sam'l Holten's bill for keeping Bredget Weab in her last sickness and 38 weeks board,.................	8	2	10½
	£58	8	8

The amount of orders drawn for the Support of the Poor from March the 1st, 1767, to March the 1st, 1768, were £154, 2 shil., 1d. L money.

The New England colonies passed numerous laws for the regulation and support of special classes of poor people, e.g., the sick and insane. The problem of admitting and caring for sick immigrants, especially those having contagious diseases, was a serious one because of the likelihood that they would become chargeable. The health conditions on immigrant ships were often unbelievably bad, due to overcrowding, insufficient, poor, or entire lack of food, and lack of medical care. Sometimes one-half or more immigrants on a passenger ship were ill on arrival, many perhaps having a contagious disease.

As early as 1642 Plymouth colony provided that shipmasters or others bringing in diseased persons must discharge the town of all responsibility of expense.[86] Massachusetts passed several acts due to the "mischief" of ships coming in with smallpox and other infectious diseases and provided for general quarantine.[87] On October 31, 1741, the sloop, "Seaflower," from Belfast for Philadelphia with 106 passengers arrived in Boston harbor. Because of storms and lack of provisions and water many had starved to death. The selectmen of Boston boarded the vessel and found that the immigrants were reduced

to such Miserable Circumstances that they were Obliged in Order to Sustain Life to feed upon the Bodys of Six Persons that Died in the Passage, that as they were cutting up the Seventh, they Espied the Success Man of War Capt. Thompson Commander who came up to them and supplied them with Men and Provisions sufficient to bring 'em into this Port, they having been out Sixteen Weeks, Forty-Six People having Died on the Passage. The Select Men also find that there is now about Thirty Persons that are in very low Circumstances and not Capable of taking Care for themselves but require the Speediest Care to be taken of them to preserve Life, and they Earnestly Pray suitable Provision may be made for them or else they must Perish.[88]

In this case the governor and council were consulted. Because there were "Sixty-five Passengers most of them in a sickly and weak Condition," the council ordered the selectmen to transfer them to the hospital at Ramsford's Island and when restored to health call on the owners of the vessel to pay the charges or "sell their Service for a reasonable time for the Payment thereof." By the next February the selectmen declared that some of these passengers were "proper Objects of Publick Charity" and ordered draughts on the town for £21 5s. "at the Charge of the Province" for boarding, nursing, dieting, and even burying some of these unfortunates.[89]

An example of a bond required by the selectmen for the admission of persons as inhabitants who might become a charge on the town will illustrate this method of lessening the burden of poor relief.

Voted, That Martha Hooker with her two Children who were lately Imported into this Town in the Ship Leghorn, Thomas Templer Master from London be admitted Inhabitants, Upon Condition that Mr. Roger Hardcastle give Bond to the Town Treasurer in the Sum of Three Hundred Pounds to Indemnify the Town from any Charge upon their Acct. for Five Years.[90]

On the other hand, the selectmen aided a stranded sailor from North Carolina, who had been captured by Spaniards and put ashore with the result that through exposure and lack of food he got a "great Cold which hath fell into one of his Leggs and renders him unable of getting a Maintenance, that he hath no Money nor Friends to support him." He was considered a "proper object of Publick Charity" and was placed in the almshouse at the charge of the province.[91]

Persons who had gained the right of inhabitancy were supported by the town, if sick, as other poor persons.[92] Contracts were entered into with doctors to cure such persons at town expense. At a Braintree, Massachusetts, town meeting (1707) the selectmen were instructed to "discourse (and agree)" with Samuel Bullard for the care and cure of Abigail Neall. The instructions show that the canny townsmen wanted to be sure that the town got its money's worth, for no cure, no pay.

That is to lay down Twenty shillings in order to said cure and to engage no more for keeping than eighteen pence per week. If in case a cure be performed that may prove sound for one whole year, then to give satisfaction for said cure not exceeding Ten Pounds, not to pay said Sum untill Twelve months are expired after the Cure and said Twenty shillings to be part of said sum, and if no cure be performed to pay no more than said Twenty Shillings and for her keeping.[93]

The insane poor were disposed of as other poor persons. Massachusetts provided (1693) that if an inhabitant "fall into distraction and become *non compos mentis*, the selectmen must take effectual care for their relief and safety."[94] Braintree, for example, voted in 1689 that Samuel Speers should build a "litle house 7 foote long and 5 foot wide and set it by his house to secure his Sister and good wife Witty being distracted and provide for her." The town agreed to bear all expenses, "to see him wel payed and sattisfied."[95] The selectmen were also ordered to see about Ebenezer Owens' "distracted daughter" and give Josiah Owen twenty pounds, provided he gave bond "to cleare the Town (forever of said girle)."[96] However, the town continued to make provision for this same girl as late as 1706.[97]

In conclusion it may be observed that the English poor law had been in operation nearly a generation when the Pilgrims and Puritans migrated and established the Plymouth, Massachusetts Bay, Connecticut, and other New England colonies. The colonists were inheritors of that great fund of English poor relief experience and legislation upon which they might draw in establishing their own systems. It is not surprising, therefore, that the more important English principles of poor relief reappear in their legislation. These were, briefly, the responsibility of the state for the relief of the poor; the right to compel those with property to help support the dependent classes through a system of general taxation; the responsibility of each local community, the town, for its own poor; special officers for administering poor relief, overseers of the poor; differentiation between classes of the poor, the setting up of workhouses for the able-bodied poor and the provision of materials for work. While the idea persisted that vagrants and vagabonds were criminals, yet the old notion, that the impotent poor should be provided for privately and were criminals, was rejected. Such persons were considered to be a public charge worthy of serious attention. Thus humanitarian ideas made their appearance. On the other hand, great determination was shown in the endeavor to protect society from the excessive burden of supporting idlers and the able-bodied poor.

It is clear that the New England colonies laid great stress on excluding those likely to become chargeable—both those entering as immigrants and after entrance those seeking the right of residence. If entrance was accomplished, an effort was made to place the burden on those responsible for bringing in or entertaining chargeable persons. If this failed, the towns resorted to the practice of warning out prospective paupers and the colony adopted the plan of deporting them. The towns seem to have been reasonably generous in their support of the poor if we may judge from such examples as those of Boston and Danvers. The system of auctioning off the poor to the lowest bidder was begun before the revolution and, with its attendant evils, became widespread at a later period.

As compared with Virginia, the New England colonies were fortunate in that they were not seriously affected by a large number of indentured servants and mulattos who became free negroes, both classes furnishing prospective paupers. Illegitimate children and orphans were accordingly less of a problem in New England. Both regions, however, accepted responsibility for the support of their poor and there is little evidence of real suffering for lack of support. The chief weaknesses in the system were the workhouses and the failure to solve the vagrant problem. The former was never successful and in the case of the latter each town endeavored to place the burden on some other town, with Boston the chief sufferer. The care of the insane and defectives were also weak spots in the system. On the whole, however, a distinct impression of humanitarianism and sympathy for the poor and unfortunate is much more in evidence than one of neglect or cruelty.

BIBLIOGRAPHICAL NOTE

The form of the notes appended to these studies makes it unnecessary to add a formal bibliography. In the references to the various chapters will be found the essential data for identifying the manuscript, original printed and secondary sources. Since the special topics chosen for study are those on which relatively little has been published, there are few references to secondary sources. No comprehensive comparative study for the colonial period has yet appeared on the general title given to this volume nor, indeed, on any one of the topics considered.

Of the various types of sources used, attention may be called particularly to the files of the colonial newspaper press, particularly the *South Carolina Gazette* and the *Virginia Gazette*. A nearly complete file of the former is to be found in the Charleston Library Society. The importance of the colonial newspaper press for the economic and social phases of our history is still but dimly realized by most of the historians of this period. This is no doubt due to the fact that it is a laborious process to turn the pages of these scattered and relatively inaccessible storehouses of material. The advertisements on the topics treated, as may be seen from the samples given, constitute a gold mine that has yet to be worked on a large scale. Another type of printed sources, of which much use has been made, is the codes of law of the various colonies, the best collection being found in the Pennsylvania Historical Society, the Charlemagne Tower Collection, of which there is a bibliography. In the laws, one finds set forth the theory of the economic and social control of the slave, servant, apprentice, and poor class, as it existed at a particular date. The relation between the session laws of the individual colonies and their codes has often resulted in a misapprehension of the law in force, as is illustrated in chapters vi and vii. The printed sermons preached before the Society for the Propagation of the Gospel in Foreign Parts, with the appended abstracts of the proceedings of the Society, are of great value for a picture of religious conditions in the southern colonies. A complete set may be found in the Newberry Library, Chicago.

Of manuscript material much use was made of the vestry books and other sources found in numerous Virginia parishes. This material is indispensable for a study of public poor relief and the apprenticeship system in the South, since by law the parish was the principal unit both for support and administration. Paralleling these sources are the archives of the counties. The latter had much to do with the administration of the poor laws and the apprenticeship laws. The Virginia State Library has a number of transcripts of county court records, but the author has used the original manuscript records of numerous Virginia counties (see notes to chap. xi) as well as some in Massachusetts. The town records of New England as well as the county court records are still largely unpublished.

Use has been made of the one important printed series (Essex County, Massachusetts) as well as published and unpublished town records.

Among the important contemporary observers and writers who have discussed some of the topics included in these studies are the following: Robert Beverley, *The History of Virginia* (London, 1722); Hugh Jones, *The Present State of Virginia* (London, 1724); John Brickell, *Natural History of North Carolina* (London, 1731); Alexander Hewatt, *An Historical Account of the Rise and Progress of South Carolina and Georgia* (London, 1779); Morgan Godwyn, *The Negro's and Indian's Advocate*, etc. (London, 1680); David Humphreys, *An Historical Account of the Incorporated Society for the Propagation of the Gospel in Foreign Parts* (London, 1730); Thomas Bacon, *Two Sermons Preached to a Congregation of Black Slaves* (London, 1749); ——— *Four Sermons, upon the Great and Indispensable Duty of All Christian Masters and Mistresses To Bring Up Their Negro Slaves in the Knowledge and Fear of God* (London, 1750); Samuel Davies, *The State of Religion among the Protestant Dissenters in Virginia, in a Letter to the Reverend Joseph Bellamy*, etc. (Boston, 1757); ——— *Letters from the Rev. Samuel Davies and Others, Showing the State of Religion in Virginia, Particularly among the Negroes*, etc. (2d ed.; London, 1757); ——— *The Duty of Christians To Propagate Their Religion among Heathens, Earnestly Recommended to the Masters of Negro Slaves in Virginia* (London, 1758); William Eddis, *Letters from America, Historical and Descriptive* (London, 1792); Gottlieb Mittelberger, *A Journey to Pennsylvania in the Year 1750 and Return to Germany in the Year 1754* (trans. by Carl T. Eben; *Philadelphia*, 1898); John Harrower, "Diary" (of an indentured servant) in *American Historical Review*, Vol. VI.

Among the most useful documentary collections are the following: Ulrich B. Phillips, "Plantation and Frontier Documents" (Vols. I–II of J. R. Commons [ed.], *Documentary History of American Industrial Society* [Cleveland, 1910–11]); J. C. Hurd, *Law of Slavery and Bondage* (Vol. I contains abstracts of the laws governing slaves and indentured servants for each colony); W. H. Perry (ed.), *Historical Collections Relating to the American Colonial Church*, 5 vols. (especially volumes for Virginia and Maryland); C. F. Pascoe, *Classified Digest of the Records of the S.P.G.* (5th ed.; London, 1895); Elsie W. Clews, *Educational Legislation and Administration of the Colonial Governments* (New York, 1899) (consists largely of laws and extracts from the laws); "Indentures of Apprenticeship," 1695–1708, in *New York Historical Society Collections*, XVIII (New York, 1886) 563–622; "Record of Indentures of Individuals Bound Out as Apprentices and Servants, etc.," 1771–73, in *Pennsylvania German Society Proceedings*, etc., XVI (1905), 1–325 (in tabular form giving date, name, from which port, to whom indentured, residence, occupation and instruction, term, amount); *Records and Files of the Quarterly Court of Essex County, Massachusetts*, 1636–1683, 8 vols. (Salem, 1911–20); printed Vestry Books of five Virginia parishes cited in chapter xii, n. 42.

The most useful secondary sources are those cited in chap. i, nn. 2, 16; chap. ii, nn. 32, 43, 76, 151; chap. iii, n. 1; chap. iv, n. 9; chap. vi, n. 3; chap. xi, n. 2; chap. xii, nn. 2, 16, 19, 20, 85; chap. xiii, n. 12.

NOTES

1. This chapter is a tentative study of a large subject. Important aspects are but lightly treated and others not considered at all. Emphasis is placed only on South Carolina and Virginia. Since, however, nearly three-fourths of all the slaves in the South, at the opening of the Revolution, lived in these colonies, we may consider that the economic conditions described are typical of the other southern colonies. This chapter was first printed in the *American Historical Review*, Vol. XXV, No. 2 (January, 1920).

2. There is no comprehensive account of the development of manufactures in the southern colonies. For illustrations of the points in this paragraph consult in general, V. S. Clark, *History of Manufactures in the United States, 1607–1860* (Washington, 1916); R. M. Tryon, *Household Manufactures in the United States, 1640–1860* (Chicago, 1917); and J. L. Bishop, *History of American Manufactures, 1607–1860* (Philadelphia, 3 vols., 1861–68). In particular, consult P. A. Bruce, *Economic History of Virginia in the Seventeenth Century*, Vol. II., chaps. xvii and xviii, "Manufactured Supplies: Domestic"; and Clark, "Colonial Manufactures," in *The South in the Building of the Nation* (ed. J. C. Ballagh), Vol. V. On soil-exhaustion see Bruce, *op. cit.*, I, 424–25; II, 566; and A. O. Craven, *Soil Exhaustion as a Factor in the Agricultural History of Virginia and Maryland, 1606–1860*.

3. Bruce, *op. cit.*, I, 345, 389–94, 401. In 1604, the Virginia and Maryland crop amounted to 50,000 hogsheads, valued at £150,000 sterling, yet the price was so low that the planters were brought in debt £50,000 (*ibid.*, I, 391).

4. *Ibid.*, I, 459–66, 370–72, 481–82. In the winter of 1673, 50,000 cattle are said to have perished in Virginia (*ibid.*, I, 372).

5. *Virginia Gazette*, February 12, 1767. For the increase in the leather and textile industries see Clark, *op. cit.*, and Bishop, *op. cit.*, in indexes under "Maryland," "Virginia," etc.

6. R. Beverley, *The History of Virginia* (London, 1722), p. 255.

7. *Virginia Gazette*, February 12, 1767. *South Carolina Gazette*, October 29, 1764.

8. For these industries see indexes of Clark and Bishop above.

9. Hugh Jones, *Present State of Virginia* (ed. J. Sabin, 1865), London, 1724, p. 36; Beverley, *op. cit.* (1722), p. 251.

10. These acts are summarized, and their workings described, in chaps. vi–viii and x–xi of this volume.

11. Beverley, *op. cit.* See n. 2.

12. The reports of governors on the state of manufactures at various dates are summarized by Clark, in *op. cit.*, chap. ix. See also A. A. Giesecke, *American Commercial Legislation before 1789;* Jones, *op. cit.*, pp. 40–41; and Tryon, *op. cit.*, pp. 49, 102–23 (official reports of governors for 1766). See also *Journal of Board of Trade, 1700–1740* and Eleanor Lord, "Industrial Experiments in the British Colonies of North America," in *Johns Hopkins University Studies in Historical and Political Science*, Extra Vol. XVII.

13. For the slave population of the southern colonies in 1755 and 1775 see chap. ii, n. 123.

14. A few negroes imported directly from Africa may have possessed some mechanical skill. See J. A. Tillinghast, *The Negro in Africa and America*, pp. 32–33.

15. On the intelligence of the negro see chap. ii, nn. 88, 103–6.

16. This class arose from miscegenation and intermarriage of white and blacks. On this question see E. B. Reuter, *The Mulatto in the United States* (Boston, 1918).

17. Tillinghast, *op. cit.*, pp. 118–21.

18. E.g., see n. 66.

19. Their short period of indenture and the fact that they were likely to run away were two objections. See n. 24.

20. For illustrations of methods of training the slave, see Jones, *op. cit.*, p. 38, and nn. 25, 51, 55, 56.

21. *A Perfect Description of Virginia* (1649), p. 15. In Peter Force, *Tracts*, etc., Vol. II, No. 8.

22. Bruce, *op. cit.*, II, 405.

23. *Ibid.*, II, 405, 471. *Virginia Magazine of History*, III, 407–8.

24. Bruce, *op. cit.* For similar practice of training slaves as artisans in the West Indies, see F. W. Pitman, *The Development of the British West Indies, 1700–1763*, pp. 58–60.

25. Jones, *op. cit.*, pp. 38–39. For a similar statement of conditions in North Carolina, see letter of the S.P.G. missionary, Rev. John Urmstone, July 7, 1711, in F. L. Hawks, *History of North Carolina*, II (1858), 215. See also John Brickell, *Natural History of North Carolina* (1731, repr.), p. 275.

26. His will is in *Va. Mag. of Hist.*, V, 412, and inventory, *ibid.*, VI, 368.

27. *William and Mary College Quarterly Historical Magazine*, XXI, 93.

28. In B. R. Carroll, *Historical Collections of South Carolina*, II, 204. See chap. ii, n. 5.

29. Habersham to the Countess of Huntingdon, April 19, 1775, in *Georgia Historical Society Collection*, VI, 242; extract in Phillips, *Plantation and Frontier Documents*, II, 44, in J. R. Commons (ed.), *Documentary History of American Industrial Society* (Cleveland, 1910–11). See *S.C. Gaz.*, October 16, 1752, November 7, 1754.

30. This by no means exhausts the trades followed by negro slaves in this period. For example, there were shingle-makers in Georgia (*Georgia Gazette*, February 16, 1774). And in Virginia, iron-workers, including "finers, hammermen and colliers" (*Virginia Gazette* [Purdie and Dixon], August 6, 1767). Rev. John Urmstone's letter from North Carolina speaks of "tallow Chandlers," "soap makers, starch-makers and dyers" (Hawks, *op. cit.*, II, 215).

31. Illustrations of these relationships follow.

32. *S.C. Gaz.*, January 28, 1751.

33. *S.C. Gaz. and Country Journal* (supp.), April 26, 1768.

34. *S.C. Gaz.*, August 22, 1768.

35. *Ibid.*, November 25, 1732, March 21, 1743.

36. *Ibid.*, September 22, 1746, April 19, 1760, December 10, 1773.

37. *Ibid.*, February 10, 1765.

38. *Ibid.*, March 21, 1768, April 7, 1743, June 2, 1733, July 28, 1733, August 29, 1743, January 23, 1746, February 24, 1746.

39. Landon Carter hired two negro sawyers (1776) for a year at ten pounds each. Diary in *William and Mary Col. Qr. Hist. Mag.*, XV, 17.

40. *S.C. Gaz.*, July 23, 1737.

41. *Ibid.*, May 29, 1755.

42. *Ibid.*, March 8, 1770.

43. *Ibid.*, January 13, 1732.

44. *Ibid.*, June 10, 1732.

45. *Ibid.*, August 6, 1741.

46. *Ibid.*, August 27, 1737, December 25, 1740.

47. Carroll, *op. cit.*, II, 238.

48. *S.C. Gaz.*, January 14, 1764.

49. *Ibid.*, March 21, 1768. *Ibid.*, May 24, 1768.

50. Phillips, *op. cit.*, 325.

51. *William and Mary, Col. Qr. Hist. Mag.*, XI, 95.

52. Clark, *op. cit.*, p. 191.

53. Phillips, *op. cit.*, II, 314–15.

54. D. Macpherson, *Annals of Commerce*, III, 260.

55. *S.C. Gaz. and Country Journal* (supp.), May 20, 1766.

56. MS *Transcripts for South Carolina from Public Record Office.* XXIV (1750–51), 315–16.

57. *William and Mary Col. Qr. Hist. Mag.*, XXI, 169–70.

58. MS *Commons Journal of S.C.*, January 25, 1743/4, pp. 144–45.

59. MS *Trans. S.C.*, XXI (1743–44), 332–34.

60. *S.C. Gaz.*, May 6, 1751.

61. Cooper, *Statutes of S.C.*, VII, 363, 407–8.

62. *Colonial Records of Georgia* (ed. Candler), I, 58.

63. W. W. Hening (ed.), *Statutes of Va.*, XI, 59.

64. Jones, *op. cit.*, pp. 38–39. See also nn. 25, 38.

65. *Va. Hist. Soc. Coll.*, Dinwiddie Papers, I, 421.

66. *Va. Gaz.* (Purdie and Dixon), September 3, 1767.

67. *Washington's Writings* (ed. Ford), II, 147.

68. *S.C. Gaz.*, February 1, 1734/35, September 7, 1769, July 9, 1772; *South Carolina and American General Gazette*, February 7, 1770.

CHAPTER II

1. This chapter is an elaboration of certain portions of a paper read by the author at the meeting of the American Historical Association at Charleston, S.C., December, 1913, and was first printed in the *American Historical Review*, XXI, 504–27.

2. J. C. Hurd, *Law of Freedom and Bondage*, I, 160–61.

3. 7 Coke 17, Calvin's case (*Reports* [ed. 1826], IV, 29); Prescott, *Ferdinand and Isabella* (ed. Kirk, 1872), II, 468.

4. Cf. Bull of Nicholas V, January 8, 1455, referring to conquests in Guinea, and "Guineans and Other Negroes." The bull is printed in Jordão, *Bullarium Patronatus Portugalliae Regum in Ecclesiis Africae, Asiae atque Oceaniae*, etc., I, 31–34.

5. Hurd, *op. cit.*, I, 163; Alexander Hewatt, *An Historical Account of the Rise and Progress of South Carolina and Georgia* (London, 1779), in Carroll, *Historical Collections of South Carolina*, I, 353.

6. Chamberline *v.* Harvey (1697), in 5 Modern Reports 190; Prescott, *op. cit.*, p. 468.

7. Hurd, *op. cit.*, I, 166–67, n. 3, and authorities cited.

8. Isambert, Decrusy, and Taillandier, *Recueil général des anciennes lois françaises 1672–86* (Paris, 1829), XIX, 495.

9. Hurd, *op. cit.*, I, 167. But see Chamberline *v.* Harvey for contrary opinion.

10. Butts *v.* Penny (1677), 2 Levinz 201, in English Reports, LXXXIII, 518; Gelly *v.* Cleve (1694), 1 Lord Raymond 147, *ibid.*, XCI, 994; Chamberline *v.* Harvey, op. cit., p. 191. Judgment was for defendant in this case, but counsel for plaintiff argued that negroes baptized "in a christian nation, as this is, should be an immediate enfranchisement to them," etc.

11. *Archives of Maryland*, I, 526, 533.

12. *Ibid.*, II, 272. This act was still in force in 1765. T. Bacon, *Laws of Maryland*, chaps. xxiii–xxiv, for the act of 1715.

13. W. W. Hening, *Statutes of Virginia* (New York ed.), II, 260.

14. *Ibid.*, p. 283.

15. *Ibid.*, p. 491.

16. *Ibid.*, III, 447. Excepting "Turks and Moors in Amity with her majesty."

17. "Fundamental Constitutions, 1669–70," in *North Carolina Colonial Records*, I, 204; and revision of 1698, *ibid.*, II, 857; D. J. McCord, *Statutes of South Carolina*, VII, 343 (act of 1690), and 364–65 (act of 1712); *Colonial Laws of New York*, I (1706), 597–98. The New Jersey act was passed in 1704, but was disallowed (N. Trott, *Laws of the British Plantations in America*, p. 257; *Acts of Privy Council, Colonial Series, 1680–1720*, p. 848).

18. Such an act was requested in Massachusetts in a memorial to the general court from "Many Ministers of the Gospel," May 30, 1694 (*Acts and Resolves of the Province of Massachusetts Bay*, VII, 537). See n. 67.

19. The opinion is printed in Hurd, *op. cit.*, I, 185–86, n. 3. It referred, however, to slaves brought into Great Britain from the colonies. On the tendency to accept English laws as applicable to the colonies, see Hildreth, *History of the United States*, II (New York, 1863), 426. Dean Berkeley, in his sermon before the S.P.G., 1731, said that this opinion was printed in Rhode Island, "and dispersed throughout the plantations." See Updike, *History of the Episcopal Church in Narragansett, Rhode Island* (1847), p. 177.

20. *Documents relating to the Colonial History of New York*, III, 36. See also *Calendar of State Papers, Colonial, 1574–1660*, pp. 492–93.

21. *N.Y. Col. Docs.*, III, 374, also (1688), p. 547; for Virginia, Bruce, *Economic History of Virginia in the Seventeenth Century*, II, 97; for Maryland, *Archives of Maryland, 1698–1731*, XXV, 57; for North Carolina (1754), *N.C. Col. Rec.*, V, 1138.

22. E.g., Governor Bellomont (1699), *N.Y. Col. Docs.*, IV, 510–11.

23. *Arch. of Md.*, XXV, 57. See also *Abstract of the Proceedings of the Society for the Propagation of the Gospel in Foreign Parts, 1712–13*, letter of Elias Neau, catechist to the S.P.G., 1712, reporting that Governor Hunter of New York urged masters to give religious instruction to their slaves.

24. *Colonial Records of Connecticut, 1678–89*, pp. 293, 298; *Cal. St. P., Col., 1681–85*, p. 497 (Va., 1683); and *Arch. of Md.*, V (1678), 267.

25. E.g., South Carolina, 1712 and 1740; Trott, *Laws*, p. 71; and McCord, *Stat. of S.C.*, VII, 404; *St. Rec. of N.C.*, XXIII (1715), 3–4. See n. 86.

26. Hening, *Stat. of Va.* (Richmond ed.), IV, 129; same act, 1748, *ibid.*, VI, 108. Compare also the New Jersey act, 1751 (Allinson, *Acts of the General Assembly of New Jersey, 1702–76*, pp. 191–92). See n. 111.

27. *The Negro's and Indians Advocate*, etc. (London, 1680).

28. *N.Y. Col. Docs.*, VII, 362–63.

29. W. H. Perry, *History of the American Episcopal Church*, I, 138.

30. Perry, *Historical Collections relating to the American Colonial Church* (Va.), p. 112.

31. *Classified Digest of Records of the S.P.G.* (5th ed.), p. 5.

32. W. W. Kemp, *The Support of Schools in Colonial New York by the S.P.G.*, pp. 14–15.

33. The queries, with answers, for Virginia and Maryland, are printed by Perry, in *Hist. Coll. rel. to the Amer. Col. Ch.* (Va.), pp. 261–318; (Md.), pp. 190–232. See also for Maryland, 1731, pp. 303–7. See n. 119.

34. These are printed by David Humphreys, *An Historical Account of the S.P.G.*, etc. (London, 1730), pp. 250–75; the first two are in Frederick Dalcho, *An Historical Account of the Protestant Episcopal Church in South Carolina*, pp. 104–14.

35. *Classified Digest*, pp. 925–28, for charter.

36. *Abstract, S.P.G.*, 1712–13, p. 43. See also for text of instructions to missionaries and schoolmasters, with list of the former (*Classified Digest*, pp. 837–40, 844–45).

37. Humphreys, *op. cit.*, p. 252.

38. *Classified Digest*, p. 837.

39. For the school at New York see n. 134; for that in Charleston, S.C., see Dalcho, *op. cit.*, pp. 156–57, 164.

40. Humphreys, *op. cit.*, pp. 250–51. "Letter of Bishop of London to Serious Christians," etc., *Abstract, S.P.G.*, 1740–41, p. 81.

41. *Abstract, S. P. G.*, 1713–14, pp. 60–62.

42. A complete set of the sermons with abstracts is in the E. E. Ayer collection, Newberry Library, Chicago.

43. For a short account of the work of this society, see Kemp, *op. cit.*, pp. 14–15, 254–61.

44. *Ibid.*, pp. 255–56, 260, note. Benjamin Franklin was an active member of the Associates, and was chairman at their meeting in 1760. See *Writings of Franklin* (ed. Smyth), IV, 23.

45. H. E. Jacobs, *History of the Evangelical Lutheran Church*, p. 157; W. O. B. Allen and Edmund McClure, *History of the S.P.C.K.*, pp. 391–92.

46. See n. 125.

47. Humphreys, *op. cit.*, p. 265.

48. *Abstract, S.P.G.*, 1734–35, p. 50; 1741–42, p. 55; concerning slaves of rectors of St. Helen's Parish, S.C. Perry, *Hist. Coll. Amer. Col. Ch.* (Va.), p. 280; Robert Bolton, *History of the Protestant Episcopal Church in Westchester County* (N.Y.), p. 250 (Rye, 1731); pp. 62–63 (Westchester, 1729).

49. *N.C. Col. Rec.*, I, 734, letter of Mr. Adams, missionary of S.P.G., 1710; Robert Beverley, *The History of Virginia* (London, 1722), p. 227.

50. See n. 120.

51. A. C. Thomas, "The Attitude of the Society of Friends toward Slavery in the Seventeenth and Eighteenth Centuries," etc., *Papers of the American Society of Church History*, VIII, 263–99, especially pp. 277, 283.

52. George Fox, *A Collection of Many Select and Christian Epistles*, etc., I (Philadelphia, 1831), 144, epistle 153, "To Friends beyond Sea, that have Blacks and Indian Slaves."

53. *Pennsylvania Magazine of History*, XIII, 265–70.

54. Thomas, *op. cit.*, p. 269. See also the letter of the yearly meeting of Friends of

Pennsylvania, 1754, printed in Thomas Clarkson, *History of the Rise, Progress and Aboli-tion of the African Slave-Trade,* I (London, 1808), 142.

55. Thomas, *op. cit.,* p. 287. See also Stephen B. Weeks, *Southern Quakers and Slav-ery,* p. 200, for meeting of 1757.

56. Thomas, *op. cit.,* p. 290.

57. J. S. Bassett, *Slavery and Servitude in North Carolina* (Johns Hopkins University Studies in History and Political Science, Ser. XIV), pp. 219–20. Cf. Weeks, *op. cit.,* p. 206.

58. Thomas, p. 279. Elihu Coleman, the Quaker preacher of Nantucket, declared (1753) that Friends told their slaves to be Christians and be baptized "and so they do" (*Friends Review,* V, 102). Friends in Newport, R.I., sometimes took their slaves to church with them (Edward Peterson, *History of Rhode Island,* pp. 104–5).

59. Peter Kalm, *Travels into North America,* 1748. "The quakers alone scrupled to have slaves: but they are no longer so nice and they have as many negroes as other people." In John Pinkerton, *Voyages,* etc., XIII (London, 1812), 501. See also Ralph Sandiford, *Brief Examination,* etc. (1729), as quoted by George H. Moore, *Notes on the History of Slavery in Massachusetts,* pp. 80–81. An indirect endowment of a monthly meeting of Friends in Maryland, 1702, is cited by Thomas, *op. cit.,* pp. 283–84.

60. Perry, *Historical Collections,* etc. (Del.), p. 46.

61. Bolton, *op. cit.,* p. 250. For negligence of Quakers in North Carolina see Journal of Benjamin Ferris, the Quaker missionary, in *Friend's Miscellany,* XII, 255–57, and John Woolman's *Journal* (1757, ed. Whittier, 1873), pp. 117–18.

62. E. R. Turner, *The Negro in Pennsylvania,* p. 44.

63. Quoted by Moore, *op. cit.,* p. 37, note. Cotton Mather accuses masters of neg-lect, and says they "deride, neglect, and oppose all due means of bringing their poor negroes unto our Lord" (*Magnalia,* etc., I, Book III [Hartford, 1855], 581; first pub-lished in London, 1702). See n. 138.

64. J. H. Trumbull (ed.), *Memorial History of Hartford County,* II, 406. See also F. M. Caulkins, *History of Norwich* (1749), p. 328. Negro slaves were owned by such noted clergymen as Rev. John Davenport of New Haven; Rev. Jonathan Edwards of Northampton, Mass.; and Rev. Ezra Stiles of Newport, R. I.; and many others. See W. C. Fowler, "Historical Status of the Negro in Connecticut," *Historical Magazine Notes and Queries,* 3d. ser., III, 13.

65. William Goodell, *Slavery and Anti-Slavery,* etc. (1852), pp. 41–43, about 1769.

66. C. B. Gillespie, *A Century of Meriden* (Conn.), Part I, p. 244. Cotton Mather was greatly interested in the conversion and baptism of negro slaves. Cf. his *Diary,* in *Massachusetts Historical Society Collections,* 7th ser., VIII (1716–18), 379, 442, 478, 532. Ezra Stiles preached to a meeting of about 40 negroes in Rhode Island, February 19, 1770. See his *Diary,* I, 39, see also pp. 204, 247–48. See n. 140.

67. *Acts and Res. of the Prov. of Mass. Bay,* VII, 537. See n. 18.

68. *The Records of the General Association of the Colony of Connecticut, 1738–99* (Hart-ford, 1888), p. 6.

69. John Robinson, *Testimony and Practice of the Presbyterian Church in Reference to American Slavery,* p. 10. In 1774 a committee was appointed to report on slavery, but the synod agreed to defer the matter to their next meeting. It was not until 1787 that definite action opposing slavery was taken (S. J. Baird, *Collection of Acts, etc., of the Presbyterian Church* [Philadelphia, 1885], pp. 817–18).

70. See his letter of October 2, 1750, Perry, *Hist. Coll. Amer. Col. Ch.* (Va.), pp. 368–71; see also letter of 1756; n. 125, *infra*.

71. *William and Mary College Quarterly*, XI (1759), 109; XII (1753), 4, 9. James Wetmore reports, 1727/8, that at Rye, New York, "Some Presbyterians will allow their servants [negroes] to be taught, but are unwilling they should be baptized" (Bolton, *op. cit.*, p. 250).

72. *Wm. and Mary Col. Qr.*, XII (1763), 10.

73. Luke Tyerman, *Life of Whitefield*, II, 272–73, letter dated March 22, 1751. See also his plea for the religious instruction of negroes, in the *New England Weekly Journal*, April 29, 1740.

74. *Minutes of the Methodist Conferences annually held in America, 1773–1813*, I (New York, 1813), 5–6. It was not until 1780 that action was taken disapproving slavery (*ibid.*, pp. 25–26).

75. H. N. McTyeire, *History of Methodism*, p. 310.

76. Francis Asbury, *Journal*, I (New York, 1852), 141. See also J. B. Earnest, *The Religious Development of the Negro in Virginia*, p. 48.

77. W. T. Thom, *Struggle for Religious Freedom in Virginia* (Johns Hopkins University Studies in Historical and Political Science, Ser. XVIII), pp. 505–7, 515–17; Robert Semple, *History of Baptists* (ed. Beale), pp. 291–92.

78. *N.C. Col. Rec.*, VII, 164. A resolve of a Baptist denomination in North Carolina in 1783 gives one of the earliest expressions of opinion of any considerable body of Baptists on the duties of the master of a slave. It is to the effect that he should give slaves liberty to attend "the worship of God in his family" and exhort slaves to this end (L. Burkitt and Jesse Read, *Concise History of the Kehukee Baptist Association* [Halifax, 1803], p. 70).

79. H. E. Jacobs, *History of Evangelical Lutheran Church in the United States*, pp. 150, 167–68; P. A. Strobel, *The Salzburgers*, pp. 30, 80, 102–3.

80. Jacobs, *op. cit.*, pp. 167–68; Strobel, *op. cit.*, p. 104. This was also advised by Urlsperger. "If you take slaves in faith, and with the intent of conducting them to Christ, the action will not be a sin, but may prove a 'benediction' " (*ibid.*).

81. Jacobs, *op. cit.*, p. 168. Compare letter of Boltzius to the Society for the Promotion of Christian Knowledge, in 1761, in Allen and McClure, *History of S.P.C.K.*, p. 392. In 1774–75 the church of Ebenezer owned a negro boy and girl (Strobel, *op. cit.*, pp. 190–91).

82. Jacobs, *op. cit.*, p. 231. Heinrich Muhlenberg baptized 3 negro slaves at New Providence, Pa., in 1745 (*Halle Reports* [Philadelphia, 1882, ed. W. J. Mann], p. 57). For the attitude of the Lutherans in New York see Jacobs, *op. cit.*, p. 119.

83. The attitude of the Moravians, Catholics, and minor denominations is omitted for want of space.

84. Morgan Godwyn, *The Negro's and Indians' Advocate*, p. 39.

85. Moore, *op. cit.*, p. 93, quoting from the *Athenian Oracle*, II (1705), 460–63.

86. *South Carolina Historical and Genealogical Magazine*, V, 26, reports of Mr. Thomas to S.P.G., 1705; Hewatt, *op. cit.*, I, 354 (see chap. i, n. 28); Bolton, *op. cit.*, (1729), pp. 62–63. See n. 25.

87. Hugh Jones, *Present State of Virginia* (ed. of 1865) (1724), pp. 70–71; John Brickell, *The Natural History of North Carolina* (reprint by J. B. Grimes), pp. 272–74 (1737); Hewatt, *op. cit.*, pp. 351–52; 355–56; *Abstract*, *S.P.G.*, 1712–13, p. 43; Thomas Bacon, *Four Sermons, upon the Great and Indispensable Duty of all Christian Masters and Mis-*

tresses to bring up their Negro Slaves in the Knowledge and Fear of God (London, 1750), pp. 81–82; Samuel Davies, *The Duty of Christians to propagate their Religion among Heathens, earnestly recommended to the Masters of Negroe Slaves in Virginia* (sermon 1757, London, 1758), p. 37. See n. 145.

88. Godwyn, *Advocate*, etc., pp. 3, 10–13, 40; Humphreys, *op. cit.*, p. 235; Hewatt, *op. cit.*, p. 355. See n. 113.

89. Godwyn, *op. cit.*, pp. 38, 139–40; *Classified Digest*, p. 15; Brickell, *op. cit.*, p. 48. The danger from contagious diseases is one of the less-known evils of the slavery system.

90. Kalm, *op. cit.*, p. 503. See also Edward McCrady, "Slavery in South Carolina," *Report, Amer. Hist. Assoc., 1895*, p. 644.

91. Perry, *Historical Collections*, etc. (Va.), pp. 323–44; especially 332–34 (letter of Forbes on the state of religion in Virginia in 1724); F. L. Hawks, *Contributions to the Ecclesiastical History of the United States* (Va.) (1722), pp. 86–87, 92.

92. Humphreys, *op. cit.*, pp. 250–51. The reports of missionaries of the S.P.G. show that comparatively few of them took active interest in the conversion of slaves. See also Bassett, *op. cit.*, pp. 215–16.

93. Perry, *op. cit.*, Forbes letter, pp. 332–33. Devereux Jarratt wrote John Wesley that there was only one Church of England clergyman in Virginia who was not a reproach to his vocation; in M. H. Moore, *Sketches of the Pioneers of Methodism in North Carolina and Virginia*, p. 50. See also Hawks, *op. cit.*, pp., 88–90; *N.C. Col. Rec.*, VII, 106, letter of Governor Tryon (1765), who wishes "not the sweepings of the Universities . . . . but some clergy of character."

94. *Classified Digest*, p. 15; Perry, pp. 254–55. Compare the sermon of Samuel Davies (1757), p. 41; Thomas Bacon, *op. cit.*, pp. 101, 114–15.

95. Perry (Va.), p. 278; (Md.), p. 305; *Abstract, S.P.G.*, 1760–61 (N.C.); pp. 58–59; *ibid.*, 1739–40 (S.C.), pp. 56–57.

96. Perry (Md., 1731), pp. 306–7; (Va. 1724), p. 267.

97. *Ibid.* (Va.), p. 289; *N. C. Col. Rec.*, VI (1760), 265, letter of Mr. Read.

98. Perry (Md.), pp. 304–5; Hewatt, p. 352; St. John de Crèvecoeur, *Letters from an American Farmer* (1770–81, ed. Blake), pp. 165–66.

99. *Ibid.*

100. See sermon, February 16, 1710/1 (London, 1711). Humphreys, *op. cit.*, pp. 257–71.

101. The replies to queries are printed for Virginia and Maryland in Perry. See n. 33.

102. See n. 88.

103. Perry (Va.), pp. 264–65; *Abstract, S.P.G.*, 1740–41, p. 63; Brickell, *op. cit.*, p. 272; Hugh Jones, *op. cit.*, p. 71; *Journal of House of Burgesses* (Va.), May 23, 1694. This is disputed by Hugh Jones, *op. cit.*; by Thomas Bacon, *op. cit.*, pp. 90–91; and by Samuel Davies, *op. cit.*, pp. 33–34. See n. 113.

104. Perry (Va.), p. 283; (Md.), p. 227.

105. *Ibid.* (Md.), p. 192; (Va.), p. 312; *Abstract, S.P.G.*, 1723–24 (S.C.), pp. 41–42; Brickell, p. 272.

106. Perry (Md.), p. 305; see also Hugh Jones, *op. cit.*, pp. 70–71; Bacon, *op. cit.*, p. 93.

107. For these points see a description of the religious condition of the negro slave in Maryland in Thomas Bacon, *Two Sermons preached to a Congregation of Black Slaves* (London, 1749), pp. 50–55, 64.

108. Bacon, *ibid.*

109. See answers of the clergy of Virginia and Maryland, 1724, n. 33, above.

110. *Abstract, S.P.G.*, 1760–61, pp. 58–59. Cf. Thomas Bacon, *op. cit.*, p. 128. See also Davies, *The State of Religion among the Protestant Dissenters in Virginia; in a Letter to the Reverend Joseph Bellamy*, etc. (Boston, 1751), p. 23.

111. Compare *Arch. of Md.*, XIX (1695), 149, 157; Bacon, *Laws of Md.*, Act of 1723, chap. xv.; McCord, *Stat. of S.C.*, VII (1712), 352; *ibid.* (1735), p. 386; *Ga. Col. Rec.*, XVIII (1735), 135. Such acts, however, did not ordinarily prevent slaves attending church with their master's consent, Allinson, *Acts of Gen. Assem. of N.J.*, 1702–76, pp. 191–92; and the Virginia Act of 1723, though prohibiting assemblies, specifically forbids masters from prohibiting their slaves attending church on Sunday, Hening, *op. cit.* (Richmond ed.), IV, 129, and repeated in 1748, *ibid.*, VI, 108; see also *Arch. of Md.*, XXV, 57. An act of North Carolina, 1715, forbade anyone to allow slaves to build a meeting-house on his land for the purpose of worship (*St. Rec. of N.C.*, XXIII, 65).

112. On Sunday laws and labor see nn. 25, 26, 86.

113. *Journal of the House of Burgesses*, May 22, 1699.

114. *N.C. Col. Rec.*, II, 332.

115. *Ibid.*, I, 720, 858; II, 153.

116. "Letters of Samuel Thomas," missionary of S.P.G., *S.C. Hist. and Gen. Mag.*, IV, 278–85; V, 21–55 ("Documents concerning Mr. Thomas, 1702–7").

117. Humphreys, *op. cit.*, p. 111.

118. *Abstract, S.P.G.*, 1723–24, p. 40. Cf. Mr. Read's report for Craven County, N.C.; he was "afraid most of the Negroes (about a thousand) may too justly be reckoned Heathens." *Ibid.*, 1760–61, pp. 58–59.

119. See n. 33.

120. Baptism occurred in 17 parishes but numbers were small and many of these were infants. Communicants are mentioned in two parishes.

121. *Journal of House of Burgesses*, May 17, 1723, pp. 368, 370. See also the proposition sent to the Bishop of London in 1724, outlining a plan for the conversion of negroes (Perry [Va.], p. 344). The replies from the clergy of Maryland in 1724 and 1731 show that the religious condition of the negroes was very similar to that of Virginia. See n. 33.

122. The replies are not printed, but may be found in the Hawks MSS., volume for South Carolina. For mention of this material see *Report, Am. Hist. Assoc.*, 1898, pp. 59–60.

123. Perry (Va.), p. 369. The slave population of the colonies is here given for two dates, approximately 1755 and 1775. For 1755 we have in Maryland, 46,225, Virginia, 116,000, North Carolina, 20,000, South Carolina, 45,000, Georgia, 2,000—total 229,225. For 1775 we have in Maryland, 70,000, Virginia, 200,000 North Carolina, 45,000, South Carolina, 110,000, Georgia, 15,000—total, 440,000. There were about 29,000 slaves in the middle colonies, and 16,000 in New England in 1775. These estimates are based on those of Franklin Dexter, "Estimates of Population in the American Colonies," in *Proceedings, Amer. Antiq. Soc.*, N.S., V, 22–50. They must be recognized as only approximately correct, for accurate figures are unobtainable.

124. Perry (Va.), p. 369. See also Mr. Gavin's letter telling of his success in St. James's parish, Goochland, 1738. He reports 172 blacks baptized (*ibid.*, p. 360).

125. *Letters from the Rev. Samuel Davies and others, showing the State of Religion in Virginia particularly among the Negroes*, etc. (2d. ed., London, 1757), p. 20. Letter to J. F., March 2, 1756.

126. *Ibid.*, pp. 21–22. See also Davies's sermon, p. 8, n. 87, *supra*.

127. Thomas, *op. cit.*, p. 288.

128. E.g., Benjamin Ferris expressed a similar opinion; see Weeks, *op. cit.*, p. 202; see also n. 61.

129. *Abstract, S.P.G.*, 1759–60, pp. 61–62.

130. *Ibid.*, 1757–58, p. 50.

131. Hewatt, *op. cit.*, pp. 353–54. For progress in North Carolina, 1735–76, see Bassett, *op. cit.*, pp. 215–16; cf. also Brickell, *op. cit.*, p. 274; also n. 151.

132. Perry (Pa.), p. 165 (1728), cf. also pp. 184, 196.

133. *Abstract, S.P.G.*, 1725–26, pp. 37–38.

134. *Ibid.*, 1740–41, pp. 71–72. An excellent account of the Catechizing School of the S.P.G. in New York City is found in Kemp, *op. cit.*, chap. ix; see n. 39.

135. *Abstract, S.P.G.*, 1770–71, p. 24.

136. The replies from some of these parishes are printed, e.g., Westchester, Rye, and New Rochelle, in Bolton, *Hist. of the Ch. in Westchester Co.*, pp. 47–49, 227–30, 436–37; Hempstead, in *New York Genealogical and Biographical Record*, XXII, 131; and Jamaica, *Documentary History of New York*, III (1850), 185–87. The replies for other parishes (New York and Staten Island) may be found in the Hawks MSS, volume for New York. See n. 122.

137. Bolton, *op. cit.*, pp. 250, 256, 258, 266, for period 1727–35; Humphreys, *op. cit.*, pp. 209, 213.

138. Cf. Bolton (1764–69), pp. 77, 84.

139. See n. 63, and *Col. Rec. Conn.*, 1678–89, p. 298; answers to queries, 1680.

140. See n. 66, and *Abstract, S.P.G.*, 1740/1–1741/2, p. 41; and 1746–47, p. 52; James McSparran, *Letter Book and Abstract of Out Services* (Boston, 1899), pp. 4–25 (catechizing and baptism of negroes, R.I., 1743–51).

141. *Abstract, S.P.G.*, 1752–53, p. 51 (N.C.); *ibid.*, 1754–55 (N.Y.), p. 48; *ibid.*, 1759–60 (N.Y.), p. 47.

142. See n. 91.

143. Cf. letter of Mr. Taylor, missionary of S.P.G. to North Carolina, 1716, *N.C. Col. Rec.*, II, 332; Perry (Md.), pp. 306–7; *Abstract, S.P.G.*, 1753–54, p. 55; *Classified Digest*, pp. 15–16. Cf. also Davies, *Duties of Christians to propagate their Religion*, etc., pp. 38–39.

144. See n. 87.

145. Godwyn, *op. cit.*, pp. 125–27; Jones, *op. cit.*, pp. 70–71; Hewatt, *op. cit.*, pp. 355–56; Moore, *Notes on Hist. of Slav. in Mass.* (quoting writer in *Athenian Oracle*), p. 94.

146. Humphreys, *op. cit.*, p. 233.

147. Sermon before S.P.G. (1731) quoted in Wilkins Updike, *Hist. of Episc. Ch. in Narragansett, R.I.* (1847), p. 177.

148. Kalm, *Travels in North America* (ed. 1770), I, 397.

149. Weeks, *op. cit.*, p. 203; see also n. 91. So Samuel Fothergill describes conditions in Maryland, 1756. "Maryland is poor; the gain of oppression, the price of blood is upon that province. . . . I mean their purchasing, and keeping in slavery, negroes, the ruin of true religion the world over, wherever it prevails" (George Crosfield, *Memoirs of the Life and Gospel Labors of Samuel Fothergill*, p. 282, letter dated November 9, 1756; see also for North Carolina, *ibid.*, p. 283).

150. Perry (Pa.), p. 184.

151. Hewatt, *op. cit.*, p. 354. For the education of the negro see C. G. Woodson, *The Education of the Negro prior to 1861* (New York, 1915). Chapter ii deals specifically with the religious education of the negro before the Revolution. See also original documents in Appendix, pp. 337–59, and bibliographies, pp. 399–434.

CHAPTER III

1. This chapter was first printed under the title, "A Forgotten Slavery of Colonial Days," in *Harper's Monthly Magazine*, October, 1913. The more important studies of the indentured servant system are those by James C. Ballagh, "White Servitude in the Colony of Virginia" in *Johns Hopkins Studies*, etc. (Ser. X); E. I. McCormac, "White Servitude in Maryland" in *J. H. Studies* (Ser. XXII); J. S. Bassett, "Slavery and Servitude in North Carolina" in *J. H. Studies* (Ser. XIV); E. McCrady, "Slavery in South Carolina," in *Report Amer. Hist. Assoc., 1895;* K. F. Geiser, *Redemptioners and Indentured Servants in the Colony and Commonwealth of Pennsylvania* (New Haven, 1901); Frank R. Diffenderfer, *German Immigration into Pennsylvania* (Lancaster, 1900); and C. A. Herrick, *White Servitude in Pennsylvania* (Philadelphia, 1926). A short account is in P. A. Bruce, *Econ. Hist. of Va. in the Seventeenth Cent.*, Vol. I, chap. ix; Vol. II, chap. x.

2. For numbers see estimates in books listed above, especially Bruce, *op. cit.*, I, 610, and Geiser, *op. cit.*, p. 41, for estimate of 60,000 servants in Pennsylvania in 1754.

3. See chap. xii.

4. *Ibid.*, nn. 1–14 for general conditions in England and early proposals.

5. Richard Hakluyt, *Voyages, Navigations*, etc., III (London, 1599), 167–81.

6. See references, n. 1, and Hugh Jones, *Present State of Virginia* (Sabin reprint, 1865), pp. 53–54.

7. J. D. Butler, "British Convicts Shipped to American Colonies" in *Amer. Hist. Rev.*, II, 12–34, and references.

8. For regulation of traffic by King and Parliament see E. D. Collins, "Studies in the Colonial Policy of England, 1672–1680," in *Rpt. Amer. Hist. Assoc., 1900*, I, 146–48. See also *Acts of the Privy Council, Colonial*, I, 10–12, 56, 370–71; *Statutes of the Realm*, V (1662), 402, 405; (1679), p. 937; VII (1696), 274; Danby Pickering, *Statutes at Large*, XIII (1717), 471–75; XIV (1719), 292–95. See nn. 12 and 16.

9. Butler, *op. cit.*, 29, and J. T. Scharf, *Hist. of Md.*, I, 371. See references in n. 1, especially McCormac, chap. viii, "Convicts." See nn. 12–20, *infra*.

10. *Gentleman's Magazine*, XVII, 246. In 1731 "upwards of 100 convicts remained to be transported to America" (*ibid.*, I, 224). See also *ibid.*, XXXII (1762), 92. In 1732, 68 men and 50 women, "felons convict," were carried from Newgate to Black Fryars to be shipped for transportation to Virginia (*London Magazine*, I, 368).

11. *Life of Samuel Johnson* by Boswell (ed. by Hill), II, 302.

12. W. W. Hening, *Statutes of Virginia*, II (1670), 509–10. H. R. McIlwaine, *Minutes of the Council of the General Court of Virginia*, 209–10: "We apparently lose our reputation, whilest we are believed to be a place only fitt to receive such base and lewd persons." For action on a case involving the importation of ten "jailbirds" see Bruce, *op. cit.*, I, 605–6. For a letter from Virginia to the Privy Council complaining of the grave dangers of importing felons, see *Acts of the Privy Council, Colo.*, I, 553. An order in Council provided that after January 20, 1671, no more felons should be sent to Virginia, but the order was disregarded (*Acts of the Privy Council, Colo.*, I, 553; H. R. McIl-

waine, *op. cit.*, p. 252). In *Acts of the Privy Council*, I (1678), 788, is an order for 52 Scotch convicts to be transported to Virginia. See also *Pa. Colo. Recs.*, II (1728), 342. See nn. 8 and 16.

13. *Md. Gaz.*, July 30, 1767. *American Weekly Mercury* (Pa.), October 29, 1720, and February 7, 1721. Compare the lament in *ibid.*, February 14, 1721, that these "promising" plantations in America "cannot be ordered to be better populated than by such absolute villains and loose women, as these proved to be by their wretched lives and criminal actions, and if they settle anywhere in these parts can only by a natural consequence leave bad seeds amongst us." Compare also the *Va. Gaz.*, May 24, 1751. "When we see our papers filled continually with accounts of the most audacious Robberies, the most cruel Murders, and infinite other Villanies perpetuated by Convicts transported from Europe, what melancholy and what terrible Reflections must it occasion. . . . . These are some of the Favours Britain, Thou art called Mother Country; but what good Mother ever sent thieves and villains to accompany her children; to corrupt with their infectious vices and to murder the rest."

14. Alexander Brown, *The Genesis of the U.S.*, I, 456.

15. This is found in the communication signed "Americus" attributed to Franklin, *Pa. Gaz.*, May 24, 1751, in Smyth, *Writings of Franklin*, III, 45–48. See letter of Franklin to Peter Colinson, May 9, 1753. He charges that shipmasters were taking felons from German jails for the sake of profits. Franklin, *Works* (Bigelow ed.) II, 299. Franklin wrote the *London Chronicle* (1769), "Their emptying their jails into our settlements, is an insult and a contempt, the cruelest that ever one people offered to another" (*ibid.*, IV, 255). In another letter to the same magazine he lists the acts for sending criminals to America as one of the causes of discontent (*ibid.*, IV [1768], 108).

16. See nn. 8 and 12. Many acts were passed by the colonial assemblies levying heavy duties on convicts imported, but these were disallowed. See J. C. Hurd, *Law of Slavery and Bondage*, Vol. I. Compare *Archives of Md.*, II (1676), 540–41; *Pa. Statutes at Large*, III (1722), 264; XXII, 560. See *Cal. St. Papers, Colo.*, XV, 666; XVII, 347. Proprietors vetoed acts of this sort because against English law. Calvert's "Letter to the Maryland Assembly" is in *Archives of Md.*, XXXV (1724), 212. See also *ibid.*, XXXI (1756), 118. For a case of disallowance see *Acts of the Privy Council, Colo.*, V, 163, and *Pa. Colo. Recs.*, V, 499. The Virginia act of 1670 (Hening, *op. cit.*, II, 509) was confirmed by the Privy Council (*Acts*, etc., I [1671] 553) but violated nevertheless, and, finally, the act of Parliament in 1717 made legal again the transportation of convicts to the colonies (see n. 8).

17. Butler, *op. cit.*

18. Hugh Jones, *op. cit.*, pp. 53–54.

19. *Doc. Rel. Colo. Hist.*, *N.Y.*, IV, 31. Convicts were wanted for military service. See also *Cal. St. Pa., Colo.*, XV, 559; *Archives of Md.*, XXXV, 212; William Eddis, *Letters from America*, etc. (London, 1792), pp. 69–70.

20. A man was convicted of stealing a horse and sentenced to be transported to Virginia or Bermuda (*Acts of Privy Council, Colo.*, I [1662] 56).

21. Political prisoners were also called criminals. Compare Bruce, *op. cit.*, I, 608.

22. On "spiriting" and kidnaping see Butler, *op. cit.*, pp. 17–19. Verney papers in *Camden Society*, LVI, 160–62; Eddis, *Letters from America*, p. 68. *Va. Mag. of Hist.*, VI, 231 (Children); *Middlesex County Recs.* (J. C. Jeafferson, ed.), III, 337.

23. *Ibid.*, III, 337.

24. The evils are stated in a Bristol report (*Cal. St. Pa., Colo.*, 1661–68, p. 220).

25. Gottlieb Mittelberger, *Journey to Pa. in 1750*, pp. 16, 38. Diffenderfer, *op. cit.*, pp. 188, 190. John Harrower, "Diary" (of Indentured Servant) in *Amer. Hist. Rev.*, VI, 77.

26. Descriptions are found in *Pa. Mag. of Hist.*, X, 167; XXVI, 112; XXXVII, 94; XXXVIII, 65.

27. Harrower's "Diary," pp. 74–76.

28. Mittelberger, *op. cit.*, pp. 48–49.

29. *Ibid.*

30. *Pa. Statutes at Large*, V (1749–50), 94–97, and *ibid.*, VIII (1774), 369. A law of 1766 was disallowed. *Acts of Privy Council, Colo.*, IV, 763. See also *Mass. Acts and Resolves*, III (1750), 536. T. Cooper, *South Carolina Statutes at Large*, IV (1759), 78.

31. Mittelberger, *op. cit.*, pp. 20–22.

32. *Ibid.*, pp. 25–29.

33. Geiser, *op. cit.*, p. 54. Letter of Phineas Bond (1788), in *Rpt. Amer. Hist. Assoc., 1896*, I, 583, "They [passengers] are 'frequently hurried in droves, under the custody of severe brutal drivers (for these are the terms) into the Back Country to be disposed of as servants.'" For an indenture see *Md. Archives*, IV (1647), 327.

34. See records of indentures, 1771–73, *Pa. German Society Proc.*, Vol. XVI.

35. *Va. Gaz.* (Purdie and Dixon), March 28, 1771.

36. *New Jersey Archives* (newspaper extracts), XIX, 351, 353, 399, 499, etc. In the *Va. Gaz.*, 1736–39, there are 110 advertisements of runaway servants, 24.5 per cent being listed as convicts.

37. U. B. Phillips, *Plantation and Frontier Documents*, I, 346, 352, 355, 357.

38. See nn. 36 and 37 and *New Jersey Archives*, XI, 237.

39. "Md. Hist. Soc. Fund Publications," No. 36.

40. Mittelberger, *op. cit.*, p. 29. Eddis, *op. cit.*, etc., pp. 69–70.

41. J. Boucher, *A View of the Causes and Consequences of the Amer. Revolution, etc.* (London, 1797), pp. 183–84. "What is still less credible is, that at least two thirds of the little education we receive are derived from instructors, who are either *indented servants*, or *transported felons*. Not a ship arrives either with redemptioners or convicts, in which schoolmasters are not as regularly advertised for sale, as weavers, tailors, or any other trade; with little other difference, that I can hear of, excepting perhaps that the former do not usually fetch so good a price as the latter."

42. Crawford to Washington, June 8, 1774, in J. M. Hamilton's *Letters to Washington*, V, 12–14.

43. See n. 39. A digest of the laws governing the indentured servant for all the colonies is in J. C. Hurd, *The Law of Slavery and Bondage*, I.

44. See elaborate acts in T. Cooper, *Statutes at Large* (South Carolina), III (1717, 1744), 15, 621; W. W. Henning, *op. cit.* (1662–1705), II, 65; III, 449.

45. See n. 39 and Eddis, *op. cit.*, pp. 69–70. Harrower's "Diary" in *op. cit.*, Vol. VI; George Alsop, *The Character of the Province of Maryland*, 1666, in "Md. Hist. Soc. Fund Publications," No. 15, p. 94.

46. For Franklin's letter of 1751 see n. 15. See also Eddis, *op. cit.*, p. 66, and chaps. x and xi of this volume.

47. Hening, *op. cit.*, III, 87. Maryland act of 1664 is in *Md. Archives*, I, 533.

48. Geiser, *op. cit.*, p. 24.

49. John Pory, Secretary of Virginia, Letter to Sir Dudley Carlton, 1619. "All our riches for the present doe consiste in Tobacco, wherein one man by his owne labour hath in one yeare raised to himselfe to the value of 200 £ sterling; and another by the

meanes of sixe servants hath cleared at one crop a thousand pound English. These be true, yet indeed rare examples, yet possible to be done by others. Our principall wealth (I should have said) consisteth in servants: but they are chardgeable to be furnished with armes, apparell and bedding, and for their transportation, and casuall both at sea, and for their first yeare commonly at lande also: but if they escape, they prove very hardy, and sound able men (*Collecs. Mass. Hist. Soc.* [4th Ser.] IX, 9–10).

50. See n. 39; William Eddis, *op. cit.* (London, 1792), p. 66.

51. Geiser, *op. cit.*, pp. 102, 109.

CHAPTER IV

1. This chapter was first printed in the *School Review*, XXIII (May, 1915), 319–50. See M. W. Jernegan, "Factors Influencing the Development of American Education before the Revolution," in *Proc. Miss. Valley Hist. Assoc.*, V, 190–206.

2. An interesting but brief chapter on this subject may be found in E. Eggleston, *The Transit of Civilization from England to America in the Seventeenth Century* (1901), chap. v.

3. A. F. Leach, *English Schools at the Reformation, 1546–48*; F. Watson, *English Grammar Schools to 1660.*

4. J. E. G. de Montmorency, *State Intervention in English Education*, 1902.

5. N. Carlisle, *A Concise Description of the Endowed Grammar Schools in England and Wales*, 2 vols., 1818: a collection of charters, statutes, etc., of a large number of schools, with some descriptive matter.

6. Compare A. M. Stowe, *English Grammar Schools in the Reign of Queen Elizabeth*, 1908.

7. Foster Watson, *The English Grammar Schools to 1660; Their Curriculum and Practice*, 1908.

8. J. L. Sibley, *Harvard Graduates*, I, 207.

9. See the paper by Franklin B. Dexter, "Influence of the English Universities in the Development of New England," *Proc. Mass. Hist. Soc.*, 1879–80, XVII, 340–52. See also J. G. Bartlett, "Univ. Alumni Founders of New England," in *Pub. Col. Soc. of Mass.*, 1924–25, XXV, 14–23.

10. For estimates of population in the American colonies see article by Franklin B. Dexter in *Proc. Amer. Ant. Soc.*, N.S., V, 25.

11. *Rec. Co. Mass. Bay*, I, 87.

12. See M. Eggleston, "The Land System of the New England Colonies," *Johns Hopkins University Studies in Historical and Political Science*, Series IV, Nos. 11 and 12.

13. *Rec. Co. Mass. Bay*, I (March 3, 1635/36), 167.

14. For a discussion of the origin of the town see *Proc. Mass. Hist. Soc.*, 2d ser., VII, 172–263.

15. *Rec. Co. Mass. Bay*, I, 172.

16. *Ibid.*, p. 240. Previously the General Court had ordered (May 14, 1634) that in all rates and public charges towns were to levy every man according to his estate and other abilities (*ibid.*, I, 120).

17. Dexter, *op. cit.* See n. 10.

18. *Rec. Co. Mass. Bay*, I, 183.

19. Josiah Quincy, *Hist. Harv. Univ.*, I, 451. The sum amounted to £729 19s. 2d.

20. *New England's First Fruits*, London, 1643; in J. L. Sibley, *op. cit.*, p. 7. Reprinted in *Mass. Hist. Soc. Collec.*, 1792, and in *Old South Leaflets*, No. 51.

CHAPTER V

1. This chapter was first printed in the *School Review*, XXIII (June, 1915), 361–80.

2. Namely, Plymouth, Massachusetts Bay, Connecticut, New Haven, Rhode Island, and Maine. New Hampshire was absorbed by Massachusetts in 1641 and continued under her jurisdiction until 1679. Maine was also absorbed by Massachusetts in 1652. The date 1647 is taken, because on November 11, 1647, Massachusetts passed an act compelling towns of a certain population to set up town schools (*Rec. Co. Mass. Bay*, II, 203).

3. Massachusetts Bay had 32, Plymouth 10, Connecticut 9, New Haven 5, and Rhode Island 4. There were other settlements, which are not included in this list. Maine had a number, such as York, Saco, and Wells; but some were not governed as towns, and, in the case of others, records are lost, so that we have no evidence of town action on schools in Maine before 1647. There were also, in Massachusetts, "plantations" or settlements consisting of a small number of families, sometimes governed by the General Court, but which later became full-fledged towns with all the powers of self-government. (See William Hubbard, "Gen. Hist. of New Eng.," *Mass. Hist. Soc. Collec.*, 2d ser., VI, 416–17, for illustration.) Compare also, Thomas Lechford, *Plaine Dealing*, etc. (ed. by J. H. Trumbull), who speaks of "farmes or villages," pp. 40–41, 106–7. Lechford was a lawyer who resided at Boston, 1638–41. For a list of towns, with dates, for Massachusetts, and Plymouth, see C. D. Wright, *Rept. on Custody and Cond. of Pub. Rec. of Mass.* (1889), pp. 149–303. See also the list in "Good News from New England" (London, 1648), *Mass. Hist. Soc. Collec.*, 4th ser., I, 212. This contains the towns and pastors, with their salaries.

4. Population statistics of towns in this period can be gleaned only incidentally from the town records and histories.

5. See below for each of these towns.

6. There was one town in Plymouth Colony, Rehoboth, that gives some evidence of action. The proprietors, in granting land and drawing lots, allowed "The Schoolmaster" a portion. In 1643 his part is recorded as worth £50; in 1644 Lot No. 8 was assigned to him, and in 1645 Lot No. 49. But nothing further is known concerning the actual opening of a school (Leonard Bliss, *Hist. of Rehoboth*, pp. 23–34). The town of Plymouth made no provision for a town school until May 20, 1672. See *Rec. Town of Plymouth*, I (1636–75), 115, 124. See also William Bradford, *Hist. Plymouth Plantation* (1606–46; ed. by W. T. Davis), p. 170.

7. There are a few other towns that have a claim, but the evidence is so scanty and inconclusive that they are omitted from this discussion.

8. "Second Rept. Rec. Com.," *Boston Town Recs.*," *1634–60*, p. 5.

9. A meeting of the "richer inhabitants" of Boston was held August 12, 1636, when a subscription amounting to about £40 was made by forty-five persons, named, for maintaining a "free schoolmaster for the youth with us, Mr. Daniel Maud being now also chosen thereunto." This record was copied into the town records at the end of the volume. It really has no official place there, as it is not a record of a town meeting, and support of a school by voluntary subscription cannot in any sense be called town support. (See *ibid.*, p. 160.) Mr. Maud was granted a garden plot April 17, 1637, and Mr. Pormont listed "schoolmaster" a tract of land January 8, 1637/8 (*ibid.*, pp. 16, 25). The latter left Boston very soon after, and went to Exeter, New Hampshire (Jeremy Belknap, *Hist. of N.H.*, I, 37).

10. March 4, 1634/5. *Rec. Co. Mass. Bay*, I, 139.

11 *Boston Town Recs., 1634–1660*, p. 65.

12. *Ibid.*, p. 82. This order was passed at a meeting of the selectmen. On January 31, 1641/2, the town granted the use of the land to Captain Gibones "until the Towne doe let the same" (*ibid.*, p. 65).

13. *Ibid.*, p. 82, December 2, 1644. Thus the year December 2, 1643, to December 2, 1644, is the first in which there is evidence that support of the school came from town funds. Even this does not prove support by taxation.

14. On October 27, 1645, the selectmen ordered the constables to "sett off six shillings of Henry Messenger's Rates" for mending the "Schoole Masters fence" (*Boston Town Recs., 1634–1660*). This appears to be an order similar to that of December 2, 1644, and both indicate the beginnings of support by taxation.

15. The selectmen decided on the town rate and then gave orders to the constables to pay certain sums due, out of the money collected. For example, on July 25, 1644, the constables were ordered to pay £4 10s to Arthur Perry, part of £7 due him for his services in drumming. Similar payments were ordered at this same meeting (*Boston Town Recs., 1634–1660*).

16. John Winthrop, *Journal*, etc. (ed. by J. K. Hosmer), II, 224. Winthrop's failure to mention the school at Boston until 1645 is significant. He subscribed to the "subscription" school of 1636. See n. 9.

17. *Boston Town Recs., 1660–1701* (March 26, 1666), p. 30. In the list of ushers of the school the first mentioned is Mr. Hincheman, appointed in 1666 by the above vote. (H. F. Jenks, *Cat. of Bost. Pub. Lat. Sch.*, p. 16.)

18. *Boston Town Recs., 1634–1660* (March 11, 1650), p. 99.

19. Compare Jenks, *op. cit.*, p. 5. See n. 37.

20. *Charlestown Archives*, Vol. XX; MS *Town Records, 1629–64*, II, 11. (See Richard Frothingham, *Hist. of Charlestown*, pp. 1–3, for comment on the early MS records of the town, some of which are copies of originals now lost.) Mr. Witherell was granted a house plot February 11, 1636/7, had a house, as recorded, March 3, 1637, participated in a division of land April 23, 1638, and sold his house December 28, 1638 (*Town Recs.*, pp. 11, 13, 18–19, 21). Sometime in 1638 he removed to Duxbury (Justin Winsor, *Hist. of Duxbury*, pp. 263, 346).

21. *Charlestown Town Recs.*, p. 17.

22. This record is of unusual importance, and was omitted by Mr. Frothingham in the account of the school in his history of Charlestown. It reads: "About Mr Witherell it was refferred to Mr Greene and Wm. Lerned to settle his wages for the yeare past in part and part to come, and they chose Ralph Sprague for A third." In the margin is written "To provide of settling the Grammer Schoolemers Sallary" (*ibid.*, p. 17). Mr. Lerned was one of the selectmen, Mr. Greene the ruling elder of the church, and Mr. Sprague was a prosperous farmer and had been a member of the first board of selectmen (Frothingham, *op. cit.*, pp. 51–52, 79, 81).

23. *Charlestown Town Recs.*, p. 36. Lovell's Island was granted the town by the General Court, October 28, 1636 (*Rec. Co. Mass. Bay*, I, 183). "Misticke Ware" referred to a fishery in which the town had a share. Lovell's Island seems to have been rented for twenty years, and the income applied for the support of the school (see Frothingham, *op. cit.*, p. 65). In 1636 there were seventy-two men in Charlestown with wives and children (*ibid.*, p. 98). Rates had been levied by the town for the colony tax since 1630 (*ibid.*, p. 99).

24. *Charlestown Town Recs.*, p. 36.

25. Granted by the General Court, March 4, 1634/5. The land was divided, but just what proportion of the inhabitants held shares is unknown. See *Hist. of Dorchester* (by a Committee of Dorchester Antiquarian and Historical Society), p. 419. "Fourth Rept. Rec. Com.," *Dorch. Town Rec., 1633–89*, pp. 30–31 (apportionment of "other land," dated March 18, 1637/8). This is the first mention of Latin and "Maydes" in public records.

26. *Ibid.*, p. 39.

27. This document is printed in *Hist. of Dorchester*, pp. 422–24. It is signed by seventy-one persons, and a facsimile of their signatures is given by W. D. Orcutt, *Good Old Dorchester*, p. 292, and by James Blake, *Annals of Dorchester*.

28. *Dorchester Town Recs.*, pp. 54–57.

29. In the rules and orders there are interesting regulations set forth respecting the length of the school year and sessions, religious instruction, including catechizing, morals, manners, and discipline. In general, the wardens were to see that the master trained up the children of the town in "religion, learning and Civilitie."

30. The distinction between town land, viz., undivided land owned by the town as a corporate body, and divided land, viz., land owned by individuals, is important. Even if every inhabitant possessed land on the island and then conveyed it to the town, it would not be endowment by the town, but by individuals.

31. See *Hist. of Dorchester*, pp. 161–64, for the documents on this point. A petition of October 8, 1659, asserts that the loss of the island resulted in "the almost if not total overthrow of or free scoole which was soe hopefull for posterity, both our owne and neighbors also who had or might have reaped benefit thereby" (*ibid.*, p. 433).

32. See below, on this point.

33. Mr. Waterhouse was, apparently, teaching October 31, 1639, for a vote on that date relieved him from teaching writing "only to doe what he can convienently therein" (*Dorchester Town Recs.*, p. 40). He returned to England about 1642 (*Hist. of Dorchester*, pp. 479–81).

34. "Salem Town Rec. 1634–59," in *Essex Inst. Hist. Collec.*, IX, 97 ff. He evidently commenced teaching soon after for Lechford speaks of him as Schoolmaster at Salem. (See T. Lechford, *op. cit.*, p. 84.)

35. *Hist. of Salem*, I, 427–28, as quoted by J. B. Felt. The order varies as printed— "[Goodman Auger is ordered to call a general town meeting the second day of the week to see about a free school—*Waste Book*]" (*Rec. and Files of Quar. Courts of Essex Co., 1636–56*, I, 25).

36. "Salem Town Rec.," *op. cit.*, p. 132. No other vote on the school occurred before 1647.

37. The word "rate," used in connection with school support, occurs in the records of six towns before January 21, 1647, viz.: Salem, September 30, 1644; Boston, December 2, 1644; Dedham, January 1, 1644/5; Dorchester, March 15, 1645; Guilford (in New Haven Colony), October 7, 1646; and Charlestown, January 20, 1646/7. Besides these towns there were two others where payment by rate was evidently intended when such phrases were used as "common stock" of the town (New Haven, February 25, 1641/2), and "town charge" (Hartford, April, 1643). There was considerable objection to the use of a "rate" even for the support of the church up to 1643. See note in Lechford, *op. cit.*, pp. 50–51; and Hubbard, "Hist. of New Eng.," *op. cit.*, p. 373 and 412. "This new way of cessment was offensive to some."

38. *Ipswich Town Rec., 1634–50*, I (1899), 24*b*. "The First third day of the 9th

1642." In the old record book of the Grammar School is an item dated 1636: "A Grammar School is set up, but does not succeed." J. B. Felt says this has the appearance of having been copied (*Hist. of Ipswich*, p. 83.) The phrase "former grant" seems to mean that the town had aided a school before this date.

39. *Ipswich Town Rec.*, p. 26.

40. Like Salem, the notion of free education applied only to poor children; so also in the vote of Hartford, April, 1643, below. There is no other vote on schools before 1647, and there is doubt whether it existed as a town school, 1644-50. See Abraham Hammatt, "Ipswich Grammar School," in *New Eng. Hist. and Gen. Reg.*, VI, 64.

41. *Dedham Town Rec., 1636-59*, III, 92. There are fifty-one names given of those who voted on this matter.

42. *Ibid.*, p. 105. In a division of land February 4, 1644/5, eighty-three men received portions (*ibid.*, pp. 109-10). On this same date the town voted to grant the remainder of the "Training ground to the Feoffees" to be improved by them to October 31, 1650. By the same vote five men, named, were chosen feoffees. Two of them, with one of the selectmen, were appointed to set off the land in question, March 4, 1644/5 (*ibid.*, p. 108).

43. There is no other vote before 1647, and the records of the feoffees are not extant. Proof of the opening of the school before 1647 is wanting. See *Dedham Hist. Reg.*, I, 88.

44. There is but one item relating to education on the town records of Cambridge before 1647. On May 11, 1638, the town voted that two and two-thirds acres be set aside "to the Professor is to the Town's use for evr. for a publick scoole or Colledge to the use of Mr. Nath. Eaten as long as he shall be Imployed in that work," etc. Mr. Nathaniel Eaton, who was granted about two acres by the same vote, was the first teacher at Harvard College (1638-40). This is evidently aid to higher education. Elijah Corlett, master of the Grammar School at this time, or a little later, was not aided by the town until November 13, 1648 (*ibid.*, p. 77). Cambridge, therefore, cannot be properly included in the list of towns that established or aided a town school before 1647. For Eaton, see Hubbard, "Gen. Hist. New Eng.," *Mass. Hist. Soc. Collec.*, 2d ser., V, 247. Hubbard was a graduate of Harvard, class of 1642.

45. In 1639 the town of Newbury granted ten acres of land to Anthony Somerby for his "Encouragement" to keep school for one year. As no other vote occurs on this subject before 1647, it was probably conducted as a private school if in operation after this date. Mr. Somerby was town clerk of Newbury for more than thirty years (J. J. Currier, *Hist. of Newbury*, p. 395).

46. The school at Roxbury was established in 1645 by voluntary gifts of persons interested. The agreement was signed by sixty-four persons, who bound themselves, their heirs, and assignees to pay annually a sum amounting to £21 10s 8d for the support of a "free School." Those not signing the document were to have no "further benefit [of the school] thereby than other strangers shall have who are no inhabitants." The town refused to contribute to its support up to 1666 (C. K. Dillaway, *Hist. of Grammar Sch. of Roxbury*, pp. 7-13, 20, 39, 33; and Winthrop, *op cit.*, II, 224.).

47. C. H. Hoadly (ed.), *Rec. of Col. and Planta. of New Haven, 1638-49*, p. 62.

48. Hoadly, *op. cit.*, p. 120. At a court held February 8, 1643/4, Mr. Cheevers "desired 4-3-6 out of the estate of Mr. Trobridge, which is justly due to him for teaching the children" (*ibid.*, p. 124). This also seems to indicate support by rate.

49. Mr. Higginson was teacher of the church, meaning an assistant pastor, and ap-

parently had charge of the school from 1643 to 1646, supported, like the pastor, by voluntary contributions (B. C. Steiner, *Hist. of Guilford*, pp. 27, 35, 40, 60).

50. Steiner, *ibid.*, p. 394; R. D. Smith, *Hist. of Guilford*, p. 80.

51. See n. 37.

52. *Hartford Town Votes, 1635–1716*, I, 63, in *Collec. Conn. Hist. Soc.*, Vol.VI (1897).

53. *Ibid.*, p. 65.

54. *An Historical Discourse, etc.* (ed. by Elton, 1843), p. 110. This was first published in 1739 and is the only evidence we have for this vote which does not occur in the printed records surviving (S. G. Arnold, *Hist. of R.I.*, I, 145; *Collec. R.I. Hist. Soc.*, IV, 116; *R.I. Colo. Rec.*, I, 104).

55. Mr. Lenthal returned to England before March 17, 1642 (*R. I. Colo. Recs.*, p. 119). See also James Savage, *Genealogical Dictionary, etc.*, III, 78; and Lechford, *op. cit.*, pp. 57–58, 94.

56. Callender, *op. cit.*, p. 110.

57. This is estimated from the data given by Dexter, "Estimates of Population in the American Colonies," *Proc. Amer. Ant. Soc.*, N.S., V, 22–32.

58. *Rec. Co. Mass. Bay*, II, 6, June 14, 1642.

CHAPTER VI

1. This chapter was first printed in the *School Review*, XXVI (December, 1918), 731–49.

2. A table showing the dates when various states and territories passed laws involving compulsory attendance may be found in *Report of the Commissioner of Education*, 1888–89, I, 471. The earliest date given is that of Massachusetts, 1852.

3. *The Statutes of the Realm* (London), 1819, IV, 414, 962, for 5 Eliz. c. 4, and 43 Eliz. c. 2. For the apprenticeship system in England and the relationship of English laws to the Massachusetts act of 1642, see O. J. Dunlop and R. D. Denman, *English Apprenticeship and Child Labour* (London, 1912); J. F. Scott, *Historical Essays on Apprenticeship and Vocational Education* (Ann Arbor, 1914); R. F. Seybolt, *Apprenticeship and Apprenticeship Education in Colonial New England and New York* (New York, 1917).

4. Elsie Clews, *Educational Legislation and Administration of the Colonial Governments* (New York, 1899). The same criticism may be made of the article by J. W. Perrin on "Beginnings of Compulsory Education" in *Educational Review*, March, 1903, which is full of errors and hopelessly confuses compulsory education, attendance, and schools.

5. *Recs. Co. Mass. Bay*, II, 6–7 and 8–9. Two versions are given with slight variations. The seventeenth-century abbreviations and contractions have been expanded in the text given. Otherwise it is reproduced exactly.

6. 5 Eliz. c. 4; see n. 3 above.

7. The first act on apprenticeship passed by the colony of New Plymouth was dated December 7, 1641. It declared that "those that have releefe from the Townes and have children and doe not ymploy them. That then it shallbe lawfull for the Towneship to take order that those children shallbe put to worke in fitting imployment according to their strength and abillities, or placed out by the Townes" (*Recs. Col. New Plymouth*, XI, 38).

Compare also the Virginia act of 1646, "profitable trades," "avoyd sloath and idlenesse" "reliefe of such parents whose poverty extends not to give them good breeding" (Hening, *The Statutes at Large, etc.* (Virginia), I, 336–37).

8. "As every new law is made to remove some inconvenience the state was subject to before the making of it, and for which no other method of redress was effectual, the law itself is a standing, and the most authentic, evidence we can require of the state of things previous to it" (Priestly, *Lectures on History* [3d ed., 1791], p. 67). Notwithstanding a prevailing notion that town schools were established by nearly all the towns of Massachusetts almost immediately, such was not the case. We have no evidence that more than seven towns, out of the twenty-one founded up to June 14, 1642, had taken any official action on schools. Massachusetts at this date had a population of about nine thousand or more. See chap. v.

9. It may be noted that the Virginia Company agreed on February 2, 1620, that the one hundred children supplied by the city of London to be sent to Virginia should be "educated and brought upp in some good Craftes, Trades, or Husbandry" so that they might gain their livelihood by the time they were twenty-one years old, or by the time they had served their seven years' apprenticeship (Susan Kingsbury, *Rec. of Va. Co.*, I, 306). Whether this includes book education is doubtful. See chap. x.

10. For a description of the code of 1648 see the *New York Nation* of July 5, 1906. This code has been recently reprinted by the Harvard University Press (1929). See Introduction by Dr. Max Farrand. The date, 1642, indicates the time of the passage of the original law, of which this is a revision.

11. *The Book of the General Lawes and Libertyes*, etc. (Cambridge, 1660), p. 16. This code was published in facsimile, edited by W. H. Whitmore, Boston, 1889. There were several supplements to this code, probably printed in 1650, 1654, and 1657, including the laws passed within these dates, but no copies have survived. Some of these supplements were in the nature of a new code, as laws passed previous to 1648 were included which are not in the code of 1648 (*ibid.*, Introduction, pp. 112–13). The heading of the first page of the text of the code of 1660 reads: "The General Lawes of the Massachusetts Colony, Revised and Published by Order of the General Court in October, 1658."

12. There are, however, five additional sections bearing on the general training of children and their care. They have to do with disobedient children, entertaining children and apprentices in taverns, debts, unnatural severity of parents, and orphans.

13. Session of General Court, meeting October 14, 1668 (*Rec. of Co. Mass. Bay*, IV², 395–96); code of 1660 supplement, pp. 17–18; this is a reprint of the session law.

14. *The General Laws and Liberties of the Massachusetts Colony; Revised and Reprinted*, etc. (Cambridge, 1672), pp. 149–50 and 26–28. Reprinted, Boston, 1887; edited by W. H. Whitmore.

15. J. H. Trumbull (ed.), *Public Rec. of Col. of Conn. to 1665*, pp. 520–21. The only essential change is the omission of the words "or the next Country Court for that shire." Connecticut was not divided into counties at this date. This code was not published until 1822.

16. The charter was dated April 23, 1662, but New Haven was not represented by deputies in the new assembly until March, 1665, and the laws of New Haven were not actually laid aside until August 14, 1665 (*Rec. Col. and Jurisdiction of New Haven, 1653–1665*, p. 557).

17. New Haven, Milford, Stamford, Greenwich, Guilford, Branford, and Southold, the latter on Long Island, were subject to the New Haven colony for longer or shorter periods.

18. *New Haven's Settling in New England and Some Lawes for Government: Published for the Use of that Colony*, etc. (London, 1656). Reprinted by C. J. Hoadly in *Rec. of Col. and Jurisdiction of New Haven, 1653–1665*, pp. 583–84.

19. *Ibid.*, p. 376.

20. A new code was published by Connecticut in 1673. This contained the law of 1650 on the education of children, with minor changes, pp. 13–14. The title was *The Book of the General Laws, for the People within the Jurisdiction of Connecticut*, etc. (Cambridge, 1673). The copy of the laws was "viewed and approved by this Court" October 10, 1672, and ordered printed (*Pub. Rec. of Col. of Conn., 1675–1678*, p. 182). This revision of the law has one new section, "Rebellious Children and Servants," with power granted to the governor and two assistants to punish on conviction.

21. *The Compact with the Charter and Laws of the Colony of New Plymouth*, etc., edited by William Brigham (Boston, 1836), pp. 270–71. This contains *The Book of the General Laws of the Inhabitants of the Jurisdiction of New Plymouth*, etc. (Cambridge, 1672).

22. Rhode Island had one law, passed in 1662, which gave power to towns to "put out to service" those "likely to become a charge" to the town. Overseers of the poor were to inform the town council concerning the poor. The town council was then "to take such course . . . . as to them shall seem proper and needful, Agreeable to the Statute of XLIII, of ELIZABETH, Chap. 2d." Thus the apprenticing of poor children was provided for, though not compulsory, and no book or religious education was mentioned. In practice, however, an educational clause might be inserted in the indenture, and, when such was the case, could be enforced. For this act see *The Charter and the Acts and Laws of the Colony of Rhode Island* (Boston, 1719), p. 10. This act was passed at a session of the General Assembly held at Newport March 1, 1662.

CHAPTER VII

1. For the character of the government of the New England colonies compare W. B. Weeden, *Economic and Social History of New England*, I, 68–69, 76–79. See also H. L. Osgood, *The American Colonies in the Seventeenth Century*, I, 212. Professor Osgood estimates that up to 1674 only one in five of the adult male residents of Massachusetts could vote for colony officers, viz., for the men who made the laws for the colony. Anyone voting or holding office had to be a church member. This has recently been questioned by Professor S. E. Morison, in his *Builders of the Bay Colony*. This chapter was first printed in the *School Review*, XXVII (January, 1919), 24–43.

2. See chap. xiii.

3. See *Pub. Rec. Col. of Conn., 1678–89*, pp. 496–502, for the cost of the war.

4. *Ibid.*, pp. 147–48. These reasons, as stated, are found in the preamble of the act of 1684.

5. *Ibid.*, 1665–77, pp. 280–83.

6. *Ibid.*, 1678–89, p. 148.

7. An act of 1677 declared that the "welfare, civilizing and good education of the said Indians and their children" was "a matter of great concernment." Indian children apprenticed to the "English Inhabitants" were "to be taught and instructed in the Christian Religion" (*The General Laws and Liberties*, etc., 1672, reprint of 1887, with supplements to 1686, pp. 51–52).

Pub. Rec. Col. of Conn., 1678–89, contains extracts of *The Acts and Proceedings of the Commissioners of the United Colonies of New England*. At a meeting held at Hartford, September 5, 1678, an order of 1660 was revised. The new law provided for the apprenticing of Indian children to the English. With the consent of two commissioners, such children could be apprenticed to "godly masters, such as will teach them to read well, and bring them to Christian nurture.". Such masters were required, once a year, to appear before the commissioners of some colony and give account thereof; "otherwise, the said apprentices are to be taken from their masters, at the request of the parents, and placed where they may be nurtured and educated as here provided" (*ibid.*, p. 497).

8. *The Book of the General Laws of the Inhabitants of the Jurisdiction of New-Plimouth*, etc. (Boston, 1685). William Bridgham in his *The Compact with the Charter and Laws of the Colony of New Plymouth* (Boston, 1836), prints some of the laws added in the code of 1685, not found in the code of 1671. This law appears on page 297.

9. The first commission of Andros, June 3, 1686 (in Bartlett [ed.], *Rec. of R.I.*, etc., III, 212–13), included Massachusetts Bay, New Hampshire, Maine, the Narragansett Country, and New Plymouth. By the second commission of April 7, 1688, Rhode Island and Connecticut were added (*Laws of New Hampshire*, I, 226–34; ed. A. S. Batchellor). Connecticut was not included in the first commission of Andros, but he declared October 31, 1687, that by order of the King "he took into his hands the Government of this Colony of Connecticott" (*Pub. Rec. of Col. of Conn., 1678–89*, p. 248). See Viola Barnes, *The Dominion of New England*.

10. *Rec. of Conn., 1678–89*, p. 251. In the instructions to Sir Edmund Andros, April 16, 1688, laws were to remain in force and continue, within the Dominion of New England, if not contrary to the commission and instructions, and until other laws were passed. Instructions are printed in *Laws of New Hampshire*, I, 224–44.

11. *Pub. Rec. Col. of Conn., 1678–89*, pp. 427–28. This is a general law regulating duties of selectment, etc. The whole body of laws enacted by Andros and his council cover pages 402–36 of this volume. This made provision for new town governments to be set up in every town in the dominion. The selectmen, who were also appointed overseers of the poor, were required, with the consent of two justices of the peace, to levy taxes for the relief of the poor and, at monthly meetings, to make distribution of the same for three specified purposes; namely, for the maintenance of the poor, for setting the poor to work, and "for putting children apprentices." An annual accounting was to be rendered of money, stocks, etc., and "what apprentices they [have] put out and bound," to be examined and approved by two justices of the peace.

12. The charter of 1691 provided that all acts disallowed by the crown, within three years after they were laid before the Privy Council, should be, upon notice of such disallowance to the governor, repealed. A convenient reprint of this charter is in William Macdonald, *Select Charters*, etc. (New York, 1899), pp. 205–12. The continuing act is in *Acts and Resolves of the Province of Massachusetts Bay*, I, 27.

13. *Acts and Resolves*, etc., p. 99.

14. *Ibid.* See also *Acts of the Privy Council of England, Colonial Series*, II (London, 1910), 841–42.

15. *Acts and Resolves*, etc., Vols. I, VII, IX. It may be noted that the committee appointed to prepare the edition of the collected laws of 1714–26 was instructed to omit all laws repealed or expired; and the committee appointed to prepare the edition of 1724 was ordered to omit "all such laws as are expired, have been disallowed or repealed."

16. *Ibid.*, I, p. 67.

17. *Ibid.*, p. 538.

18. *Ibid.*, p. 654.

19. The law was renewed seven times at various dates, 1717, 1720, 1731, April 10, 1741, 1760, 1770, and 1773 (*Acts and Resolves*, etc., II, 74, 182–83, 579–80, 1053–54; IV, 324; V, 39, 258).

20. *Ibid.*, II, 757–58.

21. *Ibid.*, II, 1067.

22. *Ibid.*, III, 488.

23. *Ibid.*, V, 161–62.

24. *Ibid.*, IV, 178–79. This law was re-enacted in 1766, 1770, and 1775 (*ibid.*, IV, 920; V, 88, 460).

25. *Pub. Rec. Col. of Conn., 1678–89*, p. 251.

26. *Ibid., 1689–1706*, pp. 30–31.

27. *Acts and Laws of His Majesty's Colony of Connecticut in New England*, etc. (Boston, 1702). The title is "An Act for Educating of Children." The code of 1715 is a reprint of that of 1702, and this act is found on p. 16 of this code. See n. 1, p. 36 of code.

28. *Pub. Rec. Col. of Conn., 1706–16*, p. 530.

29. *Ibid., 1726–35*, pp. 202–3.

30. *Conn. Code of 1750*, pp. 20–21.

31. *Laws of New Hampshire*, II, 115.

32. *Ibid.*, II, 340.

33. *Ibid.*, III, 391.

34. That of 1662 we have referred to. Her next act was that of April 1, 1741 (*Acts and Laws of His Majesty's Colony of Rhode Island*, etc. [Newport, 1745], p. 236), which was in reality a poor law, giving power to the town council to "bind out as apprentices poor children who were likely to become Chargeable to the Town wherein they live." Indentures were made binding and effectual in law. This act was included in the code of 1767 (*Acts and Laws of the English Colony of Rhode Island* [Newport, 1767], p. 228).

35. There were numerous acts passed by the New England colonies relating to apprentices and servants jointly, involving their control, treatment, and punishment for offenses, not treated in this study, as they only remotely involved the education of children apprenticed.

36. A study of this subject by R. F. Seybolt, *Apprenticeship and Apprenticeship Education in Colonial New England and New York* (New York, 1917), a Columbia University thesis, is inaccurate, because of a failure to examine with care the colonial codes of laws. At least six important acts passed by the New England colonies on apprenticeship are not mentioned, and three of these directly involve book education. The author's failure to distinguish between the special and general acts (pp. 47–48 and p. 105) of Massachusetts, especially those of 1735, 1741, and 1771, results in an incorrect statement of the book education required in indentures of boys and girls. For all children apprenticed, except those living outside the boundaries of organized towns and districts, a relatively small number, the requirement from 1710–76 was reading and writing for boys and reading for girls, and not reading, writing, and ciphering for all boys from 1741 on and reading and writing for girls from 1771 on as is implied on p. 47. A most regrettable error is the statement (p. 48) that the "educational provisions of the Act of 1642 were re-enforced and amplified by the Poor Laws just reviewed. While these laws were primarily intended to take care of poor children, they applied to all children just as the earlier law did. Children whose education had been neglected were treated as poor children and bound out accordingly." Nothing could be further from the truth. Not only did the acts of 1703 and 1710, the latter in force throughout the colonial period, specifically state the contrary, but the act of 1735, cited apparently in support of the above statement, was limited strictly to the town of Boston. Moreover, the law of 1642 and others on parental education was disallowed by the Privy Council in 1695. See nn. 13 and 14, above.

CHAPTER VIII

1. This chapter was first printed in the *Social Service Review*, V (September, 1931), 411–45.

2. For the English background see O. J. Dunlop and R. D. Denman, *English Apprenticeship and Child Labour* (London, 1912).

3. See A. F. Leach (ed.), *Beverley Town Documents* (London: Selden Society, 1900), for examples.

4. *Records of the Borough of Leicester*, ed. Mary Bateson, III, 197: February 8, 1584.

5. *Ibid.*, p. 183: September 21, 1580. For analysis of the act of 1642 see chap. v.

6. *Transactions of the American Antiquarian Society*, VII (1885), 251 (*Thomas Lechford's Note Book*, June 27, 1638—July 29, 1641).

7. *Records of the Colony of New Haven*, I, 30. Cf. Boston vote in town meeting (1660): "All Indentures made between any master and servant shall bee brought in and enrolled in the Towne's Records within one month after the contract made" (*Boston Town Records*, II, 157). In 1672 parents were ordered to make return of the names of masters and children put out to service "with their Indenture to the Selectmen at their nexte monthly Meeting" (*ibid.*, VII, 67).

8. *Watertown Records*, I, 47.

9. H. R. Stiles, *Ancient Winsor*, I, 442. In 1647 the county court bound out a boy as an apprentice and provided that the master should teach him to read and write (*Essex County Court Records*, I, 118; see also *ibid.*, pp. 132, 163, 380). Indentures recorded in Maine provide for the teaching of apprentices "to reade and writte"; "to write and siffer"; "to write, etc., read, Legably and Audibly" (*York Deeds* [Portland, Me., 1887], II, 129: 1672); see also *ibid.*, p. 159: 1674; *ibid.*, p. 73: 1679). Hartford (Conn.) selectmen "put out" a boy as an apprentice and provided that he be taught to read the Bible and to write (*Coll. Conn. Hist. Soc.*, VI, 775).

10. *Dorchester Town Records* (1634–87), p. 306: 1651.

11. See *ibid.*, p. 165, for a contract (1669) stipulating that in the case of the child of John Stock, the master should "teach or Cause it to be taught to read p'ftly the English tongue . . . . the principles of the Christian religion. And in such housewifly employment of Spinning and Knitting . . . . [the town to pay] out of the Towne Rate the Sum of Thirty pounds." Other examples are in *ibid.*, pp. 166, 173, 171. See also *Watertown Records*, I, 107: 1671, "and to have for his incurigment fifty shillings to be paid by the town."

12. *Essex County Court Records*, V, 417.

13. An apprentice was to be sent to school until he could write (*ibid.*, II, 135). Another apprentice was to be kept at school for at least two years (*Plymouth Colony Records*, I, 36–37).

14. See chap. v.

15. *Cambridge Town Records* (1630–1703), p. 47.

16. H. A. Hazen, *History of Billerica*, p. 252. The selectmen appointed the next day to "go the rounds" to examine the teaching of children and youth according to law.

17. *Ibid.*

18. *Watertown Records*, I, 204.

19. *Ibid.*, p. 102.

20. *Ibid.*, p. 103: December 13, 1670.

21. *Ibid.*, p. 114: November 25, 1672.

22. *Dorchester Town Records*, p. 182.

23. *Lancaster Town Records* (1643–1725), pp. 95–96.

24. Sylvester Judd, *History of Hadley*, pp. 60–61.

25. Records of the County Court of Middlesex, Mass., 1649–63 (MSS), I, 194: December 27, 1659.

26. *Essex County Court Records*, IV, 212: 1668.

27. *Maine Hist. Soc. Col.*, I, 285 (extracts from "York County Court Records").

28. Essex County Court Records, 1667–79 (MSS), XXII, 78–79: July 21, 1674. (In the printed records this presentment was omitted and is here given from the original manuscript.)

29. *Ibid.*, November, 1674.

30. *Ibid.*

31. *Ibid.*

32. *New Eng. Hist. and Gen. Reg.*, V, 173.

33. A. S. Hudson, *Annals of Sudbury, Wayland and Maynard*, p. 44.

34. *Public Records of the Colony of Connecticut* (1678–89), p. 251.

35. F. M. Caulkins, *History of Norwich*, p. 92.

36. *Essex County Court Records*, IV, 219: March 29, 1670.

37. "Salem Town Records," *Essex Inst. Hist. Coll.*, IX, 132. Cf. also *Brookline and Muddy River Records*, p. 86: 1687, "Save any persons that are poor to be abated wholly or in part"; *Watertown Records*, II, 28: 1686, "Voated also that the towne will pay for such Chilldren as thear parents are not abell to pay for. The selectmen Being Judges of that mattur."

38. *Records of the Town of Plymouth* (1636–1743), II, 2.

39. *Ibid.*, I, 270. Cf. H. M. Burt, *First Century of the History of Springfield*, I, 74: 1707.

40. J. R. Trumbull, *History of Northampton*, I, 426.

41. D. P. Corey, *History of Malden*, p. 602.

42. Charlestown Town Records (MSS), VI, 92: May 2, 1712.

43. *Mass. Acts and Resolves*, I, 654.

44. Corey, *History of Malden*, pp. 402–3. For other examples see *Conn. Hist. Soc. Coll.*, VI, 175: 1703. For Rhode Island see *Early Records of Providence*, V, 146: 1696; IX, 5: 1713.

45. Charlestown Town Records, 1719–61 (MSS), VII, 180.

CHAPTER IX

1. See chap. iv. This chapter was first printed in the *School Review*, XXVII, (May, 1919), 360–76.

2. In *New-England's True Interest*, etc., Cambridge, 1670. This was an election sermon preached at Boston on April 29, 1668. See J. L. Sibley, *Harvard Graduates*, I, 207.

3. Franklin B. Dexter, "Estimates of Population in the American Colonies," *Proc. Amer. Antiq. Soc.*, V (1887), 25, 42; "Influence of the English Universities in the Development of New England," *Proc. Mass. Hist. Soc.*, *1877–80*, pp. 347, 349. See chap. iv, n. 9.

4. J. C. Ballagh, "White Servitude in the Colony of Virginia," *Johns Hopkins Studies in Hist. and Polit. Sci.*, Series X, chap. i.

5. Dexter, *op. cit.*, pp. 25, 42.

6. For the higher planter class, see P. A. Bruce, *Social Life of Virginia in the Seventeenth Century*, pp. 23–24.

7. See chap. iii, n. 1.

8. W. W. Hening, *Statutes at Large* (Virginia), II, 515, contains a report of Governor Berkeley. He gives Virginia, in 1671, 40,000 white inhabitants, 2,000 negro slaves, and 6,000 white servants. In 1683, Governor Culpepper estimates the white servants at nearly double the number of 1671 (J. A. Doyle, *English Colonies in America*, I, 385, quoting *Colonial Entry Book*, No. 83, p. 339). The white population at this date was about 50,000. There were, besides the voluntary servants, other classes, such as convict servants.

9. Dexter, *op. cit.*, p. 43. The population at this date was perhaps 275,000, of which the negro slaves numbered about 110,000.

10. Thomas Jefferson, *Notes on the State of Virginia*, 1781 (ed. of 1787), pp. 270–71.

11. *Ibid.*

12. Dexter, *op. cit.*

13. William H. Perry, *Hist. Collec. Relating to the Amer. Col. Church* (Virginia), pp. 303–7.

14. See chap. ii.

15. Hugh Jones, *The Present State of Virginia* (London, 1724), pp. 44–45.

CHAPTER X

1. We find little or no recognition of the fact that there were other agencies for education than organized schools in such general histories of American education as those by E. G. Dexter or Richard G. Boone; nor even in most state histories of education, like those of B. C. Steiner for Connecticut or R. D. Smith for North Carolina.

2. Compare A. B. Faust, *History of the German Element in the United States*, II, 203–4; G. L. Jackson, *The Privilege of Education*, p. 67.

3. See chaps. vi–viii.

4. See chap. ix.

5. See section below "Poor Children." The acts relating to orphans are concerned especially with the security of their estates. Minute regulations are set forth governing guardians, in order that the orphan might have the largest income possible from his estate and its increase, and that he might be maintained and educated in the best manner possible.

6. W. W. Hening, *Statutes at Large* (Virginia), I, 260–61 (eds.: New York, 1823, Vols. I–II; Philadelphia, 1823, Vol. III; Richmond, 1814–21, Vols. IV–VIII).

7. Hening, *ibid.*, I, 416.

8. *Ibid.*, p. 551.

9. *William and Mary College Quarterly*, V, 221.

10. An orphan's court was in existence in London in 1625/6. See *Fourth Report of Hist. Mss. Commission* (London, 1874), p. 7.

11. Henning, *op. cit.*, I, 310. The act of 1661/2 which appears in the revisal of the laws of 1661/2 (*ibid.*, pp. 41–43) was largely a re-enactment of that of 1656; that of 1672 gave power to the county courts to dispose of orphans' estates according to the best judgment of the justices, if they could not find persons to take the estates according to the regulations of previous acts; that of 1679 made justices who failed to take sufficient security for orphans' estates chargeable for all losses due to such failure (*ibid.*, II, 92–94, 295, and 444). These three acts were repealed by the act of 1705, but the main provisions were re-enacted and appear in the Virginia codes of the eighteenth century and

hence were in force throughout the colonial period. See also *A Collection of all the Acts of Assembly, now in force*, etc. (Williamsburg, 1733), pp. 186–87; *The Acts of Assembly, now in force*, etc. (Williamsburg, 1752), pp. 226–28; *The Acts of Assembly, now in force*, etc. (Williamsburg, 1769), pp. 156–59.

12. Hening, *op. cit.*, III, 375. This act repealed all previous acts on the subject. It appears in the code of 1733, pp. 186–87.

13. *Ibid.*, IV, 286; also in the code of 1733, pp. 447–48.

14. *Ibid.*, V, 100–101. The substance of this act was included in that of 1748.

15. *Ibid.*, V, 450–52, chap. vi. This act is in the code of 1752, pp. 226–28, and also appears in the code of 1769, pp. 156–59.

16. See chap. iv.

17. James D. Butler, "British Convicts Shipped to American Colonies," *American Historical Review*, II, 12–33. See chap. iii, n. 1, and McCormac, *White Servitude in Maryland*, chap. viii. J. D. Lang, *Transportation and Colonization* (London, 1837), pp. 37–38.

18. Hening, *op. cit.*, II, 170. A law of 1662 even complained that "Some dissolute masters have gotten their maides [white servants] with child" (Hening, *ibid.*, II, 167).

19. See W. W. Kemp, *The Support of Schools in Colonial New York by the Society for the Propagation of the Gospel in Foreign Parts* (New York, 1913).

20. The Virginia Company agreed February 2, 1620, that one hundred children supplied by the city of London to be sent to Virginia and apprenticed should be "Educated and brought upp in some good Craftes, Trades, or Husbandry" (Kingsbury, *Rec. of Va. Co.*, I, 306).

21. Hening, *op. cit.*, I, 156.

22. *Ibid.*, p. 157; see also *ibid.*, p. 181, for re-enactment of this law in 1632.

23. *Ibid.*, I, 290.

24. *Ibid.*, pp. 311–12. None of these four acts appears in the revisal of 1661/2, to be found in *ibid.*, II, 41–162, nor in later codes.

25. *Ibid.*, I, 336–37.

26. *Ibid.*, This act was omitted in the revisal of 1661/2, and later was replaced by that of 1668.

27. *Ibid.*, II, 266–67. This act remained in force until 1755 (code of 1733, p. 48) and was then superseded by the law of that year, which declared that the number of poor people had greatly increased of late years, and houses for their reception were proposed to help prevent "great mischiefs" arising from such numbers of unemployed poor. Vestries of every parish were given power to provide one or more houses, and provide cotton, hemp, or flax or other material for setting the poor to work. Parishes, if small, might unite to build houses, and were also given power "to levy a reasonable allowance in their parish levies, for the education of such poor children as shall be placed in the said house, or houses, until they shall be bound out according to law" (*ibid.*, VI, 475–76).

28. *Ibid.*, II, 298; also in the code of 1733, p. 57.

29. *Ibid.*, IV, 208–12, also in code of 1733, p. 397.

30. By the act of 1736 apprentices were to serve full time until they became of age, even if apprenticed in infancy, because "skill in trades, arts and industries....would be very beneficial to such apprentices and increase the number of artificers in the colony," (*ibid.*, IV, 482).

31. *Ibid.*, VI, 32 (chap. xix). This act is also in the code of 1752, pp. 303–5, and that of 1769, pp. 216–18.

32. *Ibid.*, I, 253.

33. *Ibid.*, I, 438.

34. *Ibid.*, II, 168.

35. *Ibid.*, VIII, 374–77.

36. *Ibid.*, VIII, 377.

37. *Ibid.*, III, 86–87. The same clause appears in substance in the code of 1769, p. 311, except that the word "Indians" is omitted.

38. *Ibid.*, p. 457.

39. *Ibid.*, II, 170. This was in force throughout the colonial period and is found in the code of 1769, p. 308.

40. *Ibid.*, VI, 361.

41. *Ibid.*, VIII, 133–34. This act is in the code of 1769, p. 450.

42. This does not include the acts on workhouses, those of 1646, 1668, and 1755, nor several acts relating to orphans involving the security of their estates, part of the purpose of which was to safeguard their education.

43. It may also be noted that there was some attention to the Indians. The act of March, 1655, declared that Indian children could be taken as servants, with the consent of their parents, "Provided that due respect and care be had thet thay the said Indian servants be educated and brought up in the Christian religion and that covenants for such service or services to be confirmed before two justices of the peace as aforesaid" (*ibid.*, I, 410).

44. *William and Mary College Quarterly*, V, 221.

CHAPTER XI

1. This chapter was first printed in the *School Review*, XXVIII (February, 1920), 127–42.

2. L. G. Tyler, "Education in Colonial Virginia," *William and Mary College Quarterly Historical Magazine*, V, 211. This article consists principally of extracts from the records of six county courts relating to some fifteen indentures of apprenticeship of orphans and poor children or court orders concerning the same.

P. A. Bruce, in his *Institutional History of Virginia in the Seventh Century*, I, 308–15, gives data from other counties up to 1700.

3. Tyler, *op. cit.*

4. *Ibid.*, p. 222.

5. *Ibid.*

6. MS *Records Essex County Court, 1695–99*, p. 89. (Transcript in Virginia State Library.)

7. Cf. *Virginia Magazine of History*, II, 345. Indenture of a boy, 1714 from *Princess Anne County Records*.

8. Bruce, *op. cit.*, pp. 310–11.

9. W. A. Crozier [ed.], *Virginia County Records*, I, 72–76.

10. *Records Rappahannock County Court, 1683–86*, p. 105. (Transcript in Virginia State Library.) There is, however, evidence that the laws respecting orphans were poorly enforced. For example, an order of the Stafford County Court of October 9, 1750, declared that guardians failed to appear when summoned to make up their accounts and that little care was taken throughout the county to put the acts relating to orphans into effect (*William and Mary College Quarterly Historical Magazine*, XII, 77–78).

11. W. W. Hening, *Statutes of Virginia*, I, 438.

12. Tyler, *op. cit.*, p. 220.

13. MS *Records Elizabeth City County Court, 1684–99*, pp. 29–30. (Transcript in Virginia State Library.)

14. MS *Record Book of Guardians Bonds and Accounts, Louisa County, 1767–1819*, pp. 33–34. (Original.)

15. *Ibid.*, pp. 68, 69.

16. See chap. viii.

17. Tyler, *op. cit.*, p. 220.

18. *Ibid.*

19. *Ibid.*, p. 222. Cf. also Bruce, *op. cit.*, p. 311. Another indenture, October 11, 1694, provided that the master give her "a years schooling and to have her taught to sew." MS *Records Essex County Court, 1695–99*, p. 73. (Transcript in Virginia State Library.)

20. *Recs. Essex Co., 1695–99*, pp. 102–3.

21. *Virginia Magazine of History*, II, p. 429. The Lancaster County Court, on August 10, 1719, bound out the son of a free negro woman with the provision that he was to be taught to read and write (*William and Mary College Quarterly Historical Magazine*, VIII, 82). Another class of children, sometimes given the advantage of an education, was imported servants, boys and girls who were indentured. The Lancaster County Court bound out two of this class, a girl who was to be taught to "Reade the Bible well" and a boy, an orphan, who was to be taught to "read and write" (*ibid.*).

22. MS *Records Elizabeth City County Court, 1684–97*, pp. 29–30. (Transcript in Virginia State Library.)

23. MS *Records Rappahannock County Court, 1683–86*, p. 79. (Transcript in Virginia State Library.)

24. Tyler, *op. cit.*, pp. 222–23.

25. *Ibid.*, p. 322.

26. *Ibid.*, VI, 35.

27. MS *Records Henrico County Court*, August 20, 1706, p. 48. (Original.)

28. *Virginia Magazine of History*, II, 345.

29. Tyler, *op. cit.*, V, 223.

30. MS *Records Charles City County Court, 1758–62*, p. 223. (Original.) It appears that the Charles City County Court was particularly active in enforcing the law. Thus "William Smett being summoned to show Cause why he has neglected the Education of his Children, John and Joseph Smett appeared, and Promising to take proper Care of them for the Future, the Complaint is dismist with Costs" (*ibid.*, September 7, 1756, p. 75). Cf. also cases in Lyman Chalkley (ed.), *Abstracts of Augusta County Court Records*, December 3, 1751, I, 49: "Thos. Smith fails to provide for his children in a Christian-like manner and they are to be bound out." For similar cases see November 29, 1770, and August 23, 1773 (*ibid.*, pp. 162, 175).

31. Tyler, *op. cit.*, VI, 35. Compare also the following: "Ordered that the Sherif sumon Richard Smith who it is said neglects the Education of his Children to the next Court to Shew Cause why they should not be bound out according to Law" (*Records of York County Court, 1748–52*, December 19, 1748). (Original.)

32. Chalkley, *op. cit.*, I, 157.

33. *Ibid.*, I, 163.

34. *Ibid.*, I, 176.

35. Tyler, *op. cit.*, V, 221.

36. *Records Essex County Court, 1695–99*, p. 32. (Transcript in Virginia State Library.)

37. Hening, *Statutes of Virginia*, IV, 208–13.

38. See Table II.

39. Tyler, *op. cit.*, V, 219. See also Table II.

40. The data given are made from a study of these original manuscript record books by the author.

41. One indenture was for two boys and another for a boy and a girl, with the result that we have 161 indentures for 163 boys and girls.

CHAPTER XII

1. This chapter was first printed in the *Social Service Review*, III (March, 1929), 1–18.

For economic and social conditions in Virginia consult P. A. Bruce, *Economic History of Virginia in the Seventeenth Century* (2 vols.; New York, 1896), and *Institutional History of Virginia in the Seventeenth Century* (2 vols.; New York, 1910).

2. E. P. Cheyney, *Social Changes in England in the Sixteenth Century;* A. P. Usher, *Introduction to the Industrial and Social History of England.*

3. Harriett Bradley, "The Enclosure of Open Fields in England," in *Columbia Studies in History*, Vol. LXXX.

4. C. J. Ribton-Turner, *A History of Vagrants and Vagrancy and Beggars and Begging;* Frank Aydelotte, *English Rogues and Vagabonds.*

5. J. E. T. Rogers, *History of Agriculture and Prices in England, 1259–1793*, 7 vols.

6. E. M. Leonard, *The Early History of English Poor Relief;* Sir George Nicholls, *A History of the English Poor Laws*, 3 vols.

7. 5 and 6 Edw. VI, c. 2. See also 5 Eliz., c. 3 "An Act for the relief of the Poor"; also in G. W. Prothero, *Select Statutes and Other Constitutional Documents*, pp. 41–45.

8. 5 Eliz., c. 4. See also in Prothero, *op. cit.*, pp. 45–54. Cf. J. F. Scott, *Historical Essays on Apprenticeship*, etc., chap. iii, "The Statute of Artificers"; O. J. Dunlop and R. D. Denman, *English Apprenticeship and Child Labour.*

9. Scott, *op. cit.*, p. 27.

10. *Utopia* (ed. Edward Arber, 1869), p. 40.

11. W. Cunningham, *The Growth of English Industry and Commerce*, II, 61.

12. 43 Eliz., c. 2, also in Prothero, *op. cit.*, pp. 103–5. See n. 6 and H. D. Traill, *Social England*, Vol. IV, chap. xiii, on "Pauperism, 1603–1642."

13. The "Discourse" is in the *Publications of the Prince Society* (Boston, 1903), p. 86.

14. Richard Hakluyt's "Discourse on Western Planting," is in *Maine Historical Society Collections*, II (1584), 37.

15. Alexander Brown, *The Genesis of the United States*, I, 456.

16. J. C. Ballagh, "White Servitude in the Colony of Virginia," *Johns Hopkins University Studies*, Series XIII, and "A History of Slavery in Virginia," in *Johns Hopkins University Studies*, extra Vol. XXIV; J. D. Butler, "British Convicts Shipped to American Colonies," in *American Historical Review*, II, 12–34. See chap. iii.

17. Hening, *Statutes of Virginia*, II, 248.

18. *Ibid.*, IV, 208–12.

19. J. H. Russell, "The Free Negro in Virginia, 1619–1895," in *Johns Hopkins University Studies*, Series XXXI.

20. S. L. Ware, "The Elizabethan Parish in Its Ecclesiastical and Financial Aspects," in *Johns Hopkins University Studies*, Series XXVI; P. A. Bruce, *Institutional History of Virginia*, I, chaps. vi–ix (Parish, Vestry, Church Wardens).

21. Hening, *op. cit.*, I, 224, 433.

22. *Ibid.*, II, 25.

23. *Ibid.*, p. 356.

24. *Ibid.*, I, 433.

25. *Ibid.*, V, 275. The vestry of Truro parish was dissolved by act of assembly in 1744 because some of the vestrymen were unqualified; several "pretending to act as vestrymen, are unable to read or write . . . . and imposed many hardships on the inhabitants of the parish" (*ibid.*, pp. 274–75).

26. *Ibid.*, VII (1759), p. 303.

27. F. L. Hawks, *Contributions to the Ecclesiastical History of the U.S.*, I, 84–86.

28. *William and Mary College Quarterly*, V, 200–203.

29. For analysis of this legislation and its workings see chaps. x and xi.

30. Hening, *op. cit.*, I, 336–37. The Act of 1668 also gave power to the county court "to take poore children from indigent parents to worke in those houses" (*ibid.*, II, 267).

31. *Ibid.*, II, 298.

32. *Ibid.*, IV, 208–14. This is a comprehensive act defining vagabonds and their treatment; poor and sick persons; the responsibilities of the vestry for the poor, and the method of caring for illegitimate children. See also nn. 27, 28, 31, chap. x.

33. See Bruce, *Inst. Hist. of Va.*, I, chap. v. ("Public Morals," "Bastardy and Slander"), for the seventeenth century. See also n. 1, *supra*.

34. Hening, *op. cit.*, I, 253.

35. *Ibid.*, p. 438.

36. *Ibid.*, II, 168.

37. *Ibid.*, VIII, 374.

38. *Ibid.*, p. 377. See p. 5, n. 1.

39. *Ibid.*, III, 86–87.

40. Other acts provide penalties for fornication between servants and for the "destroying and murdering of bastard children," (*ibid.*, III [1696], 139; [1710], p. 510; IV [1727], 213).

41. The act of 1756 provided that if orphans had an estate so "meane and inconsiderable that it will not reach to a free education," then he must be bound out as an apprentice (*ibid.*, I, 416).

42. *The Vestry Book of Saint Peter's Parish, New Kent County, Va., 1682–1758* (Richmond, 1905); C. G. Chamberlayne, *The Vestry Book and Register of Bristol Parish, Virginia, 1720–89* (Richmond, 1898); L. W. Burton, *Annals of Henrico Parish* contains "Vestry Book of Henrico Parish, 1730–1773" (ed. by R. A. Brock); "King William's Vestry Book, 1707–1750," is in *Virginia Magazine of History*, Vols. XI and XII; C. G. Chamberlayne, *The Vestry Book of Christ Church Parish, 1663–1767* (Richmond, 1928).

43. "King Williams's Parish V. B.," in *Virginia Magazine of History*, XII, 26, 243; XIII, 179.

44. *Bristol Parish V. B.*, pp. 3–45.

45. *St. Peter's Parish V. B.*, pp. 133–34.

46. *Bristol Parish V. B.*, p. 30. Compare the budget of *St. Peter's Parish* (1744).

47. See *William and Mary College Quarterly*, VII, 222, 236, 255, for bequests to the poor; and Bruce, *Institutional History of Virginia*, I, 26–27.

48. *William and Mary College Quarterly*, VII, 254.

49. Hening, *op. cit.*, VII, 418.

50. Bruce, *Institutional History of Virginia*, p. 88, and Robert Beverley, *History of Virginia* (1722), p. 223.

51. *Virginia Magazine of History, 1901–2*, p. 55.

52. Hening, *op. cit.*, I, 242.

53. *William and Mary College Quarterly*, V, 219, 221.

54. *St. Peter's Parish V. B.*, pp. 125–26.

55. *Bristol Parish V. B.* (1757), p. 168; (1762), p. 182.

56. *Ibid.* (1757), pp. 165–66.

57. *St. Peter's Parish V. B.*, pp. 194–96.

58. *Ibid.*, p. 67.

59. *Ibid.*, p. 23.

60. *Ibid.*, p. 26.

61. *Ibid.*, p. 40.

62. *Ibid.*, p. 43.

63. *Ibid.*

64. *Ibid.*, pp. 51, 56, 60, 66, etc.

65. *Ibid.*, p. 92.

66. *Bristol Parish V. B.*, pp. 5, 10, 17; *St. Peter's Parish V. B.*, p. 69.

67. *Bristol Parish V. B.*, p. 38.

68. *St. Peter's Parish V. B.*, p. 41. In Henrico Parish, 1737, among others, aid was given for two "impotent" persons, one old woman, one blind woman, and one "Ideot" (*Henrico Parish V. B.*, p. 42).

69. *St. Peter's Parish V. B.* (1698), p. 49

70. *Ibid.*, p. 55.

71. *Bristol Parish V. B.*, pp. 25–26.

72. *Ibid.*, p. 45.

73. *Ibid.* (1728), p. 37. So also "To Mary Harding for curing Mary Burnet of a Burn" (*Henrico Parish V. B.*, p. 8).

74. *St. Peter's Parish V. B.*, p. 108. See also *Bristol Parish V. B.*, p. 36.

75. *Ibid.* (1744), p. 116. The Vestry of King William's Parish paid 150 pounds of tobacco "for burying a poor man" (*Virginia Magazine of History*, XIII, 269).

76. *St. Peter's Parish V. B.* (1739), p. 181.

77. *Ibid.* (1744), p. 194.

78. Hening, *op. cit.*, I (Act of 1642–43), p. 242; III (1700), p. 201.

79. *Bristol Parish V. B.*, p. 1. See also *St. Peter's Parish V. B.*, p. 148.

80. *Bristol Parish V. B.*, p. 2.

81. *St. Peter's Parish V. B.*, pp. 157–58.

82. *Bristol Parish V. B.*, p. 271.

83. *Ibid.*, pp. 65–66. See *William and Mary College Quarterly*, V, 219–23, for binding out of poor children and orphans, and see above.

84. *St. Peter's Parish V. B.*, p. 151.

85. For the seventeenth century see Bruce, *Inst. Hist. of Va.*, Vol. I, chap. v, "Public Morals: Bastardy and Slander." At one meeting of Henrico Vestry, grants were

made for the support of three bastard children (*Henrico Parish V. B.* [Oct. 13, 1732], 11).

86. *St. Peter's Parish V. B.*, p. 8.

87. *Bristol Parish V. B.*, p. 2. An unusual case was "Mary Burnet's bastard child, she being an Idiot, and upon ye Parish" (*Henrico Parish V. B.* [1748], p. 83). At the same meeting aid was given "To John Jones, for keeping his Daughter, being a Fool" (*ibid.*).

88. *Bristol Parish V. B.*, pp. 18–19.

89. *Ibid.*, p. 24. The following entries seem to indicate that the parish gave aid to mulatto and negro servants, or possibly free negroes: "To Robert Cooke for the care of Susannah a Mulatto 400" (pounds of tobacco); and "To Ryland Randolph, churchwarden, for smallpox negro, £2, 17, o" (*Henrico Parish V. B.* [1758], p. 109; [1763], p. 123).

90. W. A. Crozier (ed.), *Virginia County Records*, I, 72–76. "Mr. Tho. Bott haveing an orphant boy bound to him by his mother desires the same may be confirmed by this Vestry" (*Bristol Parish V. B.*, p. 2).

91. Hening, *op. cit.*, IX, 527.

92. *Ibid.*, X, 288.

93. *Ibid.*, XI, 62.

94. *Ibid.*, XII, 27–29.

CHAPTER XIII

1. This chapter was first printed in *Social Service Review*, V (June, 1931), 175–98. See chap. xii for acts of 1562 and 1601.

2. Edw. III, c. 1, in Pickering, *Statutes at Large*, II, 26.

3. 22 Henry VIII, c. 12.

4. *Ibid.*

5. See 14 Eliz., c. 5 (1573); 18 Eliz., c. 3 (1577); 39 Eliz., c. 5 (1597).

6. 27 Henry VIII, c. 25. This act also forbade private alms-giving.

7. 5 Eliz., c. 3. For the important Statute of Artificers (1562), see chap. xii.

8. 14 Eliz., c. 5.

9. *Ibid.*

10. 18 Eliz., c. 3. Both of these principles reappear in the New England poor laws.

11. 43 Eliz., c. 2.

12. *Rec. Co. Mass. Bay*, I (1639), 264; *Plymouth Col. Rec.*, XI (1642), 40; *Conn. Col. Recs.*, I (1650), 546; *R. I. Col. Rec.*, I (1652), 245; *New Haven Colo. Recs.*, II (1656), 610. The history of poor relief in New England has been inadequately treated. A sketch of the laws only may be found in Edward W. Capen, *Historical Development of the Poor Law of Connecticut* (New York, 1910). See also John Cummings, *Poor-Laws of Massachusetts and New York* (New York, 1895). R. W. Kelso, *History of Public Poor Relief in Massachusetts, 1620–1920* (Boston, 1922), omits a number of important aspects of poor relief and is poorly organized. For general economic and social conditions in New England see W. B. Weeden, *Economic and Social History of New England*, 2 vols. (Boston, 1890).

13. *Plymouth Col. Recs.*, XI (1638), 108. Compare *R. I. Acts and Laws, 1636–1705*, p. 53.

14. *Mass. Acts and Resolves, 1700–1701*, c. 23.

15. *Ibid., 1722–23*, c. 5. *Ibid.*, II (1724), 336–37.

16. *Ibid.*, VI, 336. In 1756 shipmasters were forbidden to land sick and infirm persons unless security was given (*ibid.*, 1756, c. 4). See n. 87.

17. *Boston Selectmen's Recs., 1736–42*, p. 10 (bond for 37 Irish passengers). See also pp. 12, 54, 79, 81, 148, 181. In 1742 a captain was prosecuted who had failed to report certain immigrants (*ibid.*, p. 367). In 1743 another captain was ordered prosecuted because he had not given bond for a "chargeable Irish woman" (*ibid.*, 1742–53, p. 19).

18. *Ply. Col. Recs.*, XI, 40. Similar provisions were made by Massachusetts in 1655, because of "the very great charge arising to several towns by reason of strangers pressing in" (*Recs. Co. Mass. Bay*, III, 376).

19. The three-months' rule applied in Plymouth, Connecticut, and Massachusetts (*Plymouth Col. Recs.*, XI [1642], 40; *Conn. Code. of 1673*, p. 57; *Rec. Co. Mass. Bay*, IV, Part 1 [1659], 365. New Haven colony required a year's residence (*N.H. Col. Rec.*, II [1656], 610) and so did Massachusetts later (*Mass. Acts and Resolves*, I [1700], 453). Over 200 persons were named by the selectmen of Boston from 1670 to 1684 and certified to the county court as not admitted or approved as inhabitants of the town (*Tenth Rpt. Rec. Commis., Miscellaneous Papers*, pp. 55–62).

20. *Rec. Co. Mass. Bay*, III, 376–77. Watertown, Massachusetts, voted that "no foreigner of England or some other plantation" could settle in the town without the consent of the freemen (Henry Bond, *Genealogies and Hist. . . . . . of [Watertown]*, p. 995).

21. *Rec. Co. Mass. Bay*, I (1639), 264; *Conn. Col. Rec.*, I (1650), 546, and *ibid.*, III (1682), iij and VII (1732), 369.

22. *Rec. Co. Mass. Bay*, I (1637), 196; *New Haven Col. Recs.*, II (1656), 610.

23. *Conn. Col. Recs.*, III (1682), iii.

24. *Boston Town Recs., 1634–60*, p. 152 (1659). See J. R. Trumbull, *Hist. of Northampton*, I, 167; E. Worthington, *Hist. of Dedham*, p. 57; Charles Brooks, *Hist. of Medford*, p. 358; L. R. Paige, *Hist. of Cambridge*, p. 40. Watertown agreed in town meeting that whoever "shall receive any person or family upon their property that may prove chargeable to the town shall maintain the said persons at their own charges" (*Watertown Recs.*, pp. 1–2).

25. *Boston Town Recs.*, VII, 149.

26. *Recs. of Town of Dorchester* (1670), 166. See also *ibid.*, p. 163.

27. J. H. Benton, *Warning Out in New England*, chap. i, and pp. 51, 59–60; *Hist. Collecs. Essex Inst.*, II, 86.

28. *Conn. Code of 1673*, p. 57.

29. *Boston Selectmen's Recs., 1701–15*, pp. 54, 78, 122, etc. See *Tenth Rpt. Rec. Commis., Miscellaneous Papers*, pp. 63–82. See n. 90.

30. *Plymouth Col. Recs.*, XI (1677), 248; *Conn. Col. Recs.*, II (1667), 66. The fine was five shillings per week for Plymouth and twenty for Connecticut.

31. *Rec. Co. Mass. Bay*, IV, Part I (1659), 365.

32. *Rec. and Files of Essex Co. Court*, VI (July 14, 1676), 192.

33. *Ibid.*, VII (September 29, 1679), 271. The selectmen of Boston made a return to the Suffolk County court, 1707, of persons warned out. One was "a Mollato man being a Lame Criple," a discharged apprentice (*Tenth Rpt. Rec. Commis.*, p. 113).

34. *Rec. Co. Mass. Bay*, II, 10, 14, 16, 19.

35. *Mass. Acts and Resolves*, 1701, c. 9.

36. *Mass. Archives, Emigrants* (MS), 1651–1774, p. 258.

37. *Ibid.*, pp. 254, 278, 279. The town also assumed the expense of sending a person to another colony (*Boston Town Recs.*, VII, 112).

38. *Ply. Col. Recs.*, XI, 41. See also the act of 1683. Selectmen must relieve and provide for the poor as "nessessitie in theere discretion doth require and the Towne shall defray the charge thereof" (William Brigham, *Laws of New Plymouth Colony*, p. 201).

39. *Conn. Code of 1673*, p. 57.

40. *Conn. Code of 1702*, p. 94.

41. *Mass. Acts and Resolves, 1692–93*, c. 28.

42. *Recs. of Town and Selectmen of Cambridge*, Dec. 3, 1675, p. 224.

43. *Watertown Records*, pp. 70–71.

44. *Ibid.*, 97, 102. For similar aid see *Records of Braintree* (1699), p. 44.

45. Sylvester Judd, *Hist. of Hadley*, p. 234.

46. *Recs. of Braintree*, p. 51, "Provided the said Owen will doe it."

47. *Conn. Col. Recs.*, III, 300.

48. *Boston Town Recs.*, VII, 135.

49. *Boston, Selectmen's Recs.* (1701–15), p. 221.

50. *Ibid.*, VII, 168.

51. *Ibid.*, pp. 181–89. Compare "John Mullberry extream poor and Lame, 0–10–9" (and) "Ambrose Honnywell by reason of his wife, her sickness, and his being out of Imploy, 0–12–0" (*Tenth Rpt. Rec. Commis.*, p. 91. See pp. 92–94, 108).

52. J. Winsor, *Memo. Hist. of Boston*, II, 460.

53. C. H. Walcott, *Hist. of Concord*, p. 133. Cf. J. B. Felt, *Annals of Salem*, II, 396–98.

54. *Mass. Laws of 1660*, pp. 125, 203, 224. See *Acts and Resolves*, I, 212, and *ibid.*, pp. 45, 56–60, 65, 452. In Boston, 1704, fines, bequests, and donations were made a "stock" for the aid of the poor (*Tenth Rpt. Rec. Commis.*, p. 112).

55. *Boston Town Recs.*, XII, 121–22, 178; XIV, 222, 240.

56. *Braintree Town Recs.*, p. 428.

57. *Mass. Acts and Resolves*, III, 37. Re-enacted *ibid.*, pp. 264, 488, 647.

58. See chap. xii.

59. *Statutes of the Realm*, V, 402, 405 (14 Car. II, c. 12). In 1713 rogues, vagabonds, and study beggars could be apprenticed either in Britain or across seas for a term no longer than ten years (*ibid.*, IX, 981 [13 Anne, c. 26]).

60. D. Pickering, *Statutes at Large*, XIII, 471 (4 George I, c. 5).

61. *Rec. Co. Mass. Bay*, I, 405. In 1632 constables were ordered to see that no person spent his time "idly or unprofitably" and to present their cases to the magistrates (*ibid.*, I, 109).

62. *Ibid.*, II, 180. In Plymouth idle persons were to be brought before the magistrates or selectmen for examination (*Ply. Col. Recs.*, XI [1639], 32).

63. *Conn. Col. Recs.*, I (1650), 528; Code of 1673, p. 66; *Conn. Col. Recs.*, VI, 112. Massachusetts ordered idle persons, if convicted, to be sent to the house of correction and whipped "on the naked back, not exceeding 10 lashes," and kept at hard labor (*Mass. Acts and Resolves, 1692*, c. 28).

64. *Recs. Co. Mass. Bay*, V, 373.

65. *Suffolk County Court Recs.*, Mass. (1671–80) MS, March 13, 1682–83.

66. *Rec. Co. Mass. Bay*, IV, Part II, 43. See also *Ply. Col. Recs.*, XI (1661), 206.

67. *Mass. Acts and Resolves, 1692–93*, chap. 28, p. 7.

68. *R.I. Laws, 1636–1705*, p. 52.

69. *Conn. Col. Recs.*, III, 300.

70. *Ibid.*, V, 383.

71. *Ibid.*, VI, 82.

72. *Suffolk County Court Recs., Mass.* (1671–80) MS, November 22, 1677.

73. W. Brigham, *Laws of Plymouth*, p. 120.

74. *Boston Town Records*, VIII (1712), 93, 94.

75. *Ibid.*, p. 101.

76. *Mass. Acts and Resolves, 1735–36*, c. 4.

77. *Boston Town Recs.* (1729–42), *Rec. Com. Rpts.*, XII, 231.

78. *Mass. Acts and Resolves, 1743–44*, c. 12. Cf. Joseph Merrill, *Hist. of Amesbury*, pp. 206, 214.

79. *Braintree, Town Recs.*, pp. 281–82.

80. *Ibid.*, pp. 284–86.

81. *Mass. Acts and Resolves, 1699–1700*, c. 8.

82. *Conn. Colo. Recs.*, V, 383.

83. *Ibid.*, VII, 127. This is a copy of the Mass. Act of 1699.

84. *Ibid.*, VII, 530; X, 159, 206; XIII, 237 (Acts of 1750, 1753, and 1759).

85. *Essex Institute Hist. Collecs.*, II, 85–92, from which extracts are given.

86. *Ply. Col. Recs.*, XI, 40. Cf. *New Haven Colo. Recs.*, III, 610.

87. *Mass. Acts and Resolves*, I, 376, 469; II (1700, 1701, 1718), 91; III (1722), 124. See note 16.

88. *Boston Selectmen's Recs., 1736–42*, pp. 316–18.

89. *Ibid.*, pp. 318–20.

90. *Ibid.*, p. 320.

91. *Ibid.*, p. 319.

92. *Conn. Code of 1673*, p. 57; *Mass. Acts and Resolves*, I, 469–70.

93. *Braintree Town Recs.*, p. 65.

94. *Mass. Acts and Resolves, 1693–94*, p. 51. Connecticut copied this act, "An Act for the relieving of Idiots and Distracted Persons" (*Conn. Col. Recs.*, IV, 285). In 1727 insane persons were confined to workhouses (*ibid.*, VII, 129).

95. *Braintree Town Recs.*, p. 26.

96. *Ibid.* (1690), p. 41.

97. *Ibid.*, pp. 46, 63. There were other special classes of poor, not here treated, for which provision was made; such as illegitimate children, Indians, widows, slaves who had been freed, and others. See E. W. Capen, *The Historical Development of the Poor Law of Connecticut*, for examples.

INDEX

INDEX

Acts of assemblies: and conversion of slaves, 27–28; and poor classes, 87–99, 103–12, 143–52, 179–80. *See* Apprentices, Apprenticeship system, Educational acts, Indentured servants, Poor children, Slaves, and names of individuals

Acts of Parliament, and convicts, 49; and poor classes, 85, 176–77, 189–91

Agriculture, diversification of, 3–6, 8, 11. *See* Indentured servants, Plantation, Slaves

Anglican church. *See* Church of England

Apprentices: slaves as, 10, 14, 21; statute of (Eng.), 47, 85, 88, 117, 176, 189; acts concerning, 7, 60, 87–92, 95–96, 98–99, 103, 103–12, 108–11, 113, 143–52, 179–80; indentures of, 93, 103, 106, 113, 117–18; girls as, 91, 152, 156, 159, 162, 163–64, 166–69; quality of education given, 126; inspection of, 127–28. *See* Artisans, Indentured servants, Poor children, Slaves

Apprenticeship system: as agency for education, 84–85, 87–98, 101, 103, 157; influence of, 128, 140, 142

Asbury, Francis, and slaves, 33

Artificers. *See* Apprentices

Artisans: variety of, 7, 11–13; supply of, 8–9; slaves as, 8–10, 11–12, 15–16; indentured servants as, 10. *See* Apprentices

Associates of Dr. Bray, and negro schools, 30

Baptism, of slaves, 27, 30

Baptists, and slavery, 33–34

Berkeley, Dean, and conversion of slaves, 42

Beverley (Mass.), lack of education, 123–24

Beverley, Robert: on planters, 6; on manufactures, 8; inventory of, 11

Billerica, parental education in, 131

Bishop of London, and conversion of slaves, 29–31, 36, 39

Blackstone, and English criminal code, 49

Blair, Rev. James, commissary, and conversion of slaves, 29

Board of Trade, report to, 20

Boltzius, and slavery, 34

Boston: town school, 71–73, 81; apprenticeship act of, 105; support of poor, 197–98, 200

Bounties, for manufactures, 4

Bray, Rev. Thomas, commissary, and conversion of slaves, 29. *See* Associates, etc.

Cambridge (Eng.), University, graduates of, 64, 68, 133

Cambridge (Mass.): school at, 78; parental education in, 121

Carroll, Charles, plantation manufactures, 18

Carter, Robert, woolen and linen factory, 18

Catechizing, 29, 41, 91–92, 108–10, 122–23, 148. *See* Religious education

Charities. *See* Poor children

Charleston (S.C.): exports from, 12–13; slave artisans in, 13, 20. *See* South Carolina

Charlestown (Mass.): town school, 73, 81–82; education in, 123

Cheevers, Ezekiel, schoolmaster, 79–80

Children. *See* Poor children, Apprentices

Christianity, and slavery, 24–25

Church of England, and conversion of slaves, 29–31. *See* Missionaries, Society for the Propagation of the Gospel in Foreign Parts, Poor children

Clergy, Anglican: and slaves, 31, 36; and education, 64–65, 68. *See* Religious denominations by name

Codes of law: and indentured servants, 54; and education, 86

Cook, Ebenezer, poem on indentured servants, 53

Committee, for town schools, 73, 77–79

Compulsory education: relation to compulsory schools, 84–85, 100; laws on, 85, 87–89, 91–98, 103, 143, 155, 159–61; principles of, 113; decline of, 114. *See* Educational acts, Schools

Harrower, John, diary of (indentured servant), 51

Hartford, school at, 80, 82

Harvard College, 65, 67–68

Harvard, John, 65, 68

Headright System, 46, 134–35. *See* Indentured servants

Hewatt, Alexander, on conversion of slaves, 41, 43

Humphreys, David, and conversion of slaves, 38, 42

Idle, persons, 47, 48

Illegitimate children, education of, 151–52, 164–65, 180

Immigration, 62, 64. *See* Germans, Irish, Scotch-Irish, Slaves

Indentured servants: as artisans, 9–10, 11, 52; influence of, 45; supply of, 46–47, 50; classes of, 47; voyage over of, 50–51; advertisements of, 52; character of, 52; work of, 53–54; laws regulating, 54; and moral problems, 55; economic significance of, 55; social significance of, 56; effects of, 56; as a class in society, 134. *See* Artisans, Convicts

Indentures, of apprentices, 93, 103, 106, 113, 117–21, 127, 142, 157, 162, 166–69. *See* Apprentices, Educational acts, Poor children

Indians, education of, 102, 109–10

Industrialism, transition in America, 3

Infidels: as slaves, 24–27, 39; and conversion, 27, 39–40

Inherited attitudes, 59, 118–19

Ipswich, town school, 77

Irish: paupers, 195; servants, 55

Johnson, Dr., on convicts, 48

Jones, Hugh: on slave artisans, 11, 21; on education, 139

Kalm, Peter, on conversion of slaves, 25, 42

Keith, George, and slaves, 31

Kidnapping, 49–50

King, of England, instructions, 27, 28

Labor. *See* Apprentices, Artisans, Indentured servants, Slaves

Lancaster, and parental education, 122–23

Land: and diversification, 5; and education, 66, 71–79; and headright system, 46; endowment for schools, 60, 71–79. *See* Plantation, Slaves

Laurens, Henry, and slave artisans, 15

Laws. *See* Acts, Codes, names of colonies

Lechford, Thomas, and apprentices, 118

Leicester (Eng.), apprentices, 117–18

Lords of Trade, queries on slaves, 28

Lottery (Va.), for slave artisans, 21

Lumber products, 7–12; and slave artisans, 12–13

Lutherans, attitudes on slaves, 33–34. *See* Salzburghers

Maine: lack of schools, 70; parental education in, 99, 123

Malden, apprentices, 127

Manchester, lack of education, 123–24

Manufactures: in southern colonies, 4–5, 8; type of, 6–7; and slave artisans, 8, 13. *See* Artisans, Factories, Indentured servants, Slaves

Manufacturing Society (Va.), 18

Maryland: and conversion of slaves, 27–28, 33, 37; indentured servants in, 53–54; and miscegenation of races, 55; population in, 137. *See* Mulatto

Massachusetts: and conversion of slaves, 32; school act of 1647, 60, 68, 83, 126; attitude toward public education in, 63–65; acts promoting education in, 67; compulsory education in, act of 1642, 67, 83, 86–91, 116–17, 119; of 1648, 91; of 1668, 94; town schools in, 70–79, 83; land system of, and education, 66, 70–80; codes of law, 86; religious education in, 87–90, 102; acts for apprenticing poor children, 104–7, 127; compared with Virginia, 133, 154; acts for poor relief, 192, 198, 202; warning out in, 194–95

Masters, attitudes toward slaves, 24, 28–29, 35–36, 38–41. *See* Planters, Servants

Mather, Cotton, on slavery, 32

Mathews, Captain, plantation of, 10–11

Mechanics. *See* Artisans

Methodists, attitudes toward slaves, 33

Middlesex County Court (Eng.): and "spirits," 50; and servants, 54

Mills, grain, 6

Ministers. *See* Church, Clergy, and denominations by name

Miscegenation, of races, 55. *See* Mulatto

Date Due